Tipping Point

THE CONSPIRACY THAT MURDERED PRESIDENT JOHN KENNEDY

Larry Hancock

Mary Ferrell Foundation Press

www.maryferrell.org

ISBN-13: 978-1-7364409-0-2

ISBN-10: 1-7364409-0-X

Mary Ferrell Foundation Press

P.O. Box 723

Ipswich, MA 01938

Other Books by Larry Hancock

Someone Would Have Talked: The Assassination of President John F. Kennedy, JFK Lancer Productions and Publications, 2006 and 2010

NEXUS: The CIA and Political Assassination, JFK Lancer Productions and Publications, 2011

The Awful Grace of God: Religious Terrorism, White Supremacy, and the Unsolved Murder of Martin Luther King, with Stuart Wexler, Counterpoint Press, 2012

Shadow Warfare: The History of America's Undeclared Wars, with Stuart Wexler, Counterpoint Press, 2014

Surprise Attack: From Pearl Harbor to 9/11 to Benghazi, Counterpoint Press, 2015

Killing King: Racial Terrorists, James Earl Ray, and the Plot to Assassinate Martin Luther King, with Stuart Wexler, Counterpoint Press, 2018

Creating Chaos: Covert Political Warfare, from Truman to Putin OR Books, 2018

In Denial: Secret Wars with Air Strikes and Tanks?, Compania Partners, 2020

Contents

From the Publisher

Larry Hancock's first book, *Someone Would Have Talked*, is an important work in the voluminous literature on the assassination of our 35th president, John F. Kennedy. It directly rebuts the old canard "if there was a conspiracy, somebody would have talked." The problem has actually always been that too many people talked, but not credibly, about their supposed involvement. Larry, with his skeptical mind and painstaking attention to details and documentation, cut through the nonsense and focused on several individuals who did talk, quietly to family and colleagues, in ways that made sense and could be corroborated. Now in its third edition, the book remains a bright flashlight beyond the voluminous evidence of cover-up into the murkier world of what really happened.

The book you are about to read is the culmination of Larry's decades-long investigation to find out "what really happened." Despite all the millions of pages of declassified documents, many of them cited herein, and the thousands of books and articles and internet discussions, the crime has remained more elusive than the cover-up. With the passage of time and the obituaries piling up, it's not clear the corpus of materials to work from will grow significantly.

The recent declassifications in 2017 and 2018 have actually provided many worthwhile details in places where it counts, particularly including the anti-Castro operations which feature prominently in the present work. Significant redactions remain in those documents; we will see what emerges if and when those blackouts lift. Larry's participation in the Mary Ferrell CIA Cryptonyms Project, the "magic decoder ring" for the codewords in the CIA-JFK records, has helped lift the fog on them for himself and others.

But Larry has worked from multiple angles, most importantly including the statements, timelines, movements, and connections and associations among the people he first identified in *Someone Would Have Talked*, and some new characters as well. He and David Boylan recently wrote an essay on the Mary Ferrell Foundation website about Gene Wheaton, a security consultant peripherally involved in Iran-Contra who told the Assassination Records Review Board about statements he overheard from some of his associates, including the heretofore obscure CIA officer Carl Jenkins.

Tipping Point tells the story of why many in the anti-Castro movement, both exiles themselves as well as their case officers, came to hate President Kennedy, and the evidence that they did something about it. Whether the operation extended to major political figures of the era – "how high" it went – remains a mystery which Larry touches upon but doesn't speculate where evidence is lacking. He long ago discovered that participating in a cover-up is very distinct from being part of the crime.

I first met Larry Hancock when I was attending and often speaking at JFK Lancer's November in Dallas conferences. Larry for many years organized them with Debra Conway, as well as giving his own presentations at them. His down-to-earth practical nature made him seem credible to me from the start, and nothing since has changed my initial impression.

True story. At one Dallas conference – I can't remember the year – Larry was midway through a presentation when he said "Ok, this is the part of the talk where I'm going to name names." As if on cue, within a second or two the fire alarm bells rang and the building had to be evacuated.

Some people would spin that event into a vast conspiracy. Larry shrugged it off as just another day researching the Kennedy assassination. This book conveys the essence of what he has learned from all the time he has spent doing so. I don't know if he will inevitably be drawn back in, or whether this book is indeed Larry's last word on "Who Killed JFK?" Either way, it is worth paying attention to what he has to say.

- Rex Bradford, President, Mary Ferrell Foundation

Foreword, by Bill Simpich

Larry Hancock's premise in *Tipping Point* is that we can't trust the official investigation, the crime scene evidence, the DPD and FBI collections, and the statements of some of the FBI and Secret Service agents.

What these officers did during the first 48 hours after JFK's assassination has been obfuscated and in some instances provably manipulated. So we have to turn to other sources – as Larry says to me, "go outside the box and through the back door."

Larry has expanded his list of individuals who have admitted knowledge about in the JFK assassination to a dozen people. His list is carefully vetted and deserves even more careful scrutiny.

A good example is Larry's analysis of a statement by Secret Service agent William Patterson. Patterson had reported that in 1963, immediately following the murder of the President, FBI Agent James Hosty stated to him that "Oswald had contacted two known subversive agents about 15 days before the shooting."

That remark appears to confirm that Oswald was under some level of FBI surveillance in Dallas, beyond the routine FBI contacts acknowledged by the Bureau.

I studied this aspect of the case after reading Larry's book. Larry had mentioned that he had spoken about Patterson's statement to Hosty many years ago – and he could never get a straight answer from Hosty.

I found that the Church Committee reviewed Patterson's report in November 1975. After hearing Patterson repeat his story twelve years later, a Justice Department investigator concluded that the Warren Commission should be reopened "in the national interest."

Hosty's statement was taken right after Patterson provided his testimony. Hosty was already on the hot seat.

It had just come out in the national media that Oswald had dropped off a note to Hosty in the Dallas FBI office in mid-November 1963 – days after Oswald wrote a 11/9/63 note to the Soviet consulate in Washington DC on Ruth Paine's typewriter – and that Hosty's boss had ordered him to destroy the note after Oswald's death. The contents of the note remain a matter of dispute to this day.

I took a look at Hosty's testimony to the Church Committee in 1975. Hosty disagreed that he used the phrase "two foreign subversive agents" – he said that he had told Patterson about "two foreign contacts."

That was strange. There is a big difference between the two concepts. Hosty was denying that he had told Patterson that Oswald had contacted subversives shortly before 11/22/63.

Hosty also testified that Oswald's two foreign contacts were Valeriy Kostikov at the Soviet embassy in Mexico City and the Soviet consul in Washington DC who received Oswald's letter typed on Ruth Paine's typewriter on 11/9/63. But that doesn't make much sense for a couple of reasons.

One inconsistency is that Oswald met with no less than four Soviet officers at the embassy.

LHO didn't just meet with Kostikov – he also met with Pavel Yatskov, Oleg Nechiporenko and maybe even Nikolai Leonov.

Then, another problem asserts itself – these contacts spanned a period of two months.

Hosty's rejoinder in 1975 was that he told Patterson "two months."

But if Hosty had said to Patterson that Oswald had made these contacts "two months" earlier, why does he claim one of the two events was the November 9 letter?

To make matters worse, Patterson's 11/25/63 memo has a note stating "*Not Hosty. Didn't see Patterson between 11/21/63 to 11/27/63.*" Hosty's initials are on the bottom of Patterson's memo, indicating that the note is recording Hosty's verbal response to Patterson's note in 1963.

In Hosty's testimony in 1975, he agrees that Patterson was in the room when he met with Dallas Secret Service agent Forrest Sorrels, and that Patterson might have overheard his comment to Sorrels.

At p. 147 of Hosty's 1996 book *Assignment Oswald*, Hosty writes that "*Patterson had written a memo saying I claimed Oswald had met two 'secret agents' in Mexico City*." Patterson's memo says nothing about Mexico City. Hosty is once again misleading the reader.

Should we believe Hosty's account in 1996, which offers new inaccuracies to replace the ones of 1963 and 1975? I don't – not anymore.

I am of the opinion that certain actors dedicated themselves to inserting false stories into the narrative. I used to think that Hosty was basically a truth-teller who was burned when his boss ordered him to destroy his note after the death of Oswald. Not anymore.

This is a small fraction of what Larry has given us in this book. He is giving us tools to analyze personalities and situations that have received a free pass in the past. There is no substitute for analyzing the evidence. Not all evidence is created equal.

Nor is there any substitute for good judgment. Larry keeps coming back to the JFK case every few years and offers deeper insights every time. This book goes in the right direction in centering on key persons of interest. JFK's outreach to Cuba was a tipping point that sealed his fate. His aide Arthur Schlesinger admitted, "Whatever Havana knew, Miami knew."

I hope Larry continues to go deeper for many years to come. As my friend Bill Kelly likes to say, this work brings us closer to the bottom of the well.

- Bill Simpich

Introduction

Very few of those in my generation who experienced the murder of President Kennedy, and even fewer of those who watched on live television as Jack Ruby shot Lee Oswald the following Sunday morning, came out of that weekend without the belief that there was more to the crime than emerged in the official story of the next few months. Most, although skeptical, went on with life. Being a teenager at the time, the assassination faded from my thoughts pretty quickly, only returning as a matter of interest in the early 1990's as a couple of new books on the subject caught my attention.

What began as a mild interest evolved into something closer to an obsession, driven by the idea that if there was something more to it than a "lone nut", at least some of the people who had investigated the crime must have had suspicions of their own. And if others were involved with the actual attack, at some point they must have talked – to someone. That idea led me through several years of research and three editions of *Someone Would Have Talked*, what began as a research monograph and evolved into an actual book in 2006.

With the ongoing release of documents mandated under the JFK Records Act, my research files grew exponentially during the 1990's, with new material obtained both in large batches by mail and even larger batches though the personal visits to the National Archives by my friend Stuart Wexler. Some early questions were answered, some questions which had puzzled the earliest researchers were resolved, and a number of leads (and sources) fell by the wayside – but with new leads and new names replacing them.

Most importantly, due to the extensive work of the JFK Assassination Records Review Board staff, including the medical personnel interviews conducted by Jeremy Gunn and Douglas Horne, the picture of what had happened during the 72 hours following the assassination became disappointingly clear, to an extent that justified all the skepticism of the months immediately following the assassination. Those findings, among other new research, became part of a major expansion in content and led to the third edition of *Someone Would Have Talked,* published in 2010.

Reality Check

By 2010 it had become quite clear, to me at least, that the official history (as portrayed in the Warren Commission Report) of the Kennedy assassination was simply not credible. That conclusion was based in part on an assessment that the materials offered in support of the Warren Report were questionable in many respects – including the fact that the legal chain of evidence used to support the Report was not only broken, but contained so many questionable elements that an evidentiary approach simply did not offer a viable foundation for assessing the crime. Beyond that, the documentary record supported the conclusion that an iterative series of actions had been taken after the assassination to suppress certain items of evidence, to obfuscate witness testimony, and to preempt any contemporary investigation of conspiracy during the months immediately following the assassination.

New information had also revealed that there had been known, active threats to President Kennedy during 1963. Those threats had been significant enough that Kennedy administration staff had begun planning – with meetings ongoing in November – "damage control" protocols to be used in the event that American diplomats or political figures died under suspicious circumstances.[1] That planning had initially been based in concern about Cuban retaliation for CIA actions against Cuba. However, by fall there were also concerns in regard to threats against President Kennedy from radical Cuban exiles embittered by resolution of the Cuban Missile Crisis and suppression of exile missions against Cuba and Castro.

Fidel Castro himself publicly raised the issue that anti-Castro Cubans which the United States had trained to assassinate him could become a threat to their American sponsors. On September 7, 1963 speech Castro warned that CIA-trained Cubans might become frustrated enough to even turn on President Kennedy or his brother.[2]

Unfortunately we have no details from the meetings addressing "damage control" in response to attacks on American diplomats or political figures. We only know that they occurred. But what we do know is that one of the traditional practices related to such events has been to pre-empt panic and overreaction by taking control over the media narrative in an attempt to minimize public fears and concerns.

We have well-documented illustrations of just such practices. In one example, only a few years later, the Director of the FBI and the U.S. Attorney General immediately announced that a single "lone nut" had murdered Martin Luther King – and that he had acted alone, no others were involved. That announcement was made before any actual criminal investigation had even begun. The Attorney General would later confirm that the announcement had been nothing more than a move to minimize public reaction to the killing, an effort in media control intended to forestall retaliation and violence.

In retrospect, it appears that something similar – albeit more extensive, extending over weeks and even months – occurred almost immediately following the death of President Kennedy. As new material has emerged over the decades it has become evident that individuals at the highest levels of government had immediately suspected a communist conspiracy, with the assassination driven by actors associated either with Cuba or Russia.

As early as Saturday morning, November 23, FBI Director J. Edgar Hoover advised President Johnson that unknown parties had impersonated Lee Harvey Oswald in Mexico City only a month prior to the assassination. The entirety of what might have been discussed during that Hoover/Johnson conversation remains an open question because it cannot be verified. While a written transcript of the conversation does exist, we now know that the actual tape of the call has been totally and intentionally erased. The LBJ Library can offer no explanation for the erasure of the tape; an audio engineer who has examined it determined the erasure to be "purposeful", and the library has confirmed the erasure in writing.[3]

Within two hours of that conversation, Director Hoover ordered that all FBI offices drop the initial open-ended investigation of the crime and focus entirely on Lee Oswald as the murder suspect. Records also show that by Sunday afternoon a directive was issued for the FBI to immediately prepare a report establishing Oswald as the lone assassin, a task described in internal FBI memoranda as "difficult". That same afternoon J. Edgar Hoover advised presidential aide Walter Jenkins that it would be necessary for the incoming administration to issue something which could be used to "*convince the public that Oswald is the real assassin.*" [4]

The following day, November 25, 1963, Assistant Attorney General Nicholas Katzenbach sent a memorandum to presidential aide Bill Moyers, which said in part:

"The public must be satisfied that Oswald was the assassin; that he did not have confederates who are still at large; and that the evidence was such that he would have been convicted at trial." [5]

Katzenbach established that position for the Johnson administration on the third day following the assassination, the day after which Oswald himself had been murdered in Dallas – a point in time when any real criminal investigation of the shooting was still very much in progress. Certainly, the question of others being involved – even if it were only encouraging or enabling Lee Oswald – could not possibly have been thoroughly investigated as of the third day after the assassination of the president.

At the same time, very much behind the scenes, the FBI itself continued to pursue leads suggesting that Oswald had been acting on behalf of Cuba – and had been in contact with Fidel Castro's agents. The FBI was not alone in those suspicions, with the Director of the CIA also continuing to direct internal inquiries which focused on Lee Oswald as part of a conspiracy:

"A Headquarters cable on the 28th stated that "[w]e have by no means excluded the possibility that other as yet unknown persons may have been involved or even that other powers may have played a role. On 1 December, the station in Mexico City...was told to "continue to follow all leads and tips. The question of whether Oswald acted solely on his own has still not been finally resolved.""[6]

Two weeks later, Headquarters [CIA] was still advising Mexico City station to "*continue to watch for ... evidence of their [Soviet or Cuban] complicity*". Reportedly CIA Director McCone personally felt that Castro might have well been the force behind the assassination.

While both McCone and Hoover can now be shown to have had suspicions of Cuban involvement in the attack, Robert Kennedy suspected a much different conspiracy in the hours immediately following the shooting. McCone himself confirmed – but never explained why – RFK had personally asked him whether or not CIA officers had been involved in the attack on his brother. Beyond that we also know that RFK himself had almost immediately been moved to call a close personal friend within the Cuban exile community - not asking him, but telling him, that "your people" in the anti-Castro effort had been involved.[7]

Such suspicions remained well concealed from the public dialogue but were quite real; one of the key advisors to President Kennedy (Arthur Schlesinger) wrote in his personal diary that on December 9, 1963 he had privately talked to Robert Kennedy about his brother's death. Robert Kennedy had remarked to him that while the FBI was taking the position Oswald alone had done the shooting, CIA Director McCone was of the opinion there were two shooters. Of course, as far as the public was being told, the "lone nut" story jelled quickly, actively promoted by President Johnson, and supported by an FBI report concluding that Oswald was indeed the only person involved – a report leaked to the media within days and formally released within two weeks. [8]

In contrast, regardless of what Robert Kennedy, Director McCone or others within the highest levels of government might themselves have privately suspected, in the first meeting of the Warren Commission after which the members had taken their oaths, former CIA Director Allen Dulles passed out a book – *The Assassins* by Richard Donovan – which established a case that all assassinations of American presidents had and would be done by "loners and solitary fanatics." In offering the book to the Commission members, he advised them that it presented a pattern which he expected had been repeated in the assassination of President Kennedy.

While certainly not a matter of written record, there is ample reason to suspect that a national security decision had been reached in Washington, certainly by Sunday November 24, that "damage control" would indeed be carried out. Lee Oswald would be presented as the sole individual involved in the attack on President Kennedy. In-depth FBI investigation not involving Oswald would be forestalled, and any material too suggestive of conspiracy would be suppressed or obfuscated; such material was not intended to survive the months-long process that was about to ensue.

Dissension

After examining repeated indications of evidentiary problems which a number of dedicated researchers have identified and written about over the decades, I personally came to conclude that the body of evidence placed into the official record was not simply a matter of poor crime scene work (although there was a good bit of that), of poor Dallas police records management (no, because known records had literally disappeared), or of the FBI's rush to complete their investigation (that would not explain their destruction of materials relating to Lee Oswald and the FBI itself, as well as the actual replacement of a page in his notebook to conceal a contact with him).

I outlined many of those police and FBI evidentiary issues in *Someone Would Have Talked*, following behind other researchers such as Sylvia Meagher and Jerry Rose, as well as David Lifton, William Law, Douglas Horne, and Debra Conway, who had done groundbreaking work in documenting a number of similar problems with the practices and materials of record related to the official autopsy at Bethesda Naval Hospital.[9] [10]

Beyond the work of those individuals, the Assassinations Records Review Board (ARRB) has to be recognized for identifying and detailing problems with missing and conflicting X-rays, photographs, autopsy doctor's notes, and even multiple versions of the official autopsy report.[11] [12] In one of their most revealing pieces of work, ARRB staff interviewed the lead autopsy doctor, asking him about wounds and damage to the president's skull and brain. Towards the end of the interview staff members Douglas Horne and Jeremy Gunn remained perplexed by the fact that no wounds were marked correctly on the archived autopsy materials. At that point they asked Doctor Humes to simply indicate to them on autopsy photographs as he would have in court – Humes responded that he could not do so, referencing other photographs and X-rays which he felt must have originally existed, but which are not now in the officially archived materials from the autopsy. His only further response was to wish them luck in resolving "their" problem.

It also has to be noted that issues of evidence, of investigation and of the suppression of information were not unknown even among those directly involved with the Warren Commission's work. There was dissension within the Committee, mistrust of the FBI's work and repeated concern about exactly what should be entered into the official record – extending even to the transcripts of the Commissioners own internal meetings. Commissioners Richard Russell, Hale Boggs, John Sherman Cooper were all dissatisfied with elements of the inquiry and its final report.[13] That dissatisfaction, and suspicions of conspiracy, extended to Kennedy administration insiders including William Atwood, Arthur Schlesinger Jr., Dick Goodwin, Frank Mankiewicz and Robert

Kennedy. Such suspicions were also shared by the wife of the murdered president, Jacqueline Kennedy, as illustrated in the following quote:

"Dallas was the ideal location for such a crime.....Perhaps there was only one assassin, but he did not act alone." [14]

The Back Door

After some 15 years of my own inquiry into President Kennedy's murder, I concluded that there had indeed been a conspiracy in play – but that my initial, and preferred, evidentiary approach to the crime would remain both frustrating and fruitless. Pursuing a conspiracy by going through the front door was simply not viable. If the actual conspiracy was to be revealed, it was not going to be in the negative template created by the Warren Commission, nor in the more critical but still superficial narrative which came out of the work of the House Selected Committee on Assassinations. It was going to have to come from individuals, not from committees.

During my first decade of research, I had come across not only well-respected individuals who dissented with the official Warren Commission inquiry, but others who appeared to have credible, if limited, knowledge in regard to the conspiracy itself. Some of those individuals had been inside the government at the time, some even within the intelligence community. Others were of a different ilk, holding guilty knowledge, perhaps complicit to some extent in having withheld that evidence from law enforcement or from the follow-on, official investigations of the assassination.

Others were more deeply involved, as possible enablers or participants in the conspiracy and the attack in Dallas. Several had actually been investigated to at least a limited extent by either the Warren Commission inquiry or the House Select Committee on Assassinations. While seriously incomplete, records and documents did provide certain details on their backgrounds, and all had been provably associated with the activities and people that would have allowed them to actually have the information expressed in their private remarks.

The most interesting were individuals who could be confirmed as actually having revealed some minimal information to family, the closest of their friends, or to their lawyers. None had talked publicly. I had researched and then written about some of those individuals in *Someone Would Have Talked* – because they had talked. Research during the decade following the publication of that work added other names to the list of both sources and associates.

And as more documents were released, these sources became even more interesting. In many instances, documents relating to them had initially been mysterious and intentionally cryptic (per standard intelligence practice and operational security concerns). But year by year they were becoming more readable and much more informative. The individuals could not only be identified, but placed in a solid historical context extending over several years.

Much of that progress was due to the "crypt busting" work of several of my fellow researchers, with David Boylan, Bill Simpich and Rex Bradford playing leading roles. The creation of an extensive CIA cryptonym and alias online reference database at the Mary Ferrell Foundation also played a key function in aiding the deciphering of documents, and connecting the dots between people, places and various intelligence community activities. It also allowed the connections and associations of individuals who had "talked" to be confirmed.

The most interesting thing was that the more we learned about these sources, not just from their personal histories, but from the still ongoing release of documents and related historical research – the more credible they became. With more records, and more history, we found ourselves not only confirming elements of their remarks, but being able to expand on them.

What we also found was that irrespective of the individual and the lead, to some extent all of them shared some sort of history with the Cuban revolution of the late 1950's, the rise to power of Fidel

Castro, the Cuban resistance to his regime, the various CIA efforts to oust Castro from power, or the years-long anti-Castro resistance movement inside Cuba or among Cuban exiles in the United States.

It didn't matter whether the individuals of interest were Dallas club owners, casino figures from Las Vegas or Los Angeles, Cuban resistance figures, private American "freedom fighters," senior CIA officers, paramilitary contractors, or simply people who had worked with them in the early 1960's, or even years later. All those sources, who after extensive research and testing, proved to be most credible in offering insights into the assassination of President Kennedy, shared some history of participation in Cuban affairs. Not just in regards to Cuban affairs circa 1963, but back to the Batista era and the revolution against his regime circa 1958/59.

Perhaps most startling, not only did all the sources and associations which seemed most credible connect to Cuba in some fashion, in the end they actually pointed in the same direction that Robert Kennedy appears to have immediately suspected on the afternoon of November 22, 1963.

This work presents my observations on the conspiracy which murdered President Kennedy – as it appears to me now after some three decades of research. It offers a hypothesis as to the origins and nature of the conspiracy, scenarios as to how the attack in Dallas originated and was carried out, and speculation as to certain leads that were knowingly suppressed after the fact. Suppression carried out in order to ensure that the official story of a lone nut attacker carried the day in the media, and the history books.

To a large extent, these observations and the conspiracy scenario are rooted in, and understandable only in, the context of revolution and resistance inside Cuba – the multi-year American covert effort to force Fidel Castro from power. Indeed, many of the remarks of the sources explored in this work are only understandable in that same context. Given that, it is necessary to begin with a deep dive into the Cuban backstory, introducing the key individuals, political and social networks, and operational connections which developed over some five years from 1958 to 1963.

The Cuba Backstory

Revolutionary Cuba 1958 - 1960

From the Eisenhower administration's viewpoint, the internal Cuban revolution against the Batista government was seen as destabilizing long-standing American business relationships with Cuba. Fidel Castro's seizure of American citizens, with attempts to blackmail their corporate employers, only increased concerns among the U.S. business community. Worse yet, the Eisenhower administration perceived virtually any revolutionary activity as providing an opening for communist influence.

Due to its proximity and its long-standing trade relationships with the United States, Cuba was already an area of routine CIA foreign intelligence collections as well as political influence (anti-communist) efforts. The CIA had begun actively conducting "foreign influence" programs in Cuba in the mid 1950's, providing financial support for anti-communist groups and circulating anti-communist propaganda.[15] Given the increasing opposition to Batista, Eisenhower had tasked oversight of Cuban matters to his Special Group (a national security level body with oversight for covert actions) as early as 1958, and Cuba had become an ongoing subject of discussion within that group.

In December 1958, with revolutionary activity continuing to grow inside Cuba, President Eisenhower had instructed the Special Group to meet weekly on Cuba's evolving political crisis.[16] The CIA's position, as expressed by the attitude of its director, Allen Dulles, was that Cuba under a populist leader such as Fidel Castro would open the door to communism and to Soviet influence. During 1958 the Special Group began discussion of contingencies ranging from overt military action by American Marines to having the United States unilaterally designate a new interim junta to govern Cuba.

In support of such options, the U.S. Army began using commercial covers to secretly place officers inside Cuba to collect military intelligence.[17] As domestic Cuban resistance to the pro-American Batista government grew, an abortive U. S. government effort attempted to persuade President Fulgencio Batista to transfer power to an interim military junta – at the same time the CIA was placing agents inside both resistance groups and the Cuban military.[18] Clandestine CIA activities escalated towards the end of 1958, as CIA Western Hemisphere Chief J.C. King initiated plans to identify dissidents who were both anti-Castro and anti-Batista. Two CIA paramilitary officers were sent into Cuba to identify groups and prepare drop zones to supply them. In January 1959, two aircraft were designated and arms loads were rigged for covert supply to conservative, anti-communist resistance groups, but there is no evidence those missions were ever actually carried out.[19]

With the CIA's efforts at supplying the "right" revolutionary groups tentative and minimal at best, more radical revolutionary groups were forced to turn to private funding and weapons smuggling out of the United States. A variety of groups used ex-patriot and family connections for such activities. Well-heeled ex-Cuban politicians, such as former Cuban president Carlos Prio Socarras in Miami, as well as individuals in the well-established Cuban business community in New York City, were tapped for political support and funding – as were sympathetic anti-communist regimes in Central America.

In the spring of 1958, the revolutionary groups affiliated with Castro's 26th of July movement in the Sierra Maestra were desperate for weapons and ammunition as they attempted to move into a more intense military phase of their movement. The overall resistance movement included guerrilla groups not just in the Sierra Maestra, but across the breadth of Cuba. Supplies were critically needed for some 2,000 fighters.[20]

However, up to that point Castro's agent Alonso Hidalgo had only managed to smuggle in a few pistols out of Miami. Only one significant shipment came into Cuba that March, from Costa Rica, with the support of its president Jose Figures. The shipment was flown in by Pedro Diaz Lantz and consisted only of thirty weapons and one hundred thousand rounds of ammunition. Later that spring a shipment of weapons was organized out of the Miami area, flown into Cuba by Frank Fiorini aka Sturgis. Sturgis managed to get the shipment in but only on the third flight, having been turned back twice by the Cuban air force.[21]

During April 1958, the FBI and police in New York and Miami began aggressively moving against Cuban weapons dealers, seizing shipments in both cities. The U. S. Coast Guard also seized a boat shipment bound for Havana. The revolutionary military groups were increasingly coming under pressure from Batista's army, and Castro's representatives in Miami were proving increasingly ineffectual in obtaining and shipping weapons; the FBI was closely monitoring them not only in Miami but also in Mexico and Venezuela.[22] By the summer of 1958, several of those individuals in both New York and Miami were replaced and a new outreach was made to Carlos Prio Socarras, pleading for him to renew his support for Castro.

An American, Robert McKeown, had been close to Prio Socarras in Cuba prior to his ouster, forced out by Batista after his ascension to power. Prio Socarras had been one of the main backers of Castro's initial entry into Cuba from Mexico (he had paid for the yacht Granma, used by Castro on his return to Cuba in 1957). However, for a time after Castro's return, Socarras's demands for power sharing had led to a break between the two.

Operating out of Houston, McKeown purchased a boat (the Seabrook) in Louisiana and transported cargoes of weapons from Arkansas and Louisiana to Mexico, for transshipment to Cuba.[23] He had actually gone into Cuba to receive the weapons following Castro's return. However, by the fall of 1958 Prio once again began to use his well-established American connections (many within the gambling and casino network) to source weapons, and also re-established his dealings with Robert McKeown. While Prio turned to McKeown for new boat shipments, he also connected with Frank

Fiorini (Sturgis) who, along with Pedro Diaz Lanz, had been involved for some time in attempts to supply the revolutionary forces by air.[24] During 1958 both McKeown and Fiorini were in routine contact with Prio in Miami, and Prio had promised Castro's representatives that routine shipments of weapons and ammunition would begin by the end of summer.[25]

While the anti-Batista revolutionary forces were struggling to obtain military materials from a variety of private sources, the CIA's Havana station (operating within the American embassy and with CIA officers under consular cover) continued to work its own existing Batista regime intelligence sources inside the Cuban police and security organizations – CIA officer David Morales played a key role in those relationships. Other agents operated under private commercial covers, with David Phillips posing as an advertising and marketing professional and Anthony (Tony) Sforza as a gambler – Sforza had strong ties to the long-established American casino community as well as to the local Cuban gaming network. Following the success of the revolution against Batista, many of the CIA personnel were exposed and forced off the island, with Sforza being one of the last to come out.

While revolutionary activities presented a threat to American business interests, the large American gambling interests managed to maintain themselves through the revolution, up to the point of being nationalized by the new Castro government in 1959. Prior to the revolution their only problem had been one of image – exacerbated by considerable American media coverage of one incident, when a close friend of then Senator Richard Nixon made highly public complaints about questionable casino gaming practices during a gambling vacation in Havana. Nixon himself was a longtime participant in the Havana scene and supporter of the Batista regime; his friend claimed to have been cheated during a gambling vacation in Cuba.

That led to some very bad press for the casino owners, especially troublesome to one of the main figures involved with the Havana casino industry, Meyer Lansky. In response Lansky sent one of his most favored troubleshooters to Havana to clean things up. The assignment introduced Johnny Roselli to Cuban affairs, and added Havana to Roselli's previous resume of "consulting" successes in Hollywood and Las Vegas. Roselli's specialty was acting as a facilitator and "strategist" (as stated on his business card) – knowing all the right people and applying the right amount of leverage to make things happen for his associates and clients.

Other individuals whose names would later become associated with the Kennedy assassination also worked in the Havana casino network. Louis McWillie had been involved in Dallas gambling circles before moving to Havana in 1958 and establishing himself in the casino industry there. He first worked as a manager in Lansky's Tropicana resort, moving on to the Sans Souci, at that time under Roselli's oversight, and finally to the Deuville casino – where John Martino was employed as a technical contractor. Martino's specialty was electronics, a specialty used primarily to improve the house's odds at both the tables and in horse racing bets.

Prior to leaving Dallas, McWillie (aka Lewis Martin)[26] had been closely associated with Jack Ruby for over a decade, often traveling with him on various undisclosed business activities. McWillie's success in moving beyond the Dallas scene and into the much higher – and more glamorous – realm of the casinos greatly impressed Ruby, who reportedly idolized McWillie's success in Havana and later in Las Vegas. Ruby maintained his long-standing relationship with McWillie, traveling to Havana to visit him and engaging in various efforts to insert himself into the Cuban scene.

Ruby's efforts to involve himself in Cuban affairs were ongoing, both pre- and post-revolutionary. Prior to the actual ouster of Batista, Jack Rubenstein (aka Ruby) wrote to the State Department's Office of Munitions Controls requesting permission to negotiate for purchases of firearms and munitions from an Italian firm. That information came from an Army Intelligence report listing U.S. arms dealers.[27] Not surprisingly, while that information relating to interest in arms dealing with Cuba emerged early in the Warren

Commission investigation, the original documents themselves appear to have since disappeared.

What has not disappeared is clear evidence of Ruby's interest in Cuba, his travel there in 1959 and his connections to names that would resurface in regards to the events of 1963. While we may never know the exact nature of all Ruby's Cuban connections, he himself gave us a very clear direction in remarks to one of his club employees who visited him in jail following his shooting of Lee Oswald:

"They're going to find out about Cuba. They're going to find out about the guns, find out about New Orleans, find out about everything." [28]

While the Warren Commission appears to have avoided entangling itself with Ruby as much as possible, years later the HSCA investigation of Ruby's travels revealed that he had indeed visited Cuba multiple times in 1959, that he carried coded messages, acting as a courier and passing them through Louis McWillie – very possibly as part of an effort to arrange the bribery which eventually resulted in the release of Havana casino figure Santos Trafficante from Cuban arrest. McWillie himself verified that scenario in testifying that he had visited Trafficante in prison, and that Jack Ruby was with him on at least one visit.

How Ruby became involved in the effort to free Trafficante is unclear; he may have been recommended by McWillie as someone not part of the Havana gambling network, and likely not under FBI observation. As a plus, being from Dallas he was in a position to contact and seek an introduction from one of Castro's favorite Americans, Robert McKeown. McKeown lived outside Houston, Texas, and Castro remained so fond of him that he made a side trip to visit him in Texas during his April visit to New York and the United Nations in 1959. However, Ruby didn't just become aware of McKeown through the publicity of that visit; he had begun his efforts to obtain an introduction from McKeown with a series of "frantic" telephone calls in January of that year.

In his later testimony to both the FBI and the HSCA, McKeown described receiving a series of telephone messages from a man in Dallas, someone totally unknown to him. Then the man, Jack Ruby, visited him in person, asking for a letter of introduction to Fidel Castro. Ruby offered to pay for the introduction, claiming he had a quantity of jeeps under contract in Louisiana, and wanted to do a deal with Castro. Ruby received no written introduction, but later McKeown, who kept up his contacts with his friends in Cuba, learned that Ruby had indeed made a number of approaches there, using McKeown's name as a reference.

Perhaps not coincidentally, that year the FBI met with Jack Ruby on 9 different occasions, identifying him as a potential criminal informant. While the FBI was forced to acknowledge those contacts following the Kennedy assassination, it provided no details and no related information has ever been released. Ultimately McKeown was arrested and charged with neutrality violations – along with Carlos Prio, Jorge Sotus (a name which will resurface later in discussion of the events of 1963) and others – on a variety of charges relating to his Cuban activities in smuggling weapons to the anti-Batista revolutionaries.

During 1959, Castro began taking control of the Havana casinos, ousting American managers and employees, and for a time putting the casino business under the supervision of Frank Fiorini aka Sturgis. As with the approach from Ruby, at that point in time McKeown was also being approached by others seeking referrals to Castro. Several of those individuals were interested in the possibility of reopening the casinos under their former owners.[29] Ruby's contact stood out only because of his mention of having vehicles under consignment in New Orleans and wanting to do a deal which would involve shipping them to Cuba.

While McKeown apparently thought little more about Jack Ruby, we know that Ruby did go on to visit Cuba, not just connecting with McWillie but evidently with Trafficante himself, who was being held in the Trescornia detention center.[30] McWillie acknowledged visiting Trafficante along with Ruby, and independently a British journalist (also being detained there) later described a visit by Ruby to Trafficante. The journalist passed word on Ruby to the American embassy in Havana.

The details of Trafficante's release remain murky. Money may have been involved (documents show that Ruby opened and used a safe deposit box that summer; the only such use in his records). Beyond that, jeeps and other military vehicles were indeed shipped out of New Orleans that year, with Trafficante being released that August, only weeks after the visits by McWillie and Ruby to Trescornia.

The shipment of the vehicles was revealed in a New Orleans Times-Picayune newspaper article of October 1960. The article revealed that some 100 war surplus jeeps, trucks and weapons vehicles had been shipped out of the Port of New Orleans during the previous year. The refurbished vehicles had been invoiced as agricultural equipment. Louisiana Senators Eastland and Ellender were informed of the activity, with transfer of at least some of the jeeps blocked before shipment because of Ellender's intervention with the Commerce Department.

The revolution against Batista had also drawn the interest, attention and even support of a number of other Americans. At the time it seemed the sort of cause that attracted a number of private citizens – several Americans with military service, such as William Morgan, Frank Fiorini and Gerry Hemming, actually went to Cuba and joined in the effort.

A young American Marine was very much interested in the revolution in Cuba, and in the possibility of joining the cause of other democratic movements in the region. Lee Oswald discussed doing just that with his Marine friend Nelson Delgado; the men both admired William Morgan, an American who had gone to Cuba to join Castro's guerrilla forces. Oswald and Delgado were both intrigued with the revolution against Batista and the idea that perhaps they could join in the revolutionary movement – help in bringing in true popular governments. Oswald in particular was "peeved" by the idea that the United States had controlled Cuba through support of the Batista regime. Oswald began to talk more frequently about going to Cuba, joining in the revolutionary cause – he began to teach himself Spanish. Yet Delgado described Oswald as gaining only a very basic conversational use of the language, nothing more.[31]

Delgado also described Oswald's varied interests, his subscribing to Russian magazines and Oswald's visit to and contact with the Cuban consulate in Los Angeles. He testified that Oswald had related such a visit to him and that he had seen a package addressed to Oswald. In addition, he also described a visit to Oswald by two "Hispanic looking males", men Delgado thought might have been from the Cuban consulate.[32]

The CIA Cuba Project 1960 - 1961

The initial CIA effort to oust Fidel Castro, approved by President Eisenhower in March 1960, failed in its goal to produce well-armed, widespread guerrilla action against the Castro regime by the end of October 1962. That resistance, accompanied by massive propaganda and political action campaigns, was intended to have either ousted Castro or have him defending his regime against a popular uprising prior to the American elections in November. Moving dramatically away from covert action, the CIA turned to the creation and amphibious landing of a heavily armed, brigade sized, conventional infantry force – supported by tanks, armored trucks, heavy weapons units and parachute drops as well as by a Cuban volunteer air element.

The full story of that effort and its failure is available in the author's most recent work, *In Denial / Secret Wars with Air Strikes and Tanks?* Two particular legacies of the Cuba Project are of major importance in understanding the attack on President Kennedy in Dallas, Texas. The first was no more and no less a legacy of mistrust – and hate.

It has taken decades for Richard Bissell's influence on the Bay of Pigs history and the perceptions of President Kennedy's role to become apparent – including the degree to which he maneuvered the project's senior operations personnel such as Jake Esterline and Colonel Jack Hawkins into carrying the message against JFK down to Cuba Project personnel at the CIA's station in Miami, and its maritime operations base in the Florida Keys. Those individuals conveyed Bissell's emotional reaction to the military officers and Cuban volunteers involved in those maritime missions – including a select group of highly trained Cuban exiles who had been supporting covert missions into Cuba, and who would remain active in paramilitary actions against Cuba through 1962 and 1963.

At its core, that messaging can now be seen to have been nothing less than a personal campaign by certain individuals to place the blame for the failure of the Cuba Project directly on President Kennedy. That campaign simply avoided the fact that Bissell himself had turned what was intended to be a covert and deniable action into a conventional military gamble at the Bay of Pigs. Instead the failure was blamed directly, and solely, on the lack of a will to succeed at any cost by President Kennedy – when Kennedy himself had only been involved with the effort over some three months in 1961. That blame campaign can be traced directly to the actions of the project's leader Richard Bissell and his chief deputy Tracy Barnes. Specifically, it was founded in misinformation and overt lies which passed from Bissell to the project's operational leader (Jake Esterline) and Colonel Jack Hawkins, the Marine officer detailed to manage the final, amphibious landing phase of the project.[33]

In both private conversations and replies to official inquiries, Bissell and Barnes were consistent in pointing towards JFK's purported weakness and indecisiveness – in particular his failure to allow extended air strikes and direct military intervention to support the landings at the Bay of Pigs. Based on the version of events relayed from Bissell, Jake Esterline personally felt compelled to travel to Miami and share what had been presented to him as a betrayal by the president with the project's Miami Station staff, and the individuals involved with the landing effort. The following excerpt from Esterline's remarks conveys that nature of the communication:

"..I tried to call it off. It was not my fault. We were screwed by Kennedy. They made me send those men in to their slaughter" [34]

In a highly emotional state, Esterline himself described his tearful meetings with individuals in Florida; his remarks and the statements to key CIA officers, contract employees and military detailees solidified views among the participants that they had no fault in the planning or conduct of the operation, but rather that disaster was totally due to a failure of will and character on the part of the president.

Those receiving the contrived version of events would have included key Cuba Project Miami Station staff including Robert Moore (head of maritime operations – Moore had served as Hawkin's deputy and succeeded him on Hawkin's return to the Marines), Gordon Campbell and Carl Jenkins (maritime operations), and David Morales (trainer for the Cuban intelligence groups prepared for deployment inside Cuba) as well as the paramilitary officers who had been personally involved in the disastrous landing at the Bay of Pigs (Rip Robertson and Grayston Lynch).

Those individuals were given the message that President Kennedy bore the blame for their failure – a view perhaps most openly expressed in Grayston Lynch's own book *Decision for Disaster / Betrayal at the Bay of Pigs*. Lynch's language offers us a clear insight into the depth of the disgust that resulted, a deeply emotional attitude toward President Kennedy which was carried on to the Cuban volunteers who had been working with CIA personnel such as Morales, Jenkins, Robertson, Lynch and Tony Sforza (a deep cover asset working on island inside Cuba).[35]

Lynch describes the *"decision for disaster"* as *"the president's decision to sign the death warrant of the 2506 Brigade" ... "a lack of courage and decisive leadership."* [36]

That same view of events carried on into the media and continues to be repeated in commentary and studies related to JFK and the Bay of Pigs. It has lost little of its original impact – Lynch's book, with his own extreme feelings about JFK, was published decades later, in 1998. The subtitle of the book "Betrayal at the Bay of Pigs" openly conveys his attitude, and his remarks in the book place all the blame directly on President Kennedy's lack of courage. In his introduction he extends thanks to those assisting him with information about the overall project: Richard Bissell, Admiral Arleigh Burke and Colonel Jack Hawkins. Unfortunately, as we only now know, the version of events passed on by Bissell and Burke to Esterline and Hawkins was far from complete – and far from accurate.

Commentary: The basic nature of the CIA's failure at the Bay of Pigs was certainly recognized by President Kennedy – he also understood the tragedy as it affected the Cuban volunteers and reacted to it emotionally – but even the official inquiry he ordered failed to disclose the full nature of the failure, and in particular, what many might well consider malfeasance by the project's chief, Richard Bissell.

It has only been with the release of a body of new information from the CIA's own internal inquiries and histories, as well a great deal of relatively recent oral history work, that we can begin to fully appreciate the disconnects between the mission as it was directed and understood by President Kennedy, and the actual military operation as it was carried out by Bissell and those reporting to him. Only now can we see the extent of disconnect between the two, a disconnect so great that ultimately the project's military leaders (Esterline and Hawkins) were forced to conclude that Bissell had failed to provide key information to the president, to reliably represent the risks associated with it, and to have actually lied to both JFK and to them in regard to key operational issues.

We can now see President Kennedy's own view of the mission, as illustrated in his actual National Security Memorandum, and in his limited but critical operational directives. Those directives clearly reveal his own views and expectations for the landing of the Cuban

Brigade at the Bay of Pigs. He viewed it as a mission to insert a force inside Cuba to stimulate on-island resistance and a mission which was to have been conducted with total deniability of any American involvement. In meetings with senior CIA officers, the president's representatives were assured that the effort would simply be the trigger for a major island uprising and that resistance fighters in the thousands would flock to quickly double and triple the size of the Cuban volunteer force, delivering the momentum for it to become the focus of an advance on Havana. Plans were made to deliver huge quantities of weapons and ammunition to supply the anticipated numbers of local recruits.

In reality, the CIA had no intelligence of any imminent uprising, was aware that the Castro regime had totally crushed the unified Cuban resistance movement (UNIDAD) weeks beforehand, and had actually cut off contacts with on-island resistance groups in pursuit of operational security. Those same briefings appear to have held no mention that main line American tanks were being landed at the beachheads – completely eliminating any pretense of deniability of American government involvement – or that the CIA was not even deploying its own Cuban volunteers for reconnaissance or to organize local resistance in the region of the landings.

Readers of this work may find a synopsis of other such disconnects in the citation noted here; full details of the overall Cuba Project under both President's Eisenhower and Kennedy are examined in the authors separate work – *In Denial / Secret Wars with Air Strikes and Tanks?* [37]

It has to be noted that the "blame Kennedy" storyline was enabled by certain of the senior military staff supporting the project, in particular Navy officers such as Admiral Arleigh Burke. Burke had adamantly and repeatedly lobbied President Kennedy to authorize direct attacks on Cuban forces by naval units under his command – not in defense of American lives or assets but strictly in support of the officially deniable Cuban landing force. Beyond that, Burke's attitude may have also been influenced by the total failure of those same naval units to conduct the one highly significant U.S. Navy air action over the beachhead which had been directly approved by President Kennedy.[38]

The extent to which the "Kennedy blame" story became embedded both in the media as well as historical references to the Bay of Pigs might seem curious, given the fact that the Cuba project had been underway for almost a year before Kennedy became involved with it – and then only with a totally new plan involving large-scale amphibious landings in Cuba. The degree of focus and the depth of details mentioned in the popular criticism of Kennedy are also revealing given that all the official inquiries and reports were immediately classified, and officially received extremely limited circulation even within the government.[39]

The explanation for the focus on JFK appears to be largely due to the fact that certain individuals, including Bissell himself, took a quite active role in quickly positioning a story which shifted some 13 months of failure under the CIA, the National Security Council, and the Joint Chiefs of Staff onto some 3 days at the Bay of Pigs in Cuba, putting the full blame for the project's failure directly on JFK and feeding that perspective into the media. The first public indication of how that effort was going to play out appeared in a September 1961 Fortune magazine article by Charles Murphy – "Cuba, the Record Set Straight."

Murphy's article openly and strongly shifted the blame for the Bay of Pigs from the CIA officers who had managed the Cuba Project for some 13 months, directing it instead towards the White House and personally towards JFK. While the sources for Murphy's article were never fully disclosed, it appears that a good deal of it can be attributed to information leaked from Admiral Burke and supplemented with details from Richard Bissell.[40] While Admiral Burke might appear to be a peripheral source on the Cuba Project, we now have a much fuller understanding of his involvement, involvement which appears to have included Navy activities outside of presidential directives, activities not communicated to either President Kennedy or the National Security Council.[41]

In addition to leaving behind a legacy of strong emotions directed against JFK, the Cuba Project did something else which would prove seminal to the conspiracy which would come into place in the fall of 1963. The project developed a group of individuals devoted to political assassination, specifically the assassination of Fidel Castro. As part of the Cuba Project a number of CIA officers, Cuban volunteers and even private individuals became involved in a series of attempts to assassinate Castro either by poison or in rifle attacks. The identities and actions of the individuals involved in those assassination efforts only emerged years later, during the Church Committee inquiries into CIA involvement in political assassination, but at this point we are able to identify several of the individuals with either knowledge of or direct involvement. At a minimum that list includes J.C. King, Richard Bissell, Tracy Barnes, Jake Esterline, John Roselli, Anthony Varona, Robert Moore, Carl Jenkins, Anthony (Tony) Sforza, and Felix Rodriquez.[42]

Historically it should come as no shock to find political assassination as an element of the Cuba Project. Assassination had first been raised as a solution to the Cuba problem by Western Hemisphere Chief J.C. King as early as 1959. CIA Director Allen Dulles approved the tactic in concept, simply substituting the more acceptable term "elimination" in his recommendations. Both of the senior Cuba Project officers – Richard Bissell and Tracy Barnes – had previously been involved with assassination activities. Research suggests that the two men were used as "cut outs" in isolating actual assassination activities from the senior levels within the agency.[43]

In July 1960, the CIA Havana station was advised that a possible elimination of the top three Castro regime leaders was being considered. That was clearly a faux pas, as such things were not to be mentioned in official documents. A reversal was quickly inserted into the chain of correspondence. Yet that month Bissell ordered the development of a poison to be used against Castro, as well as a variety of tools which might be used to deliver it. Bissell also began searching for contacts which might be used to actually field the poison inside Cuba, ultimately turning to individuals within the old

Havana casino crowd – individuals who most definitely wanted Castro gone and renewed access to what had been a highly lucrative source of revenue. The key to an introduction to the casino crowd proved to be Johnny Roselli, Meyer Lansky's long-time troubleshooter who had been sent to improve the image of the casinos in pre-Castro Cuba.

Roselli was first asked to coordinate a sniper attack on Castro, but given the risk with Castro's increasingly effective security measures, he too felt that poison would be the most effective approach (much easier to sell to potential volunteers who would prefer to escape with their lives). Arrangements were made via an active Cuban exile leader, Antonio de Varona, to deliver the poison; however the effort was run so loosely and delayed for so long that only two last-minute efforts were actually made in the very last weeks before the landings at the Bay of Pigs. The final attempt, which actually might have worked, was frustrated by the sequestration of Varona (along with other exile leaders) during the landings in Cuba.

While the poison efforts eventually became known to the public, only recently have we come to know that a corollary effort occurred within the military element of the Cuba Project. That effort involved highly trained individuals who were being infiltrated into Cuba on very covert insertions to collect intelligence and contact on-island guerrilla groups.

During the first three months of 1961, at least two different assassination missions were planned. One mission was intended to be a sniper attack on Fidel Castro, at a location near the Bay of Pigs resort where he routinely vacationed. It appears that plan may have included details of Castro's personal travel and activities, including information from sources previously close to Castro inside Cuba such as Frank Sturgis (Fiorini). In 1959, prior to his departure from Cuba, Sturgis himself had offered to personally carry out a lethal attack on Castro; however the CIA had declined his offer at that point in time.

A second plan actually did go operational; it involved the maritime insertion of personnel who were to carry out a well-planned sniper attack on Fidel Castro at his retreat on Varadero Beach, east of Havana. The mission was supported with maps and annotated drawings of the Varadero (formerly DuPont owned) Estate. Those materials were prepared from aerial and satellite photo imagery processed by the technical staff assigned to the Miami station. We only know about these two assassination projects because certain of those personnel were later transferred to the National Photographic Interpretation Center (NPIC), and they provided information to the Church Committee on assassinations. The very limited records which describe the two plans were submitted to the Church Committee by managers at NPIC; they included statements from some eight personnel who had worked on projects related to attacks on Castro.

According to Edward Cates, the chief of the Image Exploitation Group at NPIC, "a number of our photo interpreters [8 individuals] supported Carl Jenkins of the DD/P (Deputy Directorate of Plans) concerning a plan to assassinate Castro at the DuPont Veradero Beach Estate, east of Havana. Castro was known to frequent the estate and the plan was to use a high-powered rifle in the attempt. The photo interpretation support was restricted to providing annotated photographs and line drawings of the estate." [44]

It appears that the CIA may have performed its own internal investigation of those missions in the mid-1970s. Two memoranda from June and August 1975 record the statement of a Cuban CIA officer (in 1961 a contract employee) that he participated in three abortive Cuban infiltration missions, including an effort to land him near Varadero Beach. The objective of that mission was a long-range rifle attack on Fidel Castro. One of the memos mentions the names of two Cubans involved in the mission, "Felix" and "Segundo". Based on that information, it appears that Carl Jenkins may have been transferred from his assignment heading the Cuba Project military training in order to provide the personnel used in a number of covert infiltration missions, at least one of which involved Felix Rodriquez and a sniper attack on Fidel Castro.

The “Segundo” mentioned in the CIA document is Segundo Borges Ransola. Felix Rodriquez verified Borges’s identity and role in the Castro assassination project in an interview many years later – stating that both he and Segundo trained in Panama and then were asked to volunteer for the Castro attacks. Rodriquez noted that both he and Segundo were only 19 years old when they entered training in the Panama camp under Carl Jenkins, and were later prepared and sent on special missions into Cuba prior to the Bay of Pigs. Borges would enter the record again in the summer of 1963, joining Manual Artime for a recruiting trip to Fort Benning, Georgia for a new and extremely covert anti-Castro project, carrying the code name AMWORLD. The AMWORLD effort was intended to be an autonomous and extremely deniable CIA project which would support military action against the Castro regime from locations in the Caribbean.

It is now possible to identify the vessel used to insert Rodriquez on his assassination missions as the Tejana III. A CIA-converted World War II sub chaser, the missions of the Tejana III began in late February 1961 and ended in early April. The Tejana made four trips into Cuba during that period, carrying infiltration personnel and supplies for on-island groups intended to support the planned uprising. Some 27 personnel and 60 tons of supplies were covertly transported into Cuba. It appears that Felix Rodriquez was sent in on a one-man mission in early April, a mission which was forced to abort due to an engine problem with the Tejana III.[45]

A separate CIA document, the debriefing of Felix Rodriquez prior to his separation from the CIA in 1976 (and a very unusual authorization for the public disclosure of his CIA service), records his own statement that in December 1960 he had volunteered to kill Fidel Castro, stating that it was the only solution to the Cuban problem. He also stated that he had been supplied with a special sniper weapon for missions into Cuba and that he and another CIA Cuban had made three missions into Cuba.[46] Rodriquez did not identify the CIA officer who had given them the assignments or state any details of the missions. In his own biography, Rodriquez provides more detail on the assassination plan, describing a German bolt action sniper rifle with a telescopic sight. The rifle itself was pre-sighted according to the specifics of the mission, based on the exact location in which Castro was to be attacked.

The details of those highly secret assassination activities have only emerged in the decades following the Cuba Project; none were discussed in the numerous investigations and inquiries immediately following the failure at the Bay of Pigs. What is now clear is that following the disastrous landings at the Bay of Pigs, a number of the CIA officers operationally involved in the project, as well as the Cuban volunteers they trained and supervised, had come to share both bitter feelings towards President Kennedy and considerable experience in planning and conducting assassination operations. Their early attempts against Castro had been defeated by strange combinations of chance and by constantly increasing Cuban security. However, several of them would continue in service in Miami (with Miami Station being re-designated as JMWAVE), supporting covert operations against Cuba through 1963, activities which included new efforts to kill Castro and oust his regime.[47]

Covert Action Against Cuba 1961 - 1962

For the Kennedy administration, the period from 1961-1962 involved a major reset in Cuban affairs. President Kennedy remained committed to action against Cuba, but it was going to be covert action – orchestrated at an interdepartmental level above the CIA. That program would officially begin early in the year, designated as Operation Mongoose and headed by a Kennedy appointee rather than a senior CIA officer. Unlike previous covert action projects, Mongoose was not being run by the CIA. Instead, the CIA was assigned to a support role, carried out by a relatively small group designated as Task Force W (headed by William

Harvey) and with field operations conducted by the JMWAVE domestic field station in Miami.

Harvey had previously been involved in both counter intelligence and technical intelligence activities (having originally served as CIA Chief of Base in Berlin). With anti-Castro operations gaining new life, Cuba Project trainer David Morales was promoted to chief of operations at JMWAVE.[48] And later on, Ted Shackley was designated as the new Station Chief. In turn, Shackley designated Cuba Project alumnus Robert Moore as his Deputy Chief of Station.

To a large extent, the initial missions into Cuba during 1962 were simply a continuation of the post-Bay of Pigs missions of 1961, limited in number and increasingly challenged by ever-increasing Cuban security. By May of that year, maritime operations had small boats operating from some half dozen locations from Miami down to Key West.

For obvious reasons, many 1961 missions in the months immediately following the Bay of Pigs appear to have been somewhat disorganized, suffering from both logistics issues and lack of good intelligence. One member of the Brigade's initial infiltration cadre, Victor Hernandez, continued on those missions. He later observed that throughout 1961 they seemed to accomplish nothing in particular. Worse yet, the teams would depart on a mission, open unmarked boxes for ammunition, and find that it didn't even match the weapons they had been issued – this did not endear them to the CIA. After several months of frustration, Victor Hernandez left JMWAVE operations, disgusted by the lack of offensive action and with no confidence at all in the CIA's anti-Castro effort.

The period following the failed landings in Cuba, from the spring of 1961 until the advent of the Cuban Missile Crisis in the fall of 1962, is both complex and chaotic as regards the activities of the Kennedy administration, the CIA and the anti-Castro community. Maritime missions into Cuba did continue, under control of DCS Moore (Deputy Chief of Station), managed by maritime operations personnel including Rip Robertson and Grayston Lynch, the two CIA paramilitary advisors who had gone into the Bay of Pigs with Brigade 2506.

The ongoing CIA activities following the Bay of Pigs and into early 1962 were largely focused on intelligence collection, efforts to assess the status of certain individuals inside Cuba, exfiltrating operatives left stranded on the island after the abortive landings (including Felix Rodriguez and Nestor "Tony" Izquierdo), and dealing with the politics of the Cuba Project, both internally within the agency and with the Kennedy administration. Major internal CIA concerns included the number of security leaks which had occurred, the degree to which the project had been penetrated by Cuban intelligence, and the obvious lack of information on the actual situation on the ground inside Cuba.

A memorandum of April 1961 states that the Cuba Project intelligence cadre trained by David Morales (cadre designated as AMOTS) were to be developed into an intelligence and security service based in Miami. This service was tasked with intelligence collection outside the country (Cuba and Mexico) as well as domestic activities. During this period a Miami station adjunct operation (using AMOTS) was established in Mexico City, apart from the regular CIA station there.

The following month, in May, the CIA Director of Counter Intelligence, James Angleton, was assigned to create a professional, organized, and highly motivated intelligence service to support the anti-Castro effort. Angleton spent several months on his Cuban assignment, presenting his final report to the Special Group in the fall. By the end of 1961, the AMOTs had become a key element of JMWAVE's Cuban intelligence service, used both domestically and out of the Mexico City adjunct station.

The Cuban intelligence service personnel (who continued to be referred to in documents as AMOTs) also performed training in conducting wire taps and surveillance for the contract employees of the Mexico City CIA station. In addition, regular CIA JMWAVE staff on temporary assignment, working as "outsiders," performed a variety of activities targeting the Communist Party of Mexico and supported counter intelligence and "dirty tricks" efforts against the Cuban embassy staff in Mexico City. Propaganda and counter intelligence by the CIA's Mexico City station was overseen by former Cuba Project propaganda Chief David Phillips, assigned to Mexico City in 1962 following his Cuba Project work.[49]

Tony Sforza would later be assigned to take over the AMOT unit in 1963, following his exit from Cuba.[50] Sforza had eventually been successfully exfiltrated from under very deep cover inside Cuba, where he had continued to work on activities ranging from the CIA's successful contacts with Fidel Castro's sister to ongoing efforts with on-island anti-Castro groups in efforts to assassinate Castro.[51]

As for Angleton, he returned to Cuban affairs again during 1962, offering advice and support for CIA officer William Harvey in yet another highly compartmentalized and secret effort to assassinate Fidel Castro. For the anti-Communist Cuban community, the extreme disappointment and frustration of 1961 extended well into 1962. That frustration was reflected by increasing efforts to take matters into their own hands and conduct military actions independent of the CIA and the U.S. government.[52] And as the year progressed, the surviving members of the original Cuban Expeditionary Force remained imprisoned in Cuba.

Still, a number of the highly trained infiltration cadre that had been originally trained under Carl Jenkins remained operational, although relegated to performing relatively minor missions during 1961 and 1962. The paramilitary personnel involved in those missions are of special interest because of the strength of their anti-Castro commitment, and the degree to which they remained militarily active in both sanctioned and unsanctioned efforts against the Castro regime over a number of years. A look at their histories helps in understanding both the depth of their commitments and their passion to oust the Castro regime.

They had bccn among the first of the volunteers for the Cuba Project and had become the earliest trainees, initially in the Panama training camp and then in Guatemala, both under CIA military officer Carl Jenkins. Following Guatemala, they were detached for advanced training at Belle Chase in Louisiana and finally taken to Florida to be utilized in extremely covert maritime infiltration missions into Cuba.[53]

In addition to individuals such as Felix Rodriquez and Segundo Borges, others became involved in ongoing missions during 1962 and onwards. Mission personnel included Nestor (Tony) Izquierdo, who had also been among the earliest CIA recruits, having already been a member inside Cuba of Artime's "Commandos Rurales" anti-Castro revolutionary group – a group which included Rafael Quintero and Carlos Hernandez.

Carlos Hernandez had also been an early volunteer for the Cuba Project, identified in CIA records as having had a black belt in judo and being a sharpshooter. It was his expertise in judo and his friendship with Artime that had led Artime to request Hernandez as his personal bodyguard while Artime was traveling in Latin America in 1960, before the landings in Cuba. Men such as Rodriquez, Izquierdo, Hernandez and Quintero represented some of the most highly trained and skilled paramilitary operatives coming out of the original Cuba Project.

These individuals were among those most committed not only to the anti-Castro cause, but to military action against the Castro regime. That commitment would continue into 1963 – and beyond – and their names will appear again when we turn to a discussion of the context for a conspiracy targeting President Kennedy.

They represented some of the most capable and most experienced of the CIA-trained anti-Castro Cubans – with advanced training in infantry combat, guerrilla operations, and sabotage as well as radio communications.[54] The list of these trainees includes a number of names that became ongoing figures in actions against Castro throughout the 1960's, both for the CIA and independently in unsanctioned Cuban exile operations. The list includes Felix Rodriquez, Segundo Borges, Nestor Izquierdo, Carlos Hernandez, Victor Espinosa Hernandez, Jorge Giraud, and Frank Bernardino.

Several of these individuals had been separated from the majority of the Brigade 2506 trainees in late 1960, moved from Guatemala to Belle Chase Louisiana and from there into safe houses in Florida. From there, they were deployed into highly secret missions into Cuba, managed out of the CIA's base in the Florida Keys (JMFIG).[55] Available documents of the missions they were involved in give us considerable insight into their skills and the level of risk they were routinely called on to take in covert CIA missions.[56]

While many of those maritime missions remain to be explored, we do know details of one involving an AMHAZE team, a team involving Carlos Hernandez and designated as Operation Yeast.[57] That mission was to launch from Ramrod Key and connect with DRE (AMSPELL) student resistance group elements already operating in Cuba's Oriente Province. Mission documents reveal that Operation Yeast aborted due to the presence of Castro military forces in the intended landing area. Other operations (PEPE, PATRICIO and GORDO) sent in teams including Carlos Hernandez and Jorge Giraud (AMHAZE-2524) to contact and coordinate with DRE resistance groups – all those missions aborted, reportedly compromised by Cuban counter intelligence. Such operational failures created a deep level of mistrust within the DRE organization, mistrust not of its members but of CIA/American commitment and capabilities.

Mission logistics and operations appear to have improved towards the end of 1962, but even then, most still involved only weapons drops or personnel infiltrations. The few attempts at sabotage were relatively limited. Team Cobra was put in place inside Cuba in the spring of 1962, establishing an active resistance network for a time. The AMTORRID team was sent into Oriente province in June, but was forced out within a few months, leaving only two CIA assets in place, one of them a radio operator. Sabotage operations turned to economic rather than military targcts. An abortive effort was made to bomb mining operations at Matahambre and Nicaro, with the CIA team leader captured in the effort.[58]

CIA officers Grayston Lynch and Rip Robertson personally led teams on several these covert maritime missions, and Robertson became one of the most respected mission leaders among the Cuban volunteers, known for his aggressiveness and his dedication to them. While CIA personnel were directed never to actually participate in combat missions, Robertson never sent his teams into danger on their own. And he never hesitated to go in to recover them if they came under attack.[59] The bond between Robertson and his paramilitary operatives was intense; it was an emotional experience for all those involved, and the Cuban volunteers were forced to trust their CIA case officers implicitly – normally given little or no details on their missions beforehand, and simply following orders.

Robertson's commando team leader, Ramon Orosco, described one mission where an assault team went into Cuba and failed to reappear for retrieval. Rather than wait, Robertson simply grabbed one of his most trusted men, Nestor Izquierdo, loaded a boat with rockets and recoilless rifles and went looking for them himself – once again against standing orders. He recovered the team, which was not at all surprised to see him; they had faith the "old man" would never abandon them. Orosco captured the relationship with Rip succinctly:

"I loved Rip but oh my God...he was not the kind of man you would want as your enemy...it was difficult for him to adjust...he wanted an open war and we were waging a silent one." [60]

Apart from ongoing maritime missions, the Miami Station also provided support for the reactivation of the Cuba Project's effort to assassinate Fidel Castro. That new initiative was tasked to and managed by William Harvey.[61] Harvey again reached out to Johnny Roselli, and during 1962 further attempts were made, using Roselli's former contacts with Cuban exile political figure Antonio Verona. While Harvey himself worked primarily out of Washington, field operations were carried out by the JMWAVE station, and the assassination support efforts were personally handled by station chief Shackley and operations chief Morales.[62] Documents now available suggest a particularly strong personal bond developed between Harvey, Johnny Roselli and a CIA officer designated as "Dave M", undoubtedly Morales.

The renewed Castro assassination effort once again established a connection into Cuba using the services of Tony Varona, still a major conservative figure in anti-Castro politics and a member of the U.S.-backed Cuban Revolutionary Council. The agreement with Varona offered weapons and supplies for his group in exchange for access to his contacts inside Cuba.[63] That activity reinforced the connection between Roselli and Varona, but towards the end of 1962 (following the resolution of the Cuban Missile Crisis) Varona would begin to turn both personally, and on behalf of the CRC, against Kennedy administration policies on Cuba.

A point which must also be mentioned is that beyond the Harvey/Roselli/Varona connection, the renewed assassination effort once again brought counter intelligence Chief James Angleton into Cuban affairs, both in support of the Castro assassination efforts and personally in support of William Harvey. Harvey's own 1961 notes reveal that when he was first tasked with setting up a covert political assassination capability, his initial thoughts included going to Angleton to discuss how to set up a cover for the effort within the agency.

It would have to have extreme compartmentalization, including a disguise for its funding and operational expenses. There were also issues of what resources to use; they would have to be non-CIA affiliated, even potentially foreign. Another early challenge was a protocol for creating patsies with any such assassinations, if at all possible blaming them on Soviet or other communist-associated actors.[64] Harvey's notes mention that the word "assassination" must never be used, all activities must be verbal and undocumented, all peripherally-related backstop documents must be forged and backdated and any files on the project must be disguised as counter intelligence activities.

Aside from personal advice, Angleton made introductions for Harvey to a British counter intelligence officer to discuss practices and the possibility of outsourcing activities. Beyond that, Angleton arranged for one of his own contacts inside Cuba to support Harvey as needed. Angleton's involvement in Cuban affairs has not been widely discussed; there has been a general view that Harvey and Angleton were competitors and quite distant from each other. However, using papers provided by Harvey's wife, his biographer makes a clear case that there was a strong three-way friendship between not only Harvey and Angleton, but also a bond between the two men and "David M", almost certainly David Morales. Following Harvey's retirement, he and Angleton renewed a correspondence, with letters exchanged between the two men up to the time of Harvey's death.

In terms of social bonding, it is also clear that a strong personal relationship – based in the Castro assassination project – developed between Harvey and Johnny Roselli. Even when that project was terminated at the end of 1962, the two men continued to meet. Such meetings occurred in Florida, and in Washington D.C., with Roselli staying at the Harvey home. The ongoing meetings continued even after Harvey was given specific orders to cease the relationship based on an active investigation of Roselli by the FBI and Justice Department.

Anti-Castro Activism 1961 - 1962

The CIA's failure at the Bay of Pigs and its secret, very low-profile operational activities against Cuba during 1962 left a number of anti-Castro activists, both Cubans and Americans, at loose ends. With the lack of any visible American effort against Castro following the landings in Cuba, both individuals and groups began to take action on their own. That meant seeking supplies and weapons, and conducting independent (albeit minor) boat and air missions into Cuba. Those efforts created a new series of linkages between anti-Castro activists – and those linkages began to extend beyond Florida, from Miami to New Orleans, and later to the Cuban exile communities in New York, Chicago and Dallas.

Elements of the first Cuba Project had already led to an expanded CIA presence in the New Orleans area during 1960/1961. Of course, the CIA had always had a presence in the city of New Orleans, as it does in most major metropolitan areas which have substantial international diplomatic or business activity. That presence falls under CIA Domestic Contacts, and includes efforts to use American business persons (as well as Americans who have lived overseas, particularly in nations of interest) as sources for "open" foreign intelligence collections – the sort of information which comes up during travel, during business transactions and in meetings with foreign contacts, both inside the United States and on business travel. The CIA has a long history in developing business and corporate leaders as sources (and as assets, ranging from courier duty to the provision of corporate intelligence).

Of course, prominent American business persons have always voluntarily offered intelligence to the military services, to government agencies, even directly to presidents – generally in the form of information intended to influence American foreign policy in regard to their own political views or business interests. On a less lofty level, the CIA specifically cultivated managers and employees of the international trade centers in major cities as sources. In New Orleans, an employee of its Trade Center, Clay Shaw, served as a source of foreign intelligence as well as an asset during his own international travel. As standard practice the identities of such sources are well protected by the CIA – which will identify neither its employees, contractors, detailed military personnel, or its various sources and assets.

During 1960 and early 1961, additional CIA presence in and around New Orleans involved a number of peripheral Cuba Project support activities. One of those was associated with the project's propaganda campaign. New Orleans has always had strong ties into the Caribbean and Central American nations, key targets for anti-communist and anti-Castro messaging. The individual responsible for that element of the Cuba Project was David Phillips, and in 1960 Phillips reportedly appeared in New Orleans, looking for covers and tools to support anti-Castro messaging.

Based on information from a local anti-communist figure, Gordon Novel, it appears that David Phillips appeared in New Orleans, holding meetings in late 1960 with other anti-communist figures including Guy Banister and Sergio Arcacha Smith (a Cuban exile activist). The goal was to organize a telethon showcasing the plight of a communist Cuba and presenting the case for action against Castro as supported by the exile community. It would have raised money for the Cuban exile front (the Frente); Arcacha Smith represented the leadership of that group, headquartered in Miami.[65] Novel's story of the meetings is corroborated by documents disclosing an urgent request by the CIA late in 1960 to clear Banister's business as a CIA cover company.

Beyond that propaganda initiative, the New Orleans area played an operational role only in the last three months before the landings in Cuba, almost a year after the project had been approved by President Eisenhower. Only in February 1961, some two months before the landings in Cuba, was a largely abandoned Navy facility near New Orleans hastily reopened and hurriedly equipped (under CIA contract employee Grayston Lynch) as a training facility, concentrating primarily on explosives training and the preparation of exile frogmen who would be deployed at the Bay of Pigs.[66]

And only in the last weeks before the landings was a special unit formed at Belle Chase, under Nino Diaz. Its mission was ostensibly to conduct a diversionary action in the mountains of eastern Cuba. The true nature of that unit and its mission remains somewhat mysterious; what we do know is that they loaded supplies and sailed with only marginally trained personnel only days before the landings – and Diaz failed even to put his group ashore, ultimately returning them to the United States.[67]

The Belle Chase facility only operated for some three months in early 1961 and was sanitized and abandoned by the CIA after the disaster at the Bay of Pigs.[68] The paperwork relating to the closure and sanitization of the facility was signed by David Phillips, suggesting that he was the senior CIA officer operating in the area. The location and disposition of the explosives made available for the Belle Chase training is not stated, but an incident of a few months later suggests that at least some of the explosives may have been "liberated" for future anti-Castro action.

During the Garrison investigation Gordon Novel claimed CIA privilege in not offering detailed testimony. That privilege likely related not only to his meetings with David Phillips, but also to the theft of explosives during the summer of 1961 – a theft which he claimed was actually sanctioned by his CIA contact. Those explosives (and blasting caps) were removed from a storage bunker at the Schlumberger facility at Houma Louisiana, some 50 miles southwest of New Orleans. The explosives were removed by a group of individuals including Novel, Sergio Arcacha Smith, Carlos Quiroga, and David Ferrie (among others).

Documents indicate that Ferrie was also monitored on travels to Miami that year, suspected of involvement in weapons smuggling. The extent of that investigation is unclear, but Ferrie explained his trips to Miami as innocent travel, related to scouting out potential field trips for his Civil Air Patrol trainees. Only much later did it become known that one of Ferrie's CAP trainees was Lee Harvey Oswald. Oswald reportedly first met Ferrie through attending classes, and later joined Ferrie's independent CAP squadron in 1955. While unproven, the possibility also exists that it was David Ferrie himself who visited Oswald's mother, encouraging her to let Oswald enlist in the Marine Corps.[69]

Versions of the Houma incident vary, some suggesting Novel had been given a key to the bunker, others that locks and bolts had to be cut. Reportedly the explosives were temporarily stored at Ferrie's and Guy Banister's office before being carried off to be used by exile activists in attacks against Cuba. One of the participants

(Carlos Quiroga) stated that he helped put explosives in a U-Haul trailer destined for Miami.[70] In retrospect, and given the timing of the Houma theft, well after the Bay of Pigs landings had failed, it's quite possible that the "theft" might well have been as Novel described, with guidance from a CIA officer associated with the camp. And according to Novel himself, he did have direct personal contact with the individual who eventually wrote the internal CIA summary of activities at the Belle Chase base, David Phillips.[71]

The New Orleans linkages are important for a number of reasons, including the fact that they reveal a precedent for CIA propaganda activities in New Orleans. Two years later, in 1963, we will find two individuals (George Joannides and William Kent) who worked in CIA anti-Castro political action activities; over time both men established temporary residences and conducted still-classified activities in New Orleans. Both Joannides and Kent served as CIA political/propaganda case officers for the DRE. And DRE members, including Carlos Quiroga, would become key to the pro-Castro public image of Lee Harvey Oswald which resulted from his time in New Orleans in the summer of 1963. Years later, in private remarks to his family, Kent would refer to Lee Oswald as a "useful idiot." [72]

While the Kennedy administration definitely continued its covert anti-Castro efforts during 1962, they were highly secret and as low profile as possible. Given that lack of visibility, the anti-Castro community inside the United States became increasingly frustrated.

That community had come to consist of three different factions: Cuban exiles and expatriates associated with literally dozens of organized groups (some such as the DRE with CIA support; others not), exiles and patriots acting independently and avoiding association with the CIA, and a small community of Americans with military experience. Several of the Americans had actively joined in the Cuban revolution against Batista, some serving with revolutionary forces inside Cuba. Once back in the United States they came to actively – and vocally – oppose the Castro regime that had emerged from their efforts. Beginning in 1961 they were highly visible in the Miami area (and in local news coverage), offering their services to train and support anti-Castro activists in missions against Castro's regime.

The relationships between the anti-Castro factions and activists became quite complex. As an example, Carlos Hernandez had been one of the earliest volunteers for the Cuba Project, had gone through training in Panama and Guatemala, and was selected for special training at Belle Chase, then going on to Florida for infiltration missions into Cuba. After the Bay of Pigs, he had stayed on at JMWAVE, participating in boat missions into Cuba. However, he had also been an MRR member inside Cuba, later joining the DRE and becoming an active DRE military mission leader. During 1962 Hernandez and a number of DRE members were simultaneously involved in CIA-sanctioned boat missions into Cuba under Robertson and Lynch and were also participants in unsanctioned, independent military activities.[73]

During 1962 Hernandez was serving with JMWAVE on boat missions; he also participated in a covert political action effort to disrupt an International Youth Conference in Helsinki. Upon his return to Florida, he was advised that a Miami weapons dealer was offering a great price on cannons, recoilless rifles and machine guns.[74]

That was exactly the type of weapon needed for a high-profile attack against ground installations inside Cuba, and Hernandez immediately followed up on the deal, with the result being a DRE boat mission which shelled Czech and Russian military advisors at a hotel in Miramar, Cuba – outside Havana. Hernandez and Juan Blanco Fernandez led the mission, and went on to become military leaders for the DRE.

The attack gained international attention; the Justice Department identified the participants and announced they would be prosecuted for neutrality violations.[75] In reality, Hernandez continued his service with the CIA and his membership in the DRE, and following two more non-sanctioned DRE efforts to bomb Cuba in 1963, was recruited into the new, highly secret CIA AMWORLD project in the fall of 1963.

The activist American anti-Castro community in Miami included highly public figures such as Frank Sturgis, Gerry Hemming, Roy Hargraves, William Seymour, Larry DeJoseph, Lawrence Hall, Steve Wilson, and Larry Howard. All were frequently in the news in Miami during 1962 and into 1963, either due to abortive attempts to run boat missions against Cuba or more often in publicity and fund-raising efforts. For some months in 1962 Hemming and Fiorini consolidated their efforts, forming a "virtual" commando group designated as INTERPEN (Intercontinental Penetration Force).[76] While it carried out no successful missions, it did conduct training for several of the smaller and less experienced Cuban exile groups. In contrast, groups such as DRE maintained their own military cadre, supported by CIA funding. DRE, MRR and JURE also managed to raise private monies, and maintained small anti-Castro forces both inside Cuba and elsewhere in the Caribbean.

1962 also saw new linkages between Miami and New Orleans anti-Castro activists, largely due to increasing pressure on the independent actors. While the Kennedy administration and the CIA were endeavoring to conduct "quiet" covert action against Cuba as part of the Mongoose program, individuals and groups not involved with the CIA were beginning to doubt the sincerity of the American effort, and began taking matters into their own hands.

But independent military missions against Cuba, especially those launched from Florida, were becoming increasingly challenging. The Mongoose project included an effort to control all anti-Castro action, and the CIA as well as other federal agencies (including INS and the FBI) were encouraged to discover and interdict such missions – whether conducted by boat or aircraft.

One of the alternatives to Florida-based operations which was pursued during the summer of 1962 was for the Cuban Revolutionary Council to open its only training facility in Louisiana, to be staffed by American volunteers from the INTERPEN community. To that end Frank Sturgis sent one of his aides, Larry DeJoseph, on a survey trip to New Orleans. That effort was supported by David Ferrie, who offered the use of his personal aircraft and flew missions scouting rural areas for a potential camp.[77] Unfortunately for the project, by that time INTERPEN had gotten enough local media visibility in Miami that it drew increased federal attention, and the effort aborted. Perhaps the most significant result of that brief effort was the personal involvement of David Ferrie, and the continuation of an anti-Castro linkage between New Orleans and Miami.

Somewhat surprisingly, despite all the press and media attention received by individuals such as Hemming and Fiorini/Sturgis, they actually never carried out successful penetration missions into Cuba. By 1963 only one American associated with Sturgis and Hemming actually managed to carry out a high-profile mission into Cuba. Roy Hargraves had begun to act more and more independently into 1963, and scored major media coverage with a boat mission which managed to attack Cuban security forces and capture a number of Cuban fishing boats.[78] Hargraves had distanced himself from INTERPEN, preferring to organize his own missions – working with his close Cuban friend, Felipe Vidal Santiago. Felipe Vidal was a former Cuban naval officer, and while he did not affiliate himself with the larger and more publicly visible groups, he was well respected and well networked in the anti-Castro community.[79]

As noted above, during 1962 the Kennedy administration was increasingly encouraging law enforcement efforts intended to intercept and obstruct efforts of the independent anti-Castro activists. While many missions were interdicted, highly visible attacks against Cuba were carried by DRE during August and September of 1962. Those attacks received considerable media attention and garnered a spurt of private contributions at a time when fundraising was a real challenge for all the increasingly independent Cuban exile groups.

Those raids were made possible because the DRE had managed to field a couple of its own vessels, and had also managed to maintain its long-time contacts with a number of weapons brokers, allowing it to build up an inventory of automatic weapons including machine guns and recoilless rifles. DRE held something of a special status, enhanced by the fact that during the Cuba Project, the CIA had repeatedly tried to move weapons to DRE groups inside Cuba. Following the failure of the landings at the Bay of Pigs, the DRE had been given continued support by the CIA, both for political and propaganda efforts and to regain a military auxiliary.[80]

The relationship between the CIA and the DRE was complex, with conflicting agendas on both sides. DRE military members were retained and protected by the CIA, used in sanctioned activities while continuing to pursue their own unsanctioned efforts. Yet in 1962 DRE missions became a major 1962 topic for the American press, particularly news magazines such as *LIFE* and the *Saturday Evening Post.*

Along with the media coverage of independent exile raids, the Cuban exile community did have some reason to hope that the Kennedy administration would ultimately move against Castro. The idea of direct American military action against Cuba had been growing throughout the summer of 1962. There were news stories of a large-scale American Navy-Marine military exercise in the Caribbean. Philbriglex-62 was designated as a liberation of the fictional "Republic of Vieques" from the rule of a dictator named Ortsac ("Castro" spelled in reverse). The exercise involved major elements of the U.S. Navy in the Atlantic, including 40 Navy combat and logistics vessels. The exercise included a planned landing of 7,500 marines on Vieques, an island off Puerto Rico's eastern coast.

That landing was described as an exercise to overthrow a fictional island-based dictator (obviously Castro), disposing of his regime over a two-week period. All elements of the exercise were carried out with the exception of the actual amphibious force landing – cancelled at the last minute due to the risk of a hurricane moving into the area.[81] Much of the logistics planning for the Philbriglex-62 exercise, and many of the same units, were soon integrated into a very real and imminent Cuban invasion plan, prepared in the earliest days of the Cuban Missile Crisis only months later.

While President Kennedy was active in ordering and supporting major conventional military exercises, both in SE Asia and in the Caribbean, he rejected pressure from the Joint Chiefs to turn to direct military action during the missile crisis. Ironically, it would be JFK's successor who would be the one to actually activate some of the conventional options that Kennedy had overseen in earlier exercises.[82]

Castro himself had continued to openly test the Kennedy administration. In August 1962, Cuban patrol boats had actually fired on a U.S. Navy aircraft some fifteen miles off Cuba, in international waters. In responding to that incident, as well as ongoing Cuban sponsorship of anti-government factions and communist agitation across Central America, President Kennedy had declared that the United States would use whatever means necessary to prevent Castro from exporting his revolution.[83]

At the same time, anti-Castro sources within Cuba, primarily among the DRE, had been providing intelligence on a growing Russian military buildup for some months. Then in October, the sensational revelation of Russian ballistic missiles was confirmed. The Cuban exile community universally assumed this meant the Castro regime would be removed though conventional American military action – as part of an American response to the missile threat. Instead it was shocked by an agreement which appeared to guarantee that the United States would not act against Cuba. It was a "bombshell"; interviews with members of the Cuban exile community described it as "soul shattering," and the word "traitor" was heard where anti-Castro activists congregated.[84]

During the winter of 1962/63, the Kennedy administration began a second "reset" of its anti-Castro programs following the missile crisis negotiations. It also completed its efforts to negotiate the return of the Brigade 2506 prisoners (along with certain Americans) who had been held in Cuban prisons.[85] The primary negotiator on prisoner releases was William Donovan.

At the same time, in a public demonstration of support for the non-intervention agreement, orders went out to all agencies of the U.S. government to interdict any further missions against Cuba – by any anti-Castro group. Even sanctioned groups such as the DRE, which had enjoyed something of a hands-off policy in its military efforts, were directed to cease action against Cuba.

Within months, what had seemed to be the certainty of American action against Castro simply evaporated, and independent groups including both DRE and Alpha 66 (a newly organized group which had launched its own missions into Cuba and was highly visible in the media promoting action against Castro prior to the Cuban Missile Crisis) faced a concentrated American government effort to prevent their military activities.

To some extent the return of the Brigade 2506 prisoners to Miami in December 1962 only served to highlight frustrations within the exile community. While the Kennedy administration had worked on their release for some two years, the United States had accomplished virtually nothing more in the cause for which the Brigade volunteers had been recruited. It had conducted a major negotiation which obtained their freedom, but only with an agreement which involved sending Castro some $53 million worth of badly needed food and medicine, strengthening rather than weakening his regime.

President Kennedy's welcome address to the members of Brigade 2506 at the Orange Bowl in Miami included a promise that the Brigade's flag would be returned and raised in a free Havana. Yet during 1963 there would be little visible evidence that Kennedy was actually acting to deliver on that highly public promise.

Helter Skelter – 1963

As 1963 began, the focused but ineffectual interdepartmental anti-Castro effort designated as Mongoose faded away (as did Task Force W under William Harvey), replaced by another high-level working group officially under the leadership of the State Department. On January 4, 1963 JFK had requested that State consolidate all Cuban activities and reorganize an interdepartmental group for strategy and planning. That directive was paralleled by an NSC directive to restructure the anti-Castro effort. As part of the new effort, the CIA designated Desmond Fitzgerald to lead its Cuban activities. Fitzgerald headed yet one more anti-Castro team, even more neutrally named. His new group – the Special Affairs Staff (SAS) – replaced Task Force W in supporting the broader effort against Castro.

By January 25, 1963 the State Department had established the new high level Cuba group (the Cuba Coordinating Committee), headed by John Crimmins. The group worked from Washington D.C., with an office in Miami. Its activities were led by Sterling Cottrell and his deputy Bob Hurwich. Throughout 1963 high level planning to oust the Castro regime occurred within that new interdepartmental committee – with Robert Kennedy's participation.[86]

The Special Group Augmented Cuba covert action oversight group had disbanded with the dissolution of Mongoose. While covert action remained delegated to the CIA, it was carried out under oversight of the Special Group, but without RFK's direct participation. Strategy development was officially designated to the Cuba Coordinating Committee; however, its immediate and primary focus was largely limited to political and military intelligence as well as the evaluation of political action opportunities inside Cuba.

CIA maritime missions into Cuba continued, with upwards of a dozen a month, but they were almost entirely devoted to intelligence collection, infiltration, exfiltration, and weapons caching. A study of the JMWAVE message traffic shows that intelligence focused on

Cuban military movements and in particular on Soviet supply and deployment activities.

Yet as the Kennedy administration was beginning its second "reset" of covert action against Cuba, something very much unanticipated occurred. As William Donovan was wrapping up his Brigade 2506 prisoner release work, he was asked to carry a very private message back to the United States. Upon his return he informed the State Department of a striking and unexpected political outreach from Fidel Castro. Castro had extended an offer to open a dialogue with the goal of improving Cuban-American relations. Donovan outlined the Castro outreach in a confidential memo to Secretary of State Dean Rusk, copied to CIA Director McCone. Word of Castro's surprise contact was quickly passed to President Kennedy.

JFK responded with interest and openness to the Castro outreach. Kennedy directed that no conditions on discussions should be set that Castro could not fulfill and that more "flexibility" in the American approach to Cuba was in order.[87]

Donovan went back to Cuba early in April 1963, and when he returned to the U.S. he was debriefed by the CIA. Director McCone himself advised President Kennedy that Castro knew that relations with the U.S. were necessary and that Castro wanted such relations developed. President Kennedy met privately with McCone and expressed great interest in opening up communications with Castro.

McCone responded that he would be sending Donovan back to Cuba; following that visit McCone characterized Castro's tone as mild, frank, and conciliatory. He also commented that in asides, Vallejo (Castro's private physician and designated backchannel) had told Donovan that Castro realized a viable Cuba (and Cuban economy) required a rapprochement with the U.S. Castro simply did not know how to go about that, so it had been impossible to discuss the subject in any detail with Donovan.

American reporter Lisa Howard had been trying for months following the Cuban Missile Crisis to obtain an interview with Fidel Castro and finally managed to do just that in early spring. At the end of April Castro allowed Howard to record a personal interview for broadcast by the ABC network. In that interview, Castro expressed his personal openness to a change in the relationship between Cuba and the United States.

Also in April, William Harvey (who had returned to his position with Staff D technical counter intelligence work following the disbanding of Task Force W) joined John Roselli for an extended meeting in Miami, as well as a boat trip to the station's field operations in the Florida Keys. Harvey's expense report notes the meeting as being "operational," related to the ZRRIFLE program – the cover for funding the ongoing 1962/1963 efforts to assassinate Fidel Castro. The two men spent time together in Miami and at least one other person joined them – a dinner recording that was cited on Harvey's expense report.

We have no idea as to the specific identity of the third party. Likely candidates include Robert Moore (Deputy Chief of Station) and David Morales (Chief of Operations). Both men had oversight over JMWAVE maritime operations, and Moore had oversight over both SAS projects and JMWAVE operations. Maritime personnel and station paramilitary personnel had played key support roles in the highly compartmentalized Castro assassination training and missions.

What is not a matter of speculation is the fact that with the discontinuation of Mongoose, the dissolution of Task Force W, and a number of confrontations between Harvey and Robert Kennedy over field operations (and Harvey's judgment), Harvey had become extremely bitter towards both Robert and John Kennedy. In fact there is every indication that he literally hated JFK.[88]

Given the events following the Cuban Missile Crisis, and with word circulating at senior levels of the CIA (Harvey was personally close to both Helms and Angleton) about a diplomatic approach from Castro, there is little doubt that the conversations between Harvey and Roselli (including any JMWAVE personnel who might have been involved) would have included a discussion of Cuba, and the possibility of some rapprochement between Castro and the United States.

The Lisa Howard/Castro interview aired on American television on May 10, 1963. Howard had been debriefed by the CIA upon her return to the U.S. and on May 1, Richard Helms had written Director McCone a three-page memorandum on that debriefing, covering the economic problems faced by Castro and his recognition of the need for improving relations with the U.S. Helms' memorandum was copied to a number of Agency and Administration chiefs including the Defense Intelligence Agency, National Intelligence Board, State Department Intelligence, presidential National Security advisor McGeorge Bundy, Attorney General Robert Kennedy and others.

A note on the memorandum indicates that it had been read by the president. Helms also took the opportunity to insert himself into the process with negative comments on Lisa Howard's offer to serve as an intermediary. In a response to Helms' May 1 memo, McCone responded that the "Lisa Howard report be handled in the most limited and sensitive manner," and "that no active steps be taken on the rapprochement matter at this time."

There is no doubt that senior CIA officers were extremely skeptical, and would increasingly oppose any dialogue with Castro as to improving relations. The primary focus at JMWAVE remained a quest to find a new strategy for covert action to oust Castro, rather than talk with him. In contrast, no new higher-level strategy had emerged from the Cuban Coordinating Committee. The most visible new Kennedy administration initiative was the announcement of a crackdown on independent Cuban exile group missions against Cuba from the United States.

A Special Group covert action meeting on April 3 included discussion of resuming sabotage raids into Cuba – but no decisions were reached. Finally, on April 11 Fitzgerald proposed three sabotage missions to be conducted by JMWAVE during April and May. That proposal was revisited on April 18, but with the admonition that any major sabotage program would take 4-6 months more to actually implement.

Fitzgerald met with the Cuba Coordinating Committee on April 26, proposing a new covert action political initiative (intended to fragment the Castro regime), and a renewal of a sabotage program – with no conclusions reached. In a follow-on meeting of April 28, he again raised the issue to the Special Group but no actions were authorized. With no progress on the SAS proposals from Fitzgerald, on May 23 the Special Group was advised that the Army was well underway in planning for covert actions against Cuba, to be taken under military control.

As previously noted, JFK was continuing to pursue the option of handing off covert action to the military – as was being done against North Vietnam. At his direction the Joint Chiefs of Staff began actively evaluating the CIA's efforts and planning for how they would pursue a program of covert military action conducted by the Department of Defense – specifically by Commander in Chief, U.S. Atlantic Command.[89]

The covert action oversight group was told that the military plans being prepared included large scale action against Cuba, including sabotage operations.[90] At the end of May renewed strikes against Cuba remained a matter only of discussion within the coordinating committee and the Special Group. It would not be until June 8 that Fitzgerald returned with yet another proposal for covert action, including both harassment activities and major sabotage missions.

While this "churning" was going on among the different committees and agencies, Manuel Artime (who had been traveling widely in Central America during March and April, seeking support for a new effort under his leadership) had met with Desmond Fitzgerald and RFK. Artime proposed covert American funding for a new effort, with the understanding there would be no direct CIA management as in earlier Cuba projects. It was Artime's proposal that would actually jell, gaining RFK's support.

In the interim, direct involvement by President Kennedy appears to have resolved the apparent decision-making churn on covert action, and on June 19 JFK gave a high-level approval for the program proposed by Fitzgerald, authorizing both strikes and new covert political action moves which might bring about a coup against Castro (the AMTRUNK project). With that authority the Special Group reviewed specific projects; two were rejected but others were released for action in July. As it turned out the two were actually delayed into August.[91]

With a general interest in covert action against Cuba continuing in Washington, JMWAVE began to prepare its own new initiative. Based on remarks by William Shackley, the new concept was a creation of he and David Morales, with Morales handpicking a very select group of Cuban mission personnel to go into special training for extremely compartmentalized maritime sabotage missions. The missions would be carried out with a hand-picked group of the most experienced JMWAVE Cuban operators, individuals such as Nestor "Tony" Izquierdo and others who had previously conducted missions under Rip Robertson and Grayston Lynch.[92]

However, the increasing pace of operations, combined with the recruiting of some experienced JMWAVE personnel into the AMWORLD project, did bring new recruits into play. At least one of those individuals, Remegio Arce, had not been involved in the earlier Cuba Projects but apparently became quite trusted by Robertson. Arce was transferred from the new maritime missions into AMWORLD, and then became one of the very select cadre whom Robertson selected to go on a highly classified mission into the Congo in 1964.

Special high-performance boats were obtained, including two "ghost" mother ships which would operate out of Florida ports. Yet in what would appear to be a direct contradiction of Kennedy administration directives to move missions against Cuba offshore, the two new ships, Rex and Leda, were based out of Port Everglades and West Palm Beach, flagged as Nicaraguan and captained / crewed by Cuban volunteers. The ships carried radar, electronics, and a variety of weapons – which were stored in port and only mounted at sea. They also carried special high-speed boats to be used in the actual sabotage missions. In addition to new military missions, the Rex and Leda were also used to support routine infiltration and caching activities, missions which continued to average some dozen per month.[93]

Going beyond operational logistics, Morales himself utilized his own social network, including contacts in Guatemala, to create a cover for the new sabotage missions – which were conducted by a group newly designated as Commando Mambises. The group was entirely a creation of Morales, using Rafael Martinez Pupo, a wealthy Cuban businessman living in Guatemala, as the public face of the group. Pupo met with the media claiming a new military effort against Castro, with victories in attacks on port facilities, a metal processing plant and an air raid on a refinery. Special Group documents do reflect two of the claimed raids but it appears a third may also have been conducted using both sea and air assets – the source of the aircraft used is totally undocumented.[94]

Pupo continued to carry on a media campaign for Commando Mambises, speaking of secret bases in the Caribbean and cells inside Cuba. A September 23 report to the Special Group on two Commando Mambises raids was well received, although some security issues were mentioned. Of course, news of the raids generated a great deal of discussion within the Cuban community, especially given that none of its many leaders or groups had any knowledge of a group led by Pupo, of anyone who might be fighting with it, or of any new bases. Following oversight reviews, new missions were authorized for October and November; the first was to be synchronized with a list of JMWAVE missions which JFK had himself approved only in early October.

The JMWAVE Commando Mambises missions, operating from Florida, continued through 1963 and on into 1964, even after being exposed to the media when an attack team was ambushed by Castro forces during a mission on October 21. During that mission, infiltration personnel previously inserted into Cuba were identified and monitored by Cuban forces, which then attacked during a pick-up effort by the Rex. Two paramilitary personnel were killed, one was wounded, and four captured.

The Rex managed to flee but was tracked back to Florida, and as part of the Cuban response, its aircraft mistakenly strafed a U.S. flag bauxite freighter transiting the same coastal waters. Within days Castro had called out the U.S. involvement, identified the CIA ships and even broadcast the locations of the Florida ports from which they operated.[95] Reporters flocked to those locations and broadcast extended interviews about the comings and goings of the "ghost ships." [96] In something of a fruitless effort, JMWAVE then "sold" the ships through cut outs, repainted and relocated them, while continuing with their missions and giving Castro the opportunity to call out the United States on their follow-on missions which continued under President Johnson.

Ironically the Commando Mambises missions, launched out of Florida, continued at the same time that millions of dollars were being poured into the entirely separate and extremely deniable Artime/AMWORLD project. That project would spend heavily in establishing bases and a logistics chain in the Caribbean, launching its first boat missions only in the spring 1964.

Objectively it has to be said that during the summer of 1963, certainly by July and August, the state of clandestine military activity against Castro and Cuba can hardly be described as anything less than chaotic, regardless of how it appeared within the Cuban Coordinating Committee or the covert action oversight Special Group. JMWAVE was establishing a compartmentalized and highly secret covert mission capability, using far superior boats and weapons than deployed in previous years. Shackley and Morales had even come up with their own political cover for Commando Mambises, using Morales' connections to a Guatemalan businessman. Yet the group's missions operated from Florida ports, and the existence of the CIA ghost ships would be exposed and touted in Cuban propaganda within their first four months of operations.

We also have good reason to suspect that neither the Special Group nor the Cuban Coordinating Committee – and neither RFK nor JFK – were aware of exactly how independently JMWAVE itself had begun to operate by the summer of 1963. That is especially evident in one extremely high-risk July mission which was carried out using extensive JMWAVE support; support including operations by one of the new "ghost" mother ships. That mission appears never to have been approved by or even discussed with any of the highest-level decision makers within the Kennedy administration.

While JMWAVE Chief of Station Shackley often complained about the burden imposed by detailed mission approvals and reporting up the chain of command, in this instance none of that occurred. Approvals and reporting for what was an extremely high-risk mission (with the potential for immense political exposure) occurred only within CIA channels. There is no indication that those within the CIA chain of command brought the mission to the attention of the senior policy forums – where its sensational nature and extreme political ramifications would have certainly provoked a firestorm.

It had all begun with stories circulating months earlier, gossip within the exile community in Miami; the rumors had begun almost immediately after the compromise that resolved the missile crisis the previous fall. The rumors first appear to have come from an appearance of DRE chief Fernandez-Rocha on *The Today Show*. During his interview, Fernandez-Rocha offered details about nuclear missiles being hidden in the Yumari valley, the hills of Camaguey and at other locations inside Cuba.

He claimed that he had personally seen some of the sites where missiles had been hidden. During the following weeks and months stories of hidden Russian missiles remained in play, both in Cuban exile circles and within right-wing American political factions. Both factions promoted the idea that President Kennedy had been extremely naïve in his negotiations with the Russians – especially after Fidel Castro had effectively abrogated US/Soviet agreements to verify the removal of the missiles.

By early 1963, the stories had expanded to include the rumor that an anti-Castro resistance group (not the DRE but an unnamed and unidentified group) inside Cuba was actually sheltering Russian technicians who had defected, and who were prepared to offer concrete proof that missiles remained in Cuba. At first that story gained little traction; however, it came to be championed by John Martino, an American recently released from prison in Cuba. Martino was receiving considerable media coverage, had begun work on both a book and a record detailing his experiences in prison, and managed to gain the attention of certain conservative Florida political figures due to the "Russian technician" rumor. By that point the rumor had already been in circulation for some two to three months.

The basics of the story reached Senator James Eastland, an avowed opponent of Kennedy administration policies on Cuba. In turn Eastland took the story on to William Pawley. Pawley was famous for his early business dealings in both China and Cuba and his work with the Flying Tigers during World War II. He had served as an American ambassador in Latin American countries (Brazil and Peru) and, as a close friend of President Eisenhower, had been appointed to an ultra-select committee evaluating intelligence capabilities during the Eisenhower administration.

The "eyes only" report of that committee, which included an evaluation of the CIA, was extremely secret, strictly for Eisenhower's own use. Pawley had connections throughout the CIA and along with such political figures as Senator James Eastland was a harsh critic of Kennedy, especially in regard to the president's apparent inaction towards Cuba. Eastland made it clear to Pawley that if he could obtain information from the Russian technicians, it would be introduced to the Senate. Such a move would have been a major blow to President Kennedy's credibility, undermining confidence in his administration, and damaging his reelection efforts.

With Pawley's high-level CIA connections (Pawley was a cleared source with his own cryptonym) it was easy enough for him to take the initiative, and he pursued the matter both with Chief of Station Shackley at JMWAVE, and with Marshall Carter, Deputy CIA director. Shackley agreed to take on the mission (designated as TILT), supported by Pawley's own yacht (the Flying Tiger) and rented amphibious aircraft. The CIA also provided other assets for the mission, including radar shadowing of the overall effort by the Leda mother ship.[97] TILT was an extremely complex mission, operationally conducted under detailed JMWAVE operational protocols.

However, in a major violation of standard CIA security practices, Shackley also agreed to the participation of not only John Martino but of a group of largely unvetted Cuban volunteers, led by Eddie Perez (Bayo). Bayo (who was introduced into the mission only weeks before it launched) himself had been cleared for earlier covert Cuban infiltration missions during the Cuba Project, on the Tejuana. Following those missions, which had been carried out during February and March of 1961, Bayo was again involved with the CIA in September/October 1962. CIA records describe that involvement as a "fiasco." [98]

Related CIA documents reveal that the CIA was well aware of that previous incident in which Perez (Bayo) had tried to gain CIA support for Cuban projects, where further investigation had shown his information and claims to be highly questionable, leading to their rejection.[99] Given that history (as well as an informant evaluation of Bayo as being unreliable and providing inaccurate information) it remains quite questionable as to why Pawley was not strongly advised against any mission in which Bayo suddenly appeared as a central figure – and the only one claiming the contacts required to reach the Russian defectors inside Cuba.

In addition to issues with Bayo himself, the majority of the Cuban volunteers received only the most basic file card checks; none of them had any operational history with the CIA or JMWAVE. And they received none of the extended inquiries normally required for mission personnel background nor any counter intelligence checks.[100] As with much of the TILT mission, JMWAVE appears to have accepted Pawley's assurances, including his statement that all the men involved would be his own employees.

What is even more striking is that Shackley, operations chief Morales and DDP Marshall Carter also agreed to an arrangement which allowed a *LIFE Magazine* representative (Richard Billings) and a photo journalist to accompany and film the mission. Filming missions using CIA assets including mission specialists was strictly prohibited. And TILT included several officers and CIA employees who were participating in the mission, including Rip Robertson and Tony Sforza (crypt Oliver Fortson aka alias Max de Cordova).

Surprisingly we actually find documents containing the correspondence between Marshall Carter and William Pawley, relating Carter's dialogue with George P. Hunt, the *LIFE* Magazine managing editor. Based in that correspondence, it appears that CIA approval for the coverage was agreed to on nothing more than demands from Martino and the Cubans involved. The only rules were that the CIA officers were not to be identified by name, and while *LIFE* was allowed to carry the story of the mission the CIA was not to be mentioned in any fashion.101 TILT documents indicate Pawley was given total control over release of the story to the public via *LIFE,* although JMWAVE did insist on taking physical control over the Soviets.[102]

In the end, the TILT mission (with operations oversight by Moore and Morales) did insert a boatful of heavily armed anti-Castro fighters into Cuba. Yet even at the start of the mission, the CIA officers involved questioned the fact that the Cubans were unknown to them, and that neither the weapons nor number of personnel were consistent with simply contacting and bringing out Russian technicians. The CIA officers were advised only when at sea that several of the men planned to stay in Cuba. It was also noted in the after-action reports that there had been no preliminary work done to verify the Russian defector story via prior infiltrations or contacts.

At the time of the actual mission in July, the Russian missile story was a good six months old and the CIA did have assets inside Cuba

– but no further confirmation had been provided other than in relatively last-minute assurances from Perez (Bayo). Bayo had been unwilling (or unable) to even share the identity of the group supposedly holding the Russians. The officers' after-action reports also note that the Cubans had seemed to be particularly uninterested in any of the briefings and training on recovery procedures.[103]

When no further contact was made with the group after it was sent off from the mission ship towards Cuba, all the craft involved returned to Florida. The final CIA assessment was that the whole thing had been a scam, with the exiles feeding a line to all involved simply to get a very well-equipped and armed team into Cuba for military action.[104] A review of the weapons provided for the mission, which included explosives and grenades, certainly suggests that it was something far more than a recovery mission for Russian technicians – something that would seemingly have been obvious to the CIA officers involved.

In fact, the official follow-on assessment was that the team was so heavily armed and the small rubber boat so full of people that it most likely swamped on its way into the beach, encumbered by ammo belts and weapons – the Cubans might not even have made it to shore. Other than admitting that it had been fooled by the Cubans, the final reports are also interesting in that they note the mission itself did have a positive result – from a political perspective.

Shackley himself noted that people like Pawley, political figures such as J. G. Sourwine, and even Senator Eastland himself would be impressed by how responsive the CIA had been, and how willing it was to work outside the box, even to take unusual risks. He also thought that *LIFE* magazine and the Luce media outlets were impressed and might treat the CIA more favorably in their media coverage.[105]

Certainly the total violation of security protocols for the TILT mission does reflect "out of the box" behavior, as does the unique agreement with *LIFE* for a journalist and photographer to record the mission – and the approval for publication of the mission itself. The fact that the mission was actually carried out more as a political and publicity effort is further reflected in the large quantity of photographs, including ones showing CIA assets. Those photographs were taken during the mission and never vetted by the CIA. They were left in the possession of the private photographer sent on the mission – only to appear years later in print as part of a *Soldier of Fortune* magazine article on the CIA mission, which itself was also described in great detail in the accompanying text.[106]

Documents reveal that the control and censorship of the photographs was left entirely to Pawley to censor, and that the agreement for publication of material on the mission was left in place at the end of the mission.[107] That was confirmed in a follow-on call directly from Pawley to the *LIFE* magazine managing editor – although *LIFE* apparently determined not to publish its own story on the TILT effort.

At the same time that the TILT mission launched, soon to be followed by the JMWAVE Commando Mambises operations, major U.S. government actions continued to quash any Cuban exile missions against Cuba – either from new groups or those with well-established networks inside Cuba, such as the DRE. DRE members were told to cease any independent military operations. Those interested in such things should join Artime's MRR group (being used as a cover for the new AMWORLD project) and join Artime in new MRR camps. Artime was also actively describing his new effort in a variety of his media appearances, including talking of new camps in locations including Nicaragua.

Artime also began actively recruiting volunteers by late summer; he was even allowed to recruit on U.S. military installations. As a cover story for the project, Artime was repeatedly forced to denounce the United States, claiming that it had deserted the effort against Castro and that the anti-Castro community was being forced to turn to new supporters in Europe and Central America. The cover story was even used in recruiting personnel for the project, both in public appearances and at military bases where Cubans had been allowed into Army and Air Force training programs.

There is little doubt that those listening to Artime would have been led to believe that the Kennedy administration had simply walked away from Kennedy's promise to Brigade 2506 at the Orange Bowl, instead choosing to honor the new non-invasion agreement with the Soviets. Such views were reinforced by increasing efforts by all government agencies to forcefully block any independent military actions against Cuba. That effort included the Coast Guard, Immigration and Naturalization and the FBI as well as local police forces and military services – there were new orders to block all weapons sales to anti-Castro groups and interdict any mission originating in the United States.

Given that most of the exile groups had headquarters in Miami, some 600 federal agents were deployed in Florida to interdict weapons purchases and military missions. That new level of pressure, combined with the administration crackdown on missions and weapons buys, gave the general Cuban exile community reason to believe they and their cause were indeed being deserted. The feeling of apparent abandonment was illustrated in the breakdown in relations between the U.S. government and the Cuban Revolutionary Council (the leadership group which the CIA had organized prior the landings of Brigade 2506). In the beginning the CRC has been expected to declare itself as a government in exile and facilitate the formation of a new Cuban government after the ouster of the Castro regime.

Despite the disaster at the Bay of Pigs, the CRC had remained the central voice for the numerous revolutionary groups. But as early as April 1963 its chairman, Miro Cardona, had resigned – declaring that President Kennedy had chosen a path of peaceful coexistence with Castro and abandoned efforts to oust his regime.[108] In May, government funds were cut from the CRC, and a series of false announcements about its new plans for military action damaged its credibility; its new head resigned and his place was taken by Antonio de Varona. Varona himself stayed with the CRC for only a few months, ultimately departing Miami in early 1964 for New York City, where he became a car salesman. The CRC disintegrated as an organization at that point, leaving individual groups to pursue their own efforts.

Despite the Cuban community's perceptions, the Kennedy administration was actually, if extremely secretly, continuing and expanding its efforts against Castro as of the summer of 1963. Those efforts included new initiatives such as the creation of a deniable off-shore military force (AMWORLD), an effort to facilitate a coup against Castro by dissident Cuban political and military figures (AMTRUNK) – not to mention JMWAVE's Commando Mambises and its newly approved sabotage missions. Yet while the Cuba Committee and the administration as a whole was still committed to Castro's ouster, such activities were all covert, highly secret, compartmentalized, and most definitely not communicated to the public or even to the many independent anti-Castro groups not being recruited into AMWORLD.

Left to their own devices, the Cuban community felt financially abandoned, with a growing and intense competition between groups for private funding. One of the newest efforts was organized out of Chicago, headed by Paulino Sierra and designated as the JCGE, more often referred to as simply the Junta. Sierra's Junta was never able to attract a significant following among existing exile groups, even though it did raise and distribute money to a few of them. In the end it was forced to use former INTERPEN members just to transport its purchases to Florida. Conservative in its politics, the Junta claimed to be focused on returning Carlos Prio to the presidency of Cuba.

In reality its existence was largely based around the personal outreach and business contacts of Sierra himself. When he began to encounter financial difficulties, the Junta faded away within months, gone from the scene by the end of 1963. While the Junta remained largely peripheral to the exile scene, with some cash in hand it had managed to insert itself into weapons buying in the Chicago area, promising support and supplies for groups including the DRE. For reference, background and a chronology of Junta activities is cited in an extended end note.[109]

The year 1963 also saw the DRE enter into a protracted series of activities intended to maintain its independence. There were ongoing efforts to locate new sources of weapons and explosives as well as to locate new bases for operations, preferably outside the United States. In all of this, the DRE retained the broadest reach within American exile communities, and continued to pursue independent military actions (even using members who had either worked for the CIA or remained active in CIA projects). It was the DRE activities – and its visibility – which led to it being approached by someone with a history of interest in Cuba, former Marine Lee Harvey Oswald.

Among all the more established or well-known groups – MRR, JURE, Alpha 66/Commandos L, and MDC, it was the DRE's leaders and activists who stand out as increasingly attempting to initiate independent military action during 1963. DRE itself was still being actively supported by the CIA through much of 1963, with both military (David Morales) and political case officers (George Joannides and William Kent) assigned to it.

DRE also remained one of the most broadly-based organizations, years after it had begun as one of the revolutionary groups fighting against Batista. The DRE had formed as a spinoff of the Federation of University Students, originally led by Jose Antonio Echeverria. One of its early leaders was Juan Manuel Salvat (crypt AMHINT-2). The DRE had been primarily active in the Cuban cities, especially Havana.

DRE had also placed representatives in the United States throughout the revolutionary struggle, engaged in weapons sourcing and smuggling as well as fund raising. By 1958 DRE had managed to smuggle at least one cache of weapons into Havana, only to have a safehouse raided by Havana police, with the loss of the entire cache. During the Batista revolution DRE had largely followed the strategy of "hitting at the top", with the goal of assassinating Batista and his senior officials to force out his regime.[110] Many of the earliest recruits for the CIA's Cuba Project had come from the DRE.

Victor Espinosa Hernandez was one example of such a committed DRE activist. Victor Hernandez was the son of a wealthy Cuban family (ranching and agriculture). As a young man he had circulated within the Havana casinos, becoming friends with figures such as Mike McLaney and Norman Rothman, and their families. As a university student he had also become friends with Jose Echeverria and was one of the earliest recruits for the DRE's assassination activities. At the age of 20, Hernandez joined one of the four DRE assassination teams targeting Batista regime leaders; his team drew first blood, killing their target within ten days.[111]

Following that successful murder, Hernandez managed to leave Cuba, first taking refuge with Mike McLaney in Miami and then traveling to New York, where his family had long-time social and financial connections. Upon hearing of the new CIA project, he became one of the earliest volunteers, training under Carl Jenkins and selected for advance training at Belle Chase and finally for infiltration missions out of Florida. Frustrated by a lack of organization in his missions, he dropped out of JMWAVE boat penetrations, and by the summer of 1963 had become one of many DRE members simply looking for some way to pursue military action against Castro.

As a whole the DRE's experience with the CIA reflected a similar level of mistrust in the agency and its personnel. Acting on its own, the DRE had put infiltration teams into Cuba as early as 1960, and several CIA Cuba Project missions had attempted to deliver weapons and supplies to DRE teams; virtually all failed. Never totally trusting the CIA after its losses of men and leaders during the Cuba Project, the DRE continually rerouted CIA funding to military activities, even as the CIA itself was attempting to focus the DRE solely on propaganda activities.[112]

Because of its dedication, and its willingness to act independently, the DRE remained able to solicit at least limited funding from a variety of non-CIA sources, ranging from the old Havana casino crowd (such as Mike McLaney in Miami) to well-placed (and wealthy) anti-communist figures including William Pawley and the family of Henry Luce (publisher of the *TIME/LIFE* family of magazines). Its military members also maintained their links to weapons suppliers such as Sam Benton in the Miami area, as well as other gun and explosives dealers from Chicago to Dallas.

During 1962/1963 many of the original and more action-oriented DRE members were left to search for opportunities to fight against Castro. There was considerable shifting among the groups, depending on which had raised enough money to prepare or even attempt actual missions into Cuba. CIA documents reveal that DRE members and representatives even attended Alpha 66 meetings.[113] Alpha 66 itself had formed outside the United States, in Puerto Rico, and launched its missions from its base there. DRE leaders also continued their efforts to obtain weapons and explosives, either from underworld sources or from right-wing arms dealers who also catered to extremist groups such as the Minutemen.

Richard Lauchli, operating out of Illinois, was one of the long-term suppliers to independent paramilitary groups of any form. Because of his history of sales of explosives and weapons, Lauchli had been monitored by both the FBI and the ATF for almost a decade. The Bureau had also developed a number of informants who provided information on his ongoing and expanding business in sales of both weapons and explosives.[114] In some instances the sources were members of particular Cuban exile groups – often informing on the activities of other groups.

The DRE were certainly among Lauchli's most ambitious customers. As early as November 1962, Marton Marua (AMBARB-70) of Miami gave Lauchli an order for 1,000 blasting caps as well as a shopping list for other weapons and C4 explosives (the list included mortars, machine guns, bazookas, and cannons). Lauchli's associate Thomas Mosley served as a regular FBI informant on Lauchli's sales, including Salazar's weapons-shopping for DRE.[115]

In this particular instance, the FBI learned details of the pickup and transport for the blasting caps from an informant within another exile group, Jose Cardoso of the ECLA (Christian Anticommunist

Army). He related the information that Jorgc Martin Salazar (of Bellwood, Illinois) and Marua had picked up the blasting caps and planned to transport them to Miami; the source of the money for the blasting caps was not identified. although Marua stated the funds had apparently come from the Chicago area.[116] During the summer of 1962, Salazar moved from the Chicago area to Dallas, Texas and almost immediately became involved in more efforts to buy weapons and explosives for exile group military activities.

The DRE's continuing interest in military missions and its assertive public posture against U.S. restrictions brought them under continuing scrutiny by the FBI, and as early as March/April 1963 the FBI was monitoring possible preparations for DRE boat missions against Cuba, to be launched out of Miami.[117] That spring the independent attitude of the DRE became highly visible in a leaflet circulated in Miami, headlined as a "Declaration of the DRE." The handbill called out American obstruction of their efforts to overthrow Castro, stated that the United States had deserted them, asserted their right as Cuban patriots to take any measures necessary to obtain freedom for Cuba, and expressed a determination to continue the fight against Castro on their own.[118]

During 1963 the DRE's political leadership (which along with a select number of its military personnel remained on the CIA payroll) became focused on establishing an offshore military capability – both through independent action and with a new pitch for CIA support. It appears that they realized they were actually in competition with Artime's MRR group (being used as a cover for AMWORLD), which was touting its own efforts to establish new camps in Nicaragua.

By summer the ongoing competition between the various exile groups added to the overall chaos among the Cuban community. It also led to anomalies such as the June 1963 creation of a transit training camp outside New Orleans. Ostensibly the camp was to train volunteers from the Christian Democrat (MDC) group who would go on to Nicaragua to join in new missions against Cuba. As it turned out, some twenty volunteers arrived outside New Orleans, only to find a run-down house with no operating utilities – making it livable was their first order of business.[119]

Afterwards their only "training" was physical training; three or four old WWII rifles were available but with no ammunition. The rifles were never fired. The MDC camp operated for about four or five weeks before an FBI raid on another set of buildings some distance away led to a rapid evacuation – with the volunteers quickly put on a bus back to Miami.

The only contact the men had was with an American living in New Orleans, Ricardo Davis, who had helped organize the whole thing and brought food to the camp on occasion.[120] Davis had formerly been associated with Gerry Hemming, Frank Sturgis and the short-lived INTERPEN effort. Apparently he had promised the MDC major financial backing for the new training camp, none of which had never appeared.

In the meantime, DRE associates continued to do business with Lauchli – during the summer of 1963 buying and transporting explosives from Chicago to the New Orleans area. In July Victor Espinosa Hernandez purchased 2,400 pounds of dynamite and bomb casings and transported it to the McClaney farm (Mike McClaney's brother owned the property; he was a New Orleans resident) outside New Orleans, where the FBI seized the materials in a July 31 raid (the raid was based on an informant tip out of Miami).[121]

That particular purchase – and the plan for using the explosives in a bombing mission – is of considerable interest given the participants. The fact that it involved New Orleans and occurred not far from the MDC transit camp has confused a good deal of JFK research over the years (which tended to blur the two together). But what is actually most important about the explosives purchase out of Illinois is that it revealed a series of independent activities by DRE members which illustrate exactly how chaotic the anti-Castro scene was becoming by the summer of 1963.

With the reduction and changes in JMWAVE maritime missions during 1962/63, a number of the former Cuban volunteers (including some of the earliest who had gone into Cuba Project training in Panama and Guatemala) had either left JMWAVE operations or been put on inactive status. Some of them remained on the DRE military reserve list, but the CIA had begun actively discouraging DRE missions as well. All of which left some of the most activist and well-trained paramilitary activists at loose ends. By summer several of those individuals, who had originally trained under Carl Jenkins and served under either Robertson or Lynch, were essentially on their own.

In what turned out to be a long and complex story (covered in detailed in the citation noted here),[122] an offer for action and a new effort against the Castro regime came from Victor Hernandez's friend Mike McLaney. McLaney offered money to finance a new series of bombing missions against Cuba, something which could bring major new publicity to the anti-Castro effort. In turn, Victor Hernandez recruited several of his associates, a combination of DRE and MRR members, all with Cuba Project experience and most with CIA missions on their records. Their efforts were facilitated by an associate of McLaney, Sam Benton. Benton was a well-established "broker" in such activities, with the connections which would provide access to aircraft, explosives and the other necessities for the missions. He had previously been involved with similar schemes with American "adventurers" including Roy Hargraves and others from the INTERPEN association.

Given the amount of federal government focus on Miami, and the number of personnel assigned to interdict Cuban exile military missions, it is no surprise that the first bombing mission was exposed, and those involved – including both Victor and Carlos Hernandez – were cited, given warnings and travel restrictions (something common among the exiles in Miami at the time, with such restrictions generally ignored).

In response, a second effort (July 1963) was conceived, with preparation to occur far away from Miami and the intense scrutiny occurring there. That effort was complex, with explosives for bombs obtained from a dealer in Illinois, materials for bomb casings and detonators ordered from firms on the East Coast and aircraft apparently sourced out of Texas. The list of participants included a pilot (Soto) on leave from flying for the CIA in highly covert air actions in the Congo and a bomb specialist (Acelo Pedroso). The assembly point was a country residence owned by McLaney's brother in a very rural area outside New Orleans. Matters proceeded according to plan, with Victor Hernandez picking up the explosives using rental cars and trailers (Victor rented a station wagon and trailer in St. Louis) and the other participants (Carlos Hernandez / Batea, Soto and Acelo Pedroso) traveling by car to New Orleans.

Upon examination, Pedroso advised the group that the materials brought for the project were totally unsuitable for aerial bombs. And with his return to Miami, word of the effort circulated, eventually reported to the FBI. The result was an investigation by the New Orleans field office, a raid on the McLaney property, confiscation of the materials, and arrests.

During FBI interviews Pedroso related that he had seen two planes, which he believed to be B-26 Marauder medium bombers. The FBI report states it failed to locate any aircraft in the area. A July 19 search report suggested that the only location which might have served for landing the aircraft fitting Pedroso's description was a municipal airport at Houma, La. That report also notes that the U-Haul trailer actually contained the equipment needed to make live bombs of some sort. Acelo told the FBI that he had been told the bombing effort was a DRE project. In further conversation he stated the aircraft to be used were actually housed outside Louisiana, perhaps in Houston. He had been told they would be flown in and loaded when the bombs were ready. When the bombs were available the planes would not remain on the Louisiana airfield for more than four or five hours before departing on the mission.[123]

All in all, it was a relatively sophisticated operation, with multiple people covertly traveling to New Orleans from a variety of locations; the FBI report delineates the use of aliases, cut outs and other tradecraft by those involved. There was actually no indication of the project until after it was virtually complete and a technical assessment deemed the materials not useful for aerial bombs. Only a leak after the fact led to an extensive FBI investigation out of both the Miami and New Orleans offices. Yet if the plan had worked, new bombing missions would certainly have had an impact similar to or greater than the earlier, highly covered DRE boat raids.

Instead, within a month, during August 1963, the AMWORLD project had begun recruiting, and new opportunities were opening up – word was circulating more broadly about new Artime camps in Nicaragua; CIA officers would begin telling DRE leaders that their only option for military action was to have their people join Artime's effort.[124] There was some response to that, but by the end of the year only a dozen actual DRE members had joined the Artime project, and certain DRE leaders remained committed to pursuing their own plans and efforts.[125]

In contrast, during the next few months individuals now well-known from earlier sections of this work (the Cuba Project, JMWAVE maritime missions and even Commando Mambises) would begin to show up within the MRR and assume key positions in AMWORLD.[126] At that point, a number of them would essentially "go black", recruited for AMWORLD but in the process of being assigned new identities, given new training and awaiting the extremely detailed processing which would take them outside the United States, into the highly classified and autonomous offshore operations of AMWORLD. Most are literally untraceable during the fall and early winter. Only in January and February of 1964 do they begin to appear at Artime's offshore bases and camps in the Caribbean.

While the new Cuba Coordinating Committee and JMWAVE projects were kept as secret as possible, and as broad government efforts continued to suppress exile group missions, there was some news in the Cuban community in the summer of 1963 – news from New Orleans that quickly passed along the social networks to Miami and even Dallas, Texas.

Enter Lee Oswald

Walking a Tightrope

With his early interest in the revolution against Batista and his contacts with the Cuban Consulate in Los Angeles previously noted, it is perhaps not surprising to find Lee Oswald entering into Cuban affairs in 1963, first with an initial approach to the Fair Play for Cuba Committee (FPCC) in March while in Dallas, and then becoming more visibly active in pro-Cuba activities in New Orleans that summer.[127] During that period, the FBI had access to all of Oswald's correspondence with the FPCC. The FBI had its own source inside the group's office, which it used to copy both correspondence and the FPCC's membership and mailing lists. The FBI routinely prepared intelligence updates on the FPCC and copied the CIA on much of that information.

Earlier, during the period of October 1962 up to March 1963 (well before his first letter to the FPCC), Oswald and his wife Marina had been covertly checked out by the CIA's Domestic Contacts section, via a contact by Dallas CIA officer J. Walton Moore with George de Mohrenschildt.[128] De Mohrenschildt was socially networked to many individuals within the Russian community in Dallas, and provided a cover for monitoring Oswald following his return to Texas. Moore had visited with de Mohrenschildt prior to the Oswalds' arrival, and advised him that a former Marine who had worked at an electronics factory in Minsk was returning to the U.S. with a Russian wife – and the CIA had an "interest" in him.

Encouraged by de Mohrenschildt, Oswald wrote an extended memoire of his time in Russia and particularly his experiences in Minsk. Oswald actually had the memoire typed, and provided a copy to de Mohrenschildt. The memoire contains detailed observations on a number of elements of general military interest as well as considerable detail on the "Minsk Radio and Television Plant" –

including plant production numbers, staffing by job position, male/female worker breakdown, as well as additional descriptions of the facility and its operational logistics. All in all, the memoire served quite admirably as an intelligence debrief of Oswald – without the need for any direct contact with the CIA.[129]

Beyond that, Oswald's remarks captured a number of very negative personal feelings which he had developed towards the Soviet Union, as well as to the Communist Party of the United States.[130]

"The Communist Party of the United States has betrayed itself! It has turned itself into a traditional lever of a foreign power to overthrow the government of the United States, not in the name of freedom or high ideals, but in servile conformity to the wishes of the Soviet Union....The Soviets have committed crimes unsurpassed...imprisonment of their own peoples [sic]....mass extermination....The Communist movement of the United States has turned itself into a "valuable gold coin" of the Kremlin. It has failed to denounce any actions of the Soviet government when similar actions of the United States bring pious protests. [I have] many personal reasons to know and therefore hate and mistrust communism."

Oswald's personal feelings in 1962 are in dramatic contrast to his actions and written communications of the following year. They are totally opposite from the language and attitudes found in Oswald's letters to CPUSA in late September and early October 1963. Something seminal occurred with regard to Lee Oswald early in 1963; it would lead to a far different image for Oswald than we find in his memoire, prepared only months earlier. The memoire itself is actually quite consistent with Oswald's diary writings about his activities while in Russia – and totally unlike many aspects of his 1963 activities.

The range of the possible associations between Lee Oswald and various elements of the American intelligence community is far beyond the scope of this work. In order to retain a focus on the JFK conspiracy, this discussion will examine only those aspects which apply to Cuban affairs – and the pro-Castro Oswald "image" which developed in New Orleans. That "image" will be discussed in regard to its probable use in a variety of intelligence activities, as well as its possible use by the conspiracy as a "poison pill" – a form of insurance which ensured that both the CIA and FBI would withhold key information from the official inquiries rather than expose their own prior knowledge of Lee Oswald.

In regard to Oswald's own thoughts, his actions in New Orleans may not have been as inconsistent as they appear. There is good reason to accept that he was genuinely interested in the populist and socialist elements of the Cuban revolution, and that his actions in both contacting anti-Castro Cubans and then publicly supporting Cuba and its revolution were not as bipolar as they seem. Additional thoughts and commentary related to Lee in 1963 may be found in the end note cited here.[131]

As noted above, Lee Oswald was already engaged with the FPCC as a pro-Cuba/Castro supporter when he made his first contact with the local Cuban community in New Orleans – a contact with its most active anti-Castro element. That much-discussed contact began with an offer to buy "bonds" which the DRE had been selling. Because the group's leader, Carlos Bringuier, had just been notified that such sales were illegal, he immediately suspected Oswald of being involved in some sort of police or FBI effort to trap him into an illegal act.

Oswald's offer of financial support for the anti-Castro effort was immediately rejected. When he was told the bonds were no longer being sold, he offered his services as a military trainer, based on his Marine experience. Bringuier referred him to the DRE's military wing, but in the interim – concerned that he might be some sort of provocateur - sent one of his own associates (Carlos Quiroga) to contact Oswald, presenting himself as a Castro supporter in order to test Oswald's true affiliations.[132]

Oswald's landlady at the time was later interviewed and described seeing Quiroga visit Oswald, carrying what appeared to be a stack of leaflets – very possibly Fair Play for Cuba leaflets. Oswald can be shown to have requested materials from the FPCC itself, however an approach by Quiroga with FPCC materials in hand would certainly have been consistent with the visit being a test of Oswald's true affiliations.

Oswald's approach to the DRE, and Bringuier's response, would have been reported to DRE headquarters in Miami as a standard practice, a report which would also have been copied to the DRE's CIA case officer. That was important since DRE was still being funded by the CIA on a monthly basis, to collect and report intelligence (in particular on potential Castro intelligence activities), on suspected double agents, and on anything which should be considered for propaganda purposes – the primary duty assigned to DRE as of 1963.

In that regard, two CIA case officers - George Joannides and William Kent – are known to have been directly in contact with and receiving reports from the DRE organization in 1963. Both men worked DRE from Miami, but documents also show that each of them had also resided in, and worked from, New Orleans for periods of time. Kent appears to have spent time in New Orleans during the summer when Oswald made his approach to the DRE. While we know a bit about the DRE/CIA connection in 1963 (primarily due to the diligent research and legal actions of Jefferson Morley), as of this writing almost six decades later, it has been impossible to obtain some sixteen key documents relating to CIA case officer communications with the group.

Oswald's Uses

The CIA knowingly and continuously shielded elements of the Oswald/DRE contacts from all Congressional inquiries (including the DRE personal meetings with and reports to SAS staff such as Joannides and Kent). Decades later the CIA was willing to go to court to protect DRE files relating to Joannides, even in the 21st century. It has only been in recent years that the extreme degree of CIA stonewalling over the DRE and Oswald has become a matter of public attention, even in Miami.[133]

Fortunately, based on Jefferson Morley's work – which included numerous interviews with actual DRE members – and that of other researchers, we now have a much fuller story of the extent to which Lee Oswald was known within the Cuban exile community following his summer in New Orleans, a story which in itself gives the lie to the official view of Oswald as a virtually unknown "lone nut."

To fully appreciate Oswald's summer 1963 encounter with the DRE, it's important to understand that the CIA maintained its relationship with the DRE largely due to the fact that DRE had by far the largest anti-Castro organization, not only inside Cuba but extending across Latin America. Because of the youth of many of its members and its roots within the university community, the DRE also continued to participate in international youth conferences – providing a perfect cover for the CIA to conduct political action in those venues.[134]

As previously noted, just prior to his activities in the independent DRE bombing projects of 1963, CIA asset Carlos Hernandez had attended a major youth conference in Helsinki, Finland. Earlier, Hernandez had participated in the high profile 1962 DRE mission into Cuba, a mission which personally included the leaders of DRE (Salvat and Borja). During both 1962 and 1963, DRE continued to demonstrate its influence by publishing newspapers which were often cited on the Senate floor, and it maintained branches throughout both the United States and Latin America.

Given its reach and potential, there is no surprise in finding that the CIA assigned DRE case officers to make the most of its capabilities in communications and propaganda. David Phillips had initially pursued propaganda activities with the DRE during the 1960/61 Cuba Project, assisted by William Kent at Miami Station. During the interregnum of 1962, Ross Crozier served as the DRE case officer.

In early 1963, Crozier was replaced by George Joannides (pseudonym Newby) – deputy chief of psychological warfare operations against the Castro government. His prior duties had involved working against communist influence in Greece and Libya. The appointment also elevated the level of the CIA relationship with the DRE, since Joannides reported directly to JMWAVE Station Chief Shackley (pseudonym Reuteman) and Deputy Chief of Station Moore. Moore prepared performance reviews for SAS staff stationed at the Miami office even though Joannides' own designated supervisor was SAS propaganda Chief William Kent (cover name Doug Gupton and pseudonym Robert Trouchard).[135] It has to be noted that the management structure between SAS and JMWAVE was exceptionally convoluted (much as the earlier Cuba Project had been), making compartmentalization of information at the Miami base challenging at best.

Joannides himself chose to establish a personal relationship with the DRE, meeting with DRE leader Fernandez-Rocha every couple of weeks and sometimes as many as three times a week.[136] Yet regardless of such personal engagement, there was a continual conflict between CIA and DRE agendas – well described to Morley by DRE military leader Manual Salvat. Salvat was adamant that DRE was simply not going to take any orders from either the CIA or the United States as to their military activities. And as noted previously, during 1963 DRE military leaders such as 'Chilo' Borja and Manuel Salvat had become increasingly frustrated and bitter about the new Kennedy administration restraints.

In interviewing individuals willing to speak on the subject, Morley found that by the summer of 1963 attitudes inside the DRE were "extremely bitter." When talking with SAS officer Ross Crozier, he was given the impression that attitudes inside the DRE towards JFK were "scarcely less hostile" to the president than to Castro. Even in official JMWAVE memos to headquarters, station chief Shackley described the attitude within the DRE for administration policy makers as nothing less than sheer "contempt."

That contempt led to action, to the decision to proceed with plans to strike a major blow against Cuba by the end of 1963, a plan endorsed by Salvat and to be implemented by the DRE's military section, using boats and weapons cached at a base on Catalina Island, off the southern coast of the Dominican Republic. Planning and preparations for that effort would carry on during the second half of 1963; however, during July DRE leaders such as Salvat and Borja also began to receive messages on another matter from the DRE's delegate in New Orleans, Carlos Bringuier.

Bringuier was seeking direction on what to do about a former Marine named Oswald, who had showed up at the local DRE office on August 5, offering to buy DRE bonds and to help with military training. According to Borja, the response was to engage with Oswald, to test him and if necessary expose him if he was not a true anti-Castro activist. Over the course of the next few weeks, Bringuier would do just that, and continue advising DRE headquarters and its leaders of his actions.

Bringuier would later testify that one of the ways he tested Oswald was to persuade an associate to visit him and determine Oswald's true intentions – was Oswald anti-Castro or pro-Castro? Had he been trying to somehow infiltrate the DRE or was he actually trying to promote the Fair Play for Cuba Committee – for which he had begun to pass out leaflets and soliciting recruits?

Of course, true allegiances within the Cuban exile community were sometimes unclear – in 1961 Quiroga himself had been suspected of being a Castro supporter. Quiroga was monitored by the CIA as being pro-Castro, however, based on their findings they revised their opinion and then considered recruiting him during 1962.[137]

Later, District Attorney Garrison would investigate Quiroga and conduct a polygraph examination related to his knowledge of a conspiracy against JFK – Quiroga challenged its findings, which had suggested he was concealing information. Among other things, the examination had found him repeatedly lying on several subjects, including Oswald's association with individuals he refused to acknowledge or name.

What Quiroga really knew about Oswald or about a conspiracy remains uncertain. All that can surely be said is that following the assassination, he would be among many in New Orleans and Miami going to the FBI and the media with information positioning Oswald as a Castro agent – stating Oswald had boasted to him that in any conflict he would support Castro over the United States.

Regardless of all the machinations and obfuscation in play – by DRE, by the CIA, or by both - by the end of August the name Lee Oswald was well-known inside the DRE and among Cuban exiles, not just in New Orleans but from Miami to Dallas. Oswald had been in public confrontations supporting Cuba, televised on local news channels. He had been in radio debates with Bringuier, defending socialism and Marxism and the Castro regime. Sections of those radio debates had even been compiled into a propaganda record, warning of the influence of the FPCC, prepared for distribution across Latin America by the Information Council of the Americas (almost certainly a CIA propaganda outlet).

Bringuier had kept Jose Lanuza, in charge of all DRE's North American chapters, informed about Oswald's activities, and a considerable file on Oswald was accumulated at DRE headquarters in Miami – the DRE even provided background information on Oswald and his time in the Soviet Union to Bringuier for the radio debate. Following the debate, Bringuier made sure that articles on the broadcast were sent to DRE headquarters, as well as tapes of the interview itself.

In turn, DRE headquarters issued a press release calling on the U.S. Congress to investigate Oswald and the FPCC – versions of that release were also issued by five other exile organizations including Alpha 66. The DRE leadership was highly supportive; one of its military leaders, Chilo Borja, told Jefferson Morley that the CIA had most definitely been advised of the DRE actions against Oswald in New Orleans – he described it as the sort of action that would bring them credit with the CIA; it was the sort of thing they were given money to do.[138] Of course, we should know much more than just that. Morley's investigative work quite plainly shows that relevant CIA records are being withheld (that has been proven in Morley's extended legal efforts) and that others may either be missing or intentionally destroyed.[139]

Oswald's visibility to the DRE and the CIA (not to mention the FBI) in New Orleans has numerous implications. Joannides himself offered no remarks concerning Oswald and neither did Chief of Station Shackley. Others, including DCS Moore and SAS counter intelligence officers and political action staff, are also absent from the record in regard to their knowledge of Oswald.

It was only decades later that Joannides' supervisor William Kent (crypt Trouchard)[140] gave the most accurate and honest answer on the subject to his daughter.

Kent was an alumnus of the Cuba Project, stationed at the Miami station in 1960/61 and then assigned as head of the re-designated JMWAVE office's psychological warfare effort before Joannides took over that position in August 1963. A Cuba Project "old timer" like Phillips or Morales, Kent was quite familiar with the activities of the DRE. When interviewed by Jefferson Morley, Kent's daughter recalled asking her father about Lee Oswald. His only response was that Oswald had been a "*useful idiot.*" When asked who killed JFK, his response was *"It's better you don't know."* [141]

Regardless of knowledge pertaining to Oswald within SAS staff and at the JMWAVE office, one point that emerges from his time in New Orleans and his engagement with the DRE is that Lee Oswald was not an unknown. He had appeared in press releases issued by half a dozen of the major exile groups, and had been a topic of extensive discussion and interest in that community during August of 1963 – so much so that even in Dallas his name and activities had been communicated to individuals with ties to New Orleans. Sylvia Odio remarked that her uncle in New Orleans (Augustine Guitart) had discussed Oswald and his highly visible efforts in support of the

Castro regime with her. Guitart himself had personally attended, along with Bringuier, the court hearing in which Oswald faced charges related to a confrontation with DRE members while leafletting for the FPCC.

By September 1963, Oswald had become a perfect figure to be used by anyone wishing to spread concern about the influence of Fidel Castro or to cast blame on the Cuban regime, whether for propaganda purposes – or something more intense.

People in Motion – Fall 1963

The preceding material provides an overview of Cuban affairs under both the Eisenhower and Kennedy administrations, as well as the view from inside the anti-Castro, Cuban exile community as it had evolved by fall 1963. Beyond that, it introduces names and connections that become important in considering the sources I have found credible as to actual remarks about a conspiracy to attack President Kennedy.

As of fall 1963, Cuban affairs as a whole can only be described as being in a state of chaos, with radically diverse actors and agendas involving the Cuban Coordinating Committee, new CIA Special Affairs Staff projects, ongoing Miami Station maritime missions, Cuban expatriate frustration and independent anti-Castro actions. A broad variety of secret tracks were being pursued – involving the CIA, the Department of Defense, the Joint Chief's Special Activities (SACSA) staff and State Department pursuit of the first hints of possible negotiations with Castro himself.

Simply following who was doing what, where and when becomes a challenge. The following chronology and commentary related to people's movements and activities during this key period will set the stage for examining the emergence of the evolving threat to President Kennedy.

August 28: Lee Oswald wrote to the Communist Party of the USA (CPUSA) about his plans to relocate to the Baltimore/Washington D.C. area and asked for advice on whether or not he should go "underground." Oswald's letters were intercepted and copied to the FBI.

August 31: Oswald wrote to *The Worker* newspaper and discussed his planned move to the Washington area; he offered his services in photography and related work.

September 1: Oswald wrote to both the Communist Party USA (CPUSA) and the Socialist Workers Party (SWP) on his pending move (the two organizations were diametrically opposed in their political views). As noted previously, Oswald himself had earlier written, in a personal memoire, that he detested the CPUSA, viewing it as a tool of Russian nationalist geopolitical policy. He expressed the view that Russia was simply using global communist parties as vehicles for its own purposes.

In New Orleans an independent witness, present while a pregnant Marina Oswald was packing to go to Dallas and move in with Ruth Paine, reported Oswald talking of going to Washington. When asked the reason for the move he offered no real reason, but did talk about getting a gun. The FBI appears to have known of Oswald's planned move (which it should have, based on his CPUSA correspondence; all CPUSA mail was monitored). In the earliest FBI post-assassination interviews with his wife Marina, she was questioned as to her knowledge of Oswald's travel to both Washington D.C and Mexico City.

August – September

Manual Artime began to bring the first AMWORLD recruits into the project, Carlos Hernandez in September, Antonio Soto in October and Felix Rodriquez only by November. Felix Rodriquez officially did not come on board earlier due to an "illness" and his new cover ID for travel outside the U.S. was delayed. In addition to those now familiar names, the AMWORLD recruit list also included names from the independent DRE/McClaney-funded projects of summer 1963 – including Carlos Hernandez, John Koch Gene, and Jorge Navarro.

The location and movements of all those individuals recruited for AMWORLD are still hazy, but we do know there were funds made available for domestic activities such as lodging, travel and even the purchase of supplies and weapons. Only in December and January were personnel given cover identities and covertly exfiltrated out of the United States to Nicaragua and the Dominican Republic. Some of them, including Rafael Quintero, Felix Rodriquez and Nestor Izquierdo, would return to Nicaragua in the 1970's, key figures during the Oliver North/Contra era.

AMWORLD recruiting and startup activities represented a problem for the DRE, and certain of their military leaders, such as Manuel Salvat (AMHINT-2) and Juan Francisco Blanco held out from August through November, opposing any merger with Artime and MRR.[142] Increasingly out of CIA control, in mid-September Salvat used money from the CIA to travel to New York City and face off with pro-Castro students speaking at a youth conference – the resulting brawl made the front page of the New York Times. By October, DRE "independent action" would become even more significant.

Early September: Journalist Lisa Howard's friend William Attwood (an advisor with the U.S. delegation at the U.N.) read an article on Cuban relations by Lisa Howard. He called her, and after their telephone conversation he volunteered his services to establish a back channel to Castro through the Cuban U.N. delegation.

September 13: President Kennedy's fall trip to Texas was announced to the public in September 1963.[143]

September 24: William Attwood had met with President Kennedy and received his approval to proceed with the new Cuba outreach; he had also met socially with Cuban UN representative Lechuga at a cocktail party at Lisa Howard's apartment. Lechuga had been quite encouraging, suggesting that Attwood come to Havana for talks. The CIA was not initially informed of this new back channel negotiation, which was only known to three State Department personnel and to Lisa Howard – who was working the contacts with Cuba. Castro's personal physician and friend Rene Vallejo served as a key channel for Castro.

Commentary: This emerging contact between JFK and Castro was extremely risky. It is now documented that the CIA initially, in the spring of 1963, had strongly opposed the United States responding to any new approach from Castro; senior officers had even taken steps to undermine Lisa Howard as an intermediary. They would do so again in 1964 when Castro once again made a similar appeal to President Johnson.

But in the fall of 1963, JFK initially chose to bypass the CIA and the National Security Council, pursuing the Castro outreach entirely though the State Department. In doing so he made use of Cuban diplomatic contacts at the United Nations, and turned to private messages and meetings carried out with the aid of Lisa Howard.

Both Arthur Schlesinger and William Atwood understood the risk involved in this new back channel, but later admitted they had not fully considered the fact that the CIA monitored adversary nation communications at the United Nations, and the NSA monitored all private calls to Cuba. Both men came to believe the CIA had quickly become aware of the president's new initiative – something they deemed to be extremely dangerous.

Years later William Attwood told author Anthony Summers that he believed word of the impending talks might well have leaked down through the CIA to radical officers at JMWAVE, and from them to extremist Cuban exiles. He felt that they would have reacted violently – it was the end of their dreams of returning to Cuba and they might have been moved to "violent action." [144]

Late September: John Martino traveled to New Orleans on September 27.

Late September: Two men, one an American and the other using the name "Hernandez," approached Robert McKeown at his home near Houston. They first attempted to buy a variety of weapons; when that offer was rejected, they turned to a deal for four Savage rifles with scoped sights. Finally, the outrageous sum of $10,000 was offered for a single rifle. They appear not to have known that McKeown had recognized Hernandez from his earlier weapon sales into Cuba, carried out during the revolution against Batista.

Those weapons deals had resulted in McKeown's conviction; he had served time, and suspected that he was still under observation by the

FBI. McKeown was extremely suspicious of his visitors and refused to respond to the two men. Following the assassination, McKeown identified the American visitor as Lee Oswald. As partial corroboration that Oswald might indeed have visited McKeown outside Houston, there are other reports of his being in the Houston area at that time – including Oswald making an employment agency inquiry. Oswald's wife and her friend Ruth Paine were both told that Oswald would be going to Houston looking for work.[145]

Late September: Sylvia Odio, a Dallas resident and JURE supporter who had been involved in looking for weapons sources in Dallas in prior months, wrote her father (jailed in a Cuban prison for supporting an earlier attempt to assassinate Fidel Castro) about a visit from men who used his revolutionary code name to approach her for assistance. Her father wrote back to advise her that she should be extremely suspicious since no one knowing his code name would be contacting her in that fashion. The men had told her that they had just traveled from New Orleans to Dallas. Odio also mentioned the visit to her doctor, concerned that the unknown visitors might pose some sort of risk to her and her sisters.[146] Following the assassination, Odio spoke to her doctor and her sisters, identifying Lee Oswald as one of the three men. She also described a telephone call the day after the visit, in which the caller had mentioned the American during the conversation.

John Martino would later write an article which discussed Lee Oswald's efforts to infiltrate the JURE exile group. Martino had no known connections to JURE as possible sources of that information, but he was very much aware of the Odio sisters being in Dallas, and had mentioned them in remarks made in a Dallas speech during his book tour presentations. Sylvia Odio was personally close to JURE leader Manolo Ray, and had visited him and his family in Puerto Rico only months earlier. Sylvia Odio's younger sister Sarita attended a local college along with several active DRE members. Martino had actually mentioned the Odio sisters being in Dallas during a public appearance there. Other than Martino's remark, there is no other record of Oswald being in contact with JURE in any fashion.

The Odio incident has received considerable attention from the Warren Commission, the HSCA and from JFK researchers. While the visit itself very likely occurred, there is considerable uncertainty about everything from the timing to possible motives. Additional context and speculation is provided in the following end note.[147]

Late September: According to the Warren Commission, in late September, Lee Oswald traveled to Mexico City and visited both the Soviet and Cuban consulates in pursuit of a visa to travel through Cuba to Russia. Much has been written about Oswald in Mexico City (including by this author), however, further research by individuals such as David Josephs continues to raise issues and questions concerning the official chronology and record of Oswald's purported time in Mexico.

Commentary: What is clear is that someone impersonated Lee Oswald in Mexico City, on telephone calls and very possibly in person. The subject of impersonation was known and discussed in a telephone call between President Johnson and FBI Director Hoover the morning after the assassination. Hoover himself advised Johnson that something suspicious had happened in Mexico – remarking that an unknown person was "using Oswald's name" and that "it appears there is a second person who was at the Soviet Embassy down there."

Thanks to the work of Rex Bradford (and confirmation by the Johnson Presidential Library), we have good reason to suspect that the official record of the conversation is quite possibly incomplete in terms of all that may have been discussed. The actual tape (magnetic belt) of the Hoover/Johnson conversation was totally erased, so we are left with only the surviving transcript – and no absolute confirmation that it is complete or accurate. While the events of Mexico City are certainly relevant to discussions and decisions made in the 48 hours following the assassination, at this point in time so much remains in doubt about Oswald and Mexico

City that time it remains to be seen whether events there were directly germane to the conspiracy to kill JFK, or to the actual attack in Dallas.

October 1-3: John Martino visited and spoke at multiple cities in Texas, including Dallas, promoting his new book. While in Dallas he spoke at exile group meetings, and in one instance talked of knowing Amador Odio while in prison in Cuba, and knowing that the Odio sisters were in Dallas. However, research shows that Martino had never had any contact with Armador Odio, while working in Cuba or in Cuban jails. Odio was held on the Isle of Pines in a high security prison and the two men were never housed in the same jails or prisons. The question arises as to whether Martino may have learned of the Odio sisters being in Dallas while he was in New Orleans in late September.

October 3: Jack Ruby began making phone calls trying to locate R.D. Matthews, a personal acquaintance from years before in Dallas – Matthews had moved on to the Havana casino scene and had been a co-worker of both Louis McWillie and John Martino in Havana.

October 5: Dallas newspapers announced JFK's upcoming visit to that city.

October 9 – 15: Manual Salvat of the DRE made a six-day trip to Dallas (a trip carried out without informing his CIA case officer).[148] The trip involved both fundraising and launching an effort to buy weapons for a new series of missions which were going to be proposed to the CIA.

Commentary: The source of the money for the extensive weapons and explosives DRE shopping lists circulated in both Dallas and Chicago in October 1963 is unclear, given that the CIA remained adamant it was not funding DRE military activities. However, there is evidence that Paulino Sierra's JCGE (Junta) was offering funding to a variety of activist groups including DRE. Sierra was demonstrably involved with the DRE in financing for its Chicago contacts with weapons dealers that same month, and it seems reasonable that his promised money would have been in play in Dallas as well.

At that point in time, Sierra had virtually no actual followers and had turned to using other groups and actually paying individuals to move his equipment purchases. The FBI's investigation revealed that much of the earliest money provided to Sierra and the JCGE had come from backers who had previously had substantial investments in Cuba – in "hotels and other operations connected to them." The individuals first approaching Sierra with money (describing themselves as being employed in a Las Vegas casino) represented themselves as being from a "Nevada Group." When asked about their backers they referred to Jake Lansky, the brother of Meyer Lansky. Meyer Lansky was known as the chief figure in the so called "Jewish Mafia"; he had been a major figure in Havana casinos. Further investigation obtained statements that John Roselli (earlier a representative of Meyer Lansky in Havana) was directly involved in organizing the approach to the Junta.[149]

October 9-12: CIA headquarters began an effort to put assets in place to perform intelligence monitoring of Castro's personal physician, Rene Vallejo. Vallejo had never previously been an active subject of intelligence interest, even during the prisoner negotiations of the previous winter. However, only weeks earlier JFK had agreed to initiate a serious back channel contact with Fidel Castro, and in that new back channel Vallejo became a key liaison figure. Although the new contacts were being held highly secret and compartmentalized, with only the State Department and Lisa Howard involved, it appears that the CIA had become aware of Vallejo's new role – not only at the headquarters level (Director Western Hemisphere)[150] but at SAS/JMWAVE, and even at the JMWAVE subsidiary station in Mexico City. CIA memos discussed using the AMOTS – including AMOTS in Mexico City – to collect intelligence and conduct surveillance on Vallejo.[151]

Mid October: Jack Ruby made a trip to New Orleans. Several days of his trip are unaccounted for, and anecdotal reports also place him in Miami, meeting with John Roselli during that period of time.

Commentary: Although there is no documented confirmation of Roselli and Ruby meeting in Florida, this period of time is one of only two during 1963 when Roselli (who was under constant FBI surveillance in Los Angeles and Las Vegas as well as in his travels) is unaccounted for in FBI surveillance files. The other is during the period of his travel to Florida and meeting with William Harvey in April.

October 16: Lee Oswald began work at the Texas School Book Depository.

Mid October: DRE members from Miami arrived in Dallas. On several occasions, unnamed individuals addressed DRE group and public meetings. Privately they contacted local DRE members and directed them to begin searching for weapons sources. The official DRE visitors included Manuel Salvat, and Joaquin Martinez de Pinillos, and Salvat assigned a local DRE member (and Brigade 2506 survivor) recently arrived in Dallas from New York City to shop for weapons in Texas. That individual, Ferman de Goicochea (aka George Perrel) was introduced to a local gun dealer, John Thomas Masen, by Martinez, who knew Masen from previous dealings – Masen was provided with an extensive list of the DRE desired weapons.

Commentary: There is no record of all the DRE visitors to Dallas during this period other than Salvat and Martinez. There do appear to have been other unidentified individuals engaged in speaking and fundraising activities, focused on small groups of Cubans and anti-Castro activists. In one event, the unidentified speakers made extremely hostile remarks about President Kennedy while their presentation was being taped. One of the speakers aggressively insisted on confiscating the tape, threatening that he would take it by force and warning that he held a black belt in martial arts. It is impossible to identify that speaker, but for reference, DRE member Carlos Hernandez is noted in CIA documents as being both skilled in martial arts and a sharpshooter.

October 22: Jack Ruby visited the location he had been considering as the location for a new club; he was accompanied by his "decorator."

October 24: Dallas area weapons and explosives dealer John Thomas Masen (under observation by the FBI and ATF for prior dealings with ultra-right groups such as the Minutemen) found the DRE shopping list to be extensive, including machine guns and heavy weapons. In response Masen reached out to an Army contact (George Nonte) with whom Masen had been privately doing business with in a specialty area of historic, black powder weapons. Nonte immediately reported Masen and the offer to Army intelligence, and became the primary source for a sting to be run against Masen by Army intelligence and the FBI.[152] Separately, not included in that sting, the ATF was also investigating Masen for his dealings with the Minutemen. Masen proceeded to meet with DRE representatives who told him the weapons were to be used for attacks into Cuba. The FBI and ATF immediately began to monitor Masen and the DRE.

Commentary: Unable to source weapons from Nonte, Masen turned to other avenues, and became involved with a weapons theft from the Army National Guard in Terrell, Texas. The weapons from that robbery were very possibly brokered with the help of Jack Ruby. Given the involvement of three separate agencies investigating Masen as well as that of the Army 112th Regional Intelligence group, this is an extremely complex story. Readers are referred to *Someone Would Have Talked*, which explores the matter in great detail, citing both Army, FBI, and ATF records on the affair.[153]

October 24: The DRE presented the CIA with a plan for a new and ambitious series of attacks on Cuba. Some 200 men, in 14 teams, would be inserted onto the island in order to trigger an insurgency which would be broad enough to engage the Castro military. JMWAVE chief Shackley rejected the proposal in harsh terms and recommended that all funds for sustaining the DRE military cadre be cut; that included cutting the money being used to maintain its boats and supply it with ammunition. The word about the total CIA withdrawal from even minimal DRE military support was passed to the group on November 19.[154]

October 27: Martino flew back to Dallas with no known book promotion or speaking engagement. The exact nature of his trip remains unknown.

Commentary: While Martino's known close connections within the Miami anti-Castro community included Felipe Vidal, Roy Hargraves, and Frank Sturgis, it should be noted that he had worked in the same Havana casinos as Louis McWillie, Jack Ruby's longtime friend. It is certainly possible that Martino could have been used as a personal contact for passing information to and from Ruby.

October: Juan Blanco and "Hernandez" of the DRE traveled to Chicago on a weapons-buying trip.

October 30/November 1: JFK's trip to attend a Chicago-area Army-Navy game was cancelled at the last minute. Officially the cancellation was explained in terms of the coup against Diem in Vietnam; however, an incident in Chicago described by former Secret Service agent Abraham Bolden may have been the actual reason. Bolden described a warning from the FBI that individuals known to be traveling to Chicago might present some type of threat (unspecified) during the president's scheduled visit to Chicago. According to Bolden, sufficient information was provided so that the individuals could be located, and two men were picked up, questioned and ultimately released. A report on the incident was submitted to Secret Service headquarters.

Commentary: There does appear to be corroboration of a threat in Chicago, but only in terms of identifiable but missing information. HSCA investigators who contacted Chicago Secret Service office personnel and agents in Chicago were clearly stonewalled about the event and related reports (even by secretaries who had typed the reports). Years later, during the ARRB inquiries, several files relating to the president's fall travel were destroyed, in spite of explicit instructions to the contrary. We also know that a number of DRE members were being monitored at that point in time, for efforts to buy weapons in Miami and Dallas, and there are reports of harsh remarks about President Kennedy being made by DRE members.

Beyond that, there are FBI reports stating that DRE military leader Juan Blanco had traveled to the Chicago area at approximately this time, in pursuit of purchases for DRE. A Treasury Department memo references an investigation into two Miami individuals who had been in Chicago; that memo is in response to a later Chicago incident involving DRE member Homer Echeverria. Other FBI documents report that Blanco was accompanied by someone named "Hernandez," full name unknown. While speculative, it seems possible that could have been either Victor Hernandez, who traveled to Chicago and obtained explosives in July, or Carlos Hernandez, who at that point in time had joined the AMWORLD project but was simply waiting for completion of the arrangements for moving him out of the country. Both men had been involved in the abortive July DRE aerial bombing effort, including the attempt to assemble bombs near New Orleans.

October 30 – November 11: Martino's close friend and anti-Castro associate Felipe Vidal traveled from Miami to Dallas and remained for approximately a week; Vidal had never been in Dallas previously and was under INS orders not to leave the Miami area. No details on his activities in Dallas are available, although it was later suggested that he was in Dallas attempting to raise funds for missions against Cuba.

Commentary: Vidal's visit to Dallas occurred in the same time frame that a witness (Dallas Deputy Sheriff Buddy Walther's mother-in-law) reported that an individual resembling Lee Oswald was visiting a house on Harlandale Street in Dallas. The house was reportedly frequented by a series of Latino men coming and going at all hours of the day and night – both Alpha 66 and DRE members were known to be involved with that location. At least one of the individuals associated with the house was involved in attempts to purchase weapons from John Thomas Masen (photographic research has shown that there is no resemblance between Masen and Oswald; Masen had a quite distinctive appearance).[155] There are also indications that the FBI may have been maintaining surveillance on the house from another building on the same street.

November 8 (approximate): Lee Oswald was observed meeting in Dallas with two "subversives" by the FBI; that information was related by FBI agent James Hosty to Secret Service agent Patterson on November 23. Hosty stated that his superiors would surely share the details of that with the Secret Service – something which never happened.[156] In separate remarks Hosty advised a Dallas police detective that the FBI had shared no information about Oswald with the DPD prior to the assassination because Oswald was being treated as an object of security interest by the Bureau.

November 11: Castro's friend Vallejo called Lisa Howard and stressed the need for absolute security about the private communications in the back-channel contacts between JFK and Castro. As reported by William Attwood, he also said that "*Castro would go along with any arrangements we might want to make…He emphasized that only Castro and himself would be present at the talks and that no one else – he specifically mentioned Guevara – would be involved.*" Vallejo also reiterated Castro's desire for this talk and hoped to hear our answer soon.

November 11: Jack Ruby obtained his first prescription for "nerve pills"; he refilled it almost immediately.

November 12: A contingency planning memorandum discussed protocols for responding to the deaths of American diplomats or high level American political figures, either in accidents or criminal acts. The planning was a result of concerns that protocols were needed for containment of any such situation, to prevent the sort of overreaction and "knee jerk" military response that had almost occurred during the Cuban Missile Crisis. The protocols were to specifically address media control and other moves necessary to prevent overreaction.[157]

November 13: Attwood visited Howard's apartment, but when they called Vallejo at home in Cuba, there was no answer, so they sent a telegram. The following day Vallejo called Howard, and set up a phone call for November 18 when, as Attwood reported. *"Miss Howard reached Vallejo at home and passed the phone to me. I told him....of our interests in hearing what Castro had in mind.... Vallejo...reiterated the invitation to come to Cuba, stressing the fact that security could be guaranteed. I replied that a preliminary meeting was essential to make sure there was something useful to talk about, and asked if he was able to come to New York... "* Attwood and Vallejo then talked about setting "an agenda" for a later meeting with Castro.

November 14: Ralph Gruber of Los Angeles visited Jack Ruby in Dallas. It was his first contact with Ruby in ten years. He offered no explanation for the trip to Dallas other than that his business had taken him to Arkansas, which was "right next door to Jack" – so he dropped by to visit. It should also to be noted that Gruber was known to be active in the same Los Angeles gambling circles as John Roselli.

November 14-15: Antonio Varona was reportedly in New Orleans staying with his friend Augustin Guitart, Sylvia Odio's uncle.

November 15: Sometime between this date and November 21 the house on Harlandale was vacated by numbers of Cuban exiles who had been frequenting it.

November 16-18: President Kennedy made a trip to Florida, visiting both Miami and Tampa. Threats were reported in both cities; six pages of threat subjects were listed for the Miami trip alone. The Secret Service called for CIA assistance in identifying the Cuban activists felt to represent the greatest threat in regard to protests, demonstrations or some sort of violent action. The JMWAVE Cuban Intelligence Service was used in that effort, and the Tampa newspaper highlighted "Threats on Kennedy Made Here." [158]

The threat was significant enough that the Miami city government was asked to assist, and special arrangements were made to minimize the president's exposure.[159] Some 250 Dade county and Miami police were deployed to deal with a bomb threat, although

Kennedy himself was not advised of it. There is also reason to believe that the Kennedys were aware of a threat from within the exile community – that is reflected in one of the first calls made by Robert Kennedy after hearing of his brother's assassination.[160]

November 17: Ruby called his recent visitor, Al Gruber – and possibly traveled to Las Vegas the following day. Multiple sources placed Ruby in Las Vegas at that time, asking for Louis McWillie; however, the Warren Commission determined not to accept the Las Vegas investigation or the witnesses cited.

Commentary: It was at this point in time when John Roselli disappeared from FBI surveillance in Los Angeles. Normally that surveillance involved telephone taps, informants in his apartment building, the use of at least one of his women friends' sources, and the monitoring of his vehicle and movements. In this instance Roselli made his own travel arrangements, with a friend and two prostitutes (something highly unusual for Roselli), to travel to a resort in Arizona. Roselli even made sure to relate the trip to a woman friend – who was an FBI source. While the group did go to Arizona, Roselli himself appears to have departed early, and surveillance did not locate him again until after the assassination.

November 17: A purported FBI teletype noted a pending threat to President Kennedy in Dallas – from a militant revolutionary group.

Commentary: Although later denied and suppressed, the FBI advisory almost certainly did exist.[161] While its exact source is unknown, there is documentation of a threat report out of Fort Worth on November 15. That report did mention an attack on JFK during his Texas trip and came from a National States Rights Party member. The NSRP was known for its violent stance against desegregation, against the Kennedy administration's civil rights actions and against JFK personally. A similar threat warning had come out of Miami, with another NSRP member (Joseph Milteer) speaking about shooting Kennedy from a tall building. The NSRP would certainly fit the description given in an FBI threat advisory.

November 17: In Abilene, Texas, Pedro Gonzalez's neighbor reported seeing a note which read "Call Me Immediately – Urgent". The note had two telephone numbers and the name Lee Oswald on it.

Commentary: Gonzalez was an exile activist associated with Anthony "Tony" Varona of the Cuban Revolutionary Council. Varona had been the initial contact used in the Roselli poison attempts targeting Castro during both the Cuba Project and Mongoose. Varona was also a friend of Augustine Guitart (Odio's uncle) and had visited him during the fall of 1963 in New Orleans.

Immediately after the assassination Pedro Gonzalez hurriedly went to all his neighbors and friends, collecting photos and any other materials relating to him – and then immediately left Abilene with no notice. It appears he left the country and was known to have traveled to Venezuela. Gonzalez's neighbor described unknown visitors to Gonzalez who had come in cars with both Louisiana and Florida license plates. His description of the older visitor to Gonzalez closely resembles that of John Martino.

November 18: JFK made a significant speech on Cuba. One interpretation of that speech is that it served as a warning against further Cuban adventurism in Central America. Given the knowledge of the Castro back channel communications, another interpretation is that it represented a public message to Castro that Kennedy was open to a political and trade compromise, and implied the possible recognition of the Castro regime – provided that Castro abandoned his military relationship with the Soviet Union and ceased exporting revolution across Latin America.

November 19: Ruby told his attorney (Graham Koch) that he now had plenty of money. His attorney had been fighting IRS judgments on Ruby for some time, with Ruby pleading lack of funds and pursuing a settlement. For the first time, Ruby also assigned a personal power of attorney to Koch.

Commentary: There are additional sources to confirm that Ruby had suddenly come into considerable money. Multiple individuals described him talking to a realtor about a new club, discussing plans for a new apartment in an expensive neighborhood on Turtle Creek, and planning for a Caribbean cruise. Ruby's club assistant Andy Armstrong also confirmed to researcher Ian Griggs that after Ruby's arrest, he retrieved a large sum of money hidden in the club's air conditioning system, and per Ruby's instructions handed the cash over to Ruby's partner Ralph Paul. He estimated the amount of cash as a substantial, four-digit sum.[162]

In conjunction with Ruby's expressed interest in a new club, researcher Larry Haapanen has discovered the fact that Ruby might indeed have had the cash to make a down payment on a new club location (a building at 2417 Maple in Dallas, owned by a broker named Robert T. Brown). According to real estate agent Olsen Alexander, the building had a price tag of $75,000.

Haapanen notes that Ruby's notebook has an entry for R.T. Brown, phone number LA 6-8374 (Armstrong Exhibit No. 5305-G). Two pages earlier, on a list of individuals to whom Ruby "disbursed money" is the name Robert T. Brown and the same phone number LA 6-8374 next to the sum of $19,806. Given the $75,000 price tag on the building, that amount could certainly indicate a cash down payment.

November 21: A Chicago area FBI informant submitted a report that a Cuban exile, with whom he was dealing in regard to weapons purchases, had made a remark that the exiles were now well funded and prepared to move against Castro – as soon as "we" (or possibly "they") take care of Kennedy.

Commentary: This incident has been repeatedly covered in JFK literature, most often with the conclusion that it was handed off to the Secret Service and that no extended investigation was made. With the release of additional documents, we now know that to be untrue, and the FBI's follow-on, extensive investigation revealed important information about the weapons buys in Chicago, which involved both DRE members and financing offered by Paulino Sierra. Details are cited in the referenced end note. What is most significant is that the remarks allow us further insight into the sources and degree of radical talk against President Kennedy within the DRE.[163]

November 21: Felipe Vidal returned to Dallas, Texas for an undetermined period.

November 22: Early in the morning, Jack Ruby contacted a good friend and asked him if he would like to come downtown to view the president's motorcade and "watch the fireworks." The individual and Ruby watched the motorcade from the corner of Main and Houston – Ruby immediately left after the president's passage.

Commentary: The "friend" happened to be a confidential IRS informant, who made an official report to the IRS, which in turn forwarded it through its own intelligence office to the FBI office in Dallas. The intelligence office volunteered both its Group Manager and the informant for FBI interviews; however, there is no indication that the FBI gave any response at all to the IRS approach.[164]

November 22: Ruby's bank manager observed him with several thousand dollars in cash.

Commentary: Ruby's sudden possession of a substantial amount of cash is corroborated by some $3,000 in cash taken in custody following his arrest after shooting Lee Oswald.

November 22: Following the assassination of President Kennedy, Jack Ruby called Gruber in Los Angeles with news of Oswald's capture. Other than a call to his sister, that is the only call Ruby made that afternoon. However his bar manager reported an ongoing series of urgent calls coming into Ruby's club, which was closed. Following his conversation with Gruber, Ruby became physically ill and his entire demeanor changed.

Context for Conspiracy

They Talked

As mentioned in the introduction, over a number of years I examined a number of individuals who have come to researchers' attention, primarily due to the work of the various official inquiries into the Kennedy assassination. In the end, I've been left with a handful of primary and secondary sources which appear to me to be credible. In no instance did those individuals "go public" with their information; what little they had to say was disclosed only to family or to other individuals, or in a fashion that would not allow it to be attributed to them personally or publicly. In some instances, their information was offered to investigative bodies under the assumption that it would be kept confidential – only to become known due to records releases or investigative work by private researchers.

The following material provides a brief introduction to sources I find credible, as well as a synopsis of how they came to be known. Citations are given for their backgrounds, as developed both in my own works (which contain document sources and available links to online materials) as well other sources. Most importantly, it describes the limited information which they did provide. In no instances did they elaborate or claim extensive knowledge of the conspiracy or the names of those involved; the information they did provide is strictly consistent with the manner in which it was reportedly obtained.

John Martino

Martino had been arrested by Cuban authorities in 1959, while working as a technician in gaming operations at a Havana casino. He had worked in the Havana casinos for some time, becoming familiar with and known to several of the Americans working there. At the time of his arrest, he was working to smuggle certain Cubans out of the country. Upon his release he immediately began a personal crusade against Castro's regime, both in the media and with certain Cuban exiles.

Martino became something of a public figure in anti-Castro activities, both in Miami and in certain right-wing political circles. Immediately following the assassination, he was active in offering purported leads to both the FBI and the media, leads which associated the president's murder with a conspiracy initiated and enabled by Fidel Castro and Cuban intelligence. Only years later, shortly before his death, did he reveal information that pointed towards a much different conspiracy, one involving his close personal friends within the anti-Castro community in Miami.

Martino provided limited detail, based in his admission that he did have foreknowledge of the attack in Dallas and that he himself had played a support role, as a courier traveling to Dallas under the cover of his book speaking tours.[165]

According to both Martino's wife and his son, Martino was very much aware of what was about to happen to the president, remarking on it both to his wife and in front of the family during a newscast about JFK's trip to Texas.

"Flo, they're going to kill him. They're going to kill him when he gets to Texas." [166]

Martino even ordered his teenage son Edward to remain home from school on November 22, instructing him to stay in front of the television rather than leaving the house.[167]

Beyond remarks to his wife and family, Martino's knowledge of the conspiracy was also provided confidentially to two of his longtime friends shortly before his death.[168] Those friends, first anonymously and then under their true names, provided his remarks to the House Select Committee on Assassinations.[169] That committee conducted a limited inquiry, but at that point in time his wife remained silent –

only later did his wife and son confirm his involvement to researchers.[170]

Martino described anti-Castro Cuban exiles as being involved with Lee Oswald, manipulating Oswald to enhance his image as a Castro supporter. The exiles had knowledge of the fact that Oswald was in contact with the FBI – and might well have been used in some fashion by the CIA as well. Martino was told that Oswald was not the shooter; the actual shooters in Dallas were two Cuban exiles, committed anti-Castro fighters.[171]

Oswald was to be killed as part of the overall plan to point the assassination towards Castro. Oswald was in contact with the anti-Castro Cubans and had been expected to meet a contact at the Texas Theater the afternoon of November 22, 1963.

Martino was told that the overall plan for Dallas aborted when Oswald was taken into custody at the theatre. He also understood that Jack Ruby had been involved in a minor fashion, but his role was changed once Oswald was taken into custody. The attack itself was planned at a basic level prior to the arrival of the tactical team in Dallas.

John Roselli

Roselli first came to public attention in regard to his role in multiple CIA efforts to assassinate Fidel Castro.[172] He was interviewed at considerable length about those activities by a Senate inquiry, the Senate Select Committee to Study Governmental Operations with Respect to Intelligence Activities (known as the Church Committee) during 1975.[173] However, Roselli had confidentially tried to plant an assassination conspiracy story well before that – similar to what Martino had done immediately after the assassination. During the winter of 1966/67 he had used his contacts in Washington D.C. to float a Castro plot to Earl Warren, to the FBI, and Secret Service – and ultimately to President Johnson. When he got no real response, he carried the story to Jack Anderson, who publicized it as a "political H-Bomb" – suggesting that the Kennedy administration efforts (specifically led by RFK) to kill Castro had backfired, resulting in the retaliation by Fidel Castro and the president's murder.[174]

At the time, Roselli's name was withheld from this "blowback" story, however in later years Anderson did reveal him as the source. Roselli's "Castro did it" rumor was circulated in Washington as the Garrison investigation was underway in New Orleans. While Garrison's investigation of the president's assassination had not yet become public, Roselli's behind the scenes activities in Washington D.C. focused renewed attention on the assassination of JFK and led to an early interest in, and concerns about, Garrison's investigation. In the end, Roselli offered no real details or sources, but his effort did sensitize the highest levels in Washington D.C. to the possibility (and risk) that the Garrison investigation might indeed reveal challenges to the official story of Lee Oswald as a "lone nut," and trigger calls for a new, open inquiry into the assassination.

In a dramatic contrast to the Castro-did-it scenario, Roselli himself privately expressed to one of his own lawyers (Tom Warden) that he had been personally involved in the conspiracy which killed JFK. Warden shared Roselli's remarks with his law partner William Hundley, who had formerly been head of the Justice Department's Organized Crime Division.[175] Warden served as an attorney for Roselli and also for Fred Black, a Washington super lobbyist (deeply involved in the Baker/Levinson/LBJ Serve-U Corp scandal).[176] Hundley had served as a special assistant to Robert Kennedy within the Justice Department, but later became John Mitchell's lawyer during the Watergate scandal.

The conspiracy scenario that Roselli did float in Washington was that of a CIA assassination team, composed of anti-Castro exiles, which had failed in an attack on Castro inside Cuba. In some fashion they had been "turned" by Castro, and directed against President Kennedy. In essence a CIA shooter team had killed JFK, but they had been under the control of Fidel Castro.[177] Versions of this same meme have appeared in following decades, turning up in books and cable television programs as recently as within the past decade.[178]

Roselli himself certainly did have knowledge of CIA Castro assassination activities. He worked under Shackley and with Varona during the first Cuba project, then with William Harvey and David Morales under Mongoose. Poison and sniper teams had been used in efforts to kill Castro during both the original Cuba Project and during the Mongoose/Task Force W activities. Roselli's connections to Harvey, JMWAVE and the CIA were inarguable, as were his broad connections to major crime figures not only as part of the Castro assassination efforts, but also because of his long career and his financial contacts on the east coast, his social network in Los Angeles, and his business dealings in Las Vegas. In terms of Cuban affairs, his connections went back to Meyer Lansky, his time in the Havana casinos and his ongoing involvement with certain of those individuals in both Los Angeles and Las Vegas.[179]

Yet despite Roselli's inherent credibility, his outreach in 1967 met with no response at all other than from President Johnson, who did order the FBI to conduct what once again turned out to be a minimal investigation. Later, when he was called to testify to the Church Committee on assassinations, he did begin to share information on the poison plots. He was recalled to answer additional questions, but before he appeared to testify further, Roselli was brutally murdered – by parties unknown.

David Morales

David Morales first came to attention through the work of Gaeton Fonzi during the HSCA inquiry. Fonzi developed a lead towards someone referred to as "El Indio" who was a key player in JMWAVE operations. Eventually Fonzi was able to connect that nickname to someone named David Morales. However, the CIA totally stonewalled all inquiries on Morales, refusing to acknowledge his employment or any connection with the agency. Only years later did Fonzi happen to mention the name to independent researcher Robert Doff – who in turn recalled a mention of David Morales in a book by an Army officer, Bradley Ayers, who had been detailed to do paramilitary training for SAS/JMWAVE in 1963.[180]

Dorff worked with Ayers, who had known Morales during that assignment to Miami Station, and was eventually able to confirm information about Morales, as well as locate two personal associates who agreed to speak about him – his best friend in Arizona and his personal lawyer. In later years, with new records releases, it has been possible to fully detail Morales' career including his assignment history with the CIA, his personal relationships with individuals such as Tony Sforza, and his contacts with individuals such as John Martino.[181]

Over the years, extensive interviews with Morales' friend and lawyer produced significant information suggesting that Morales had been personally involved with the Kennedy assassination, perhaps the most suggestive being a simple statement – "*Well we took care of that son of a bitch, didn't we*!" [182]

Morales made that statement to both his best friend and his lawyer; later he specifically confirmed to his friend Reuben Carbajal that he had indeed been personally involved with the conspiracy which killed JFK.[183]

As Chief of JMWAVE operations in 1963, Morales worked with the most proficient of the Cuban exile paramilitary operators including Rip Robertson and Grayston Lynch. Given his lengthy history with CIA paramilitary operations and covert action (in later years he became a consultant in counter insurgency to the Joint Chiefs' staff), Morales remains a highly credible source. His very personal remarks provide us with no detail, but imply that both he and individuals he worked with were involved with the conspiracy to kill JFK – an implication directly confirmed to his friend Carbajal.[184] Multiple sources also verify that Morales had a deep personal hatred of President Kennedy, based on failed landings at the Bay of Pigs –

Morales himself had been deeply involved in the first Cuba Project.[185]

Morales named no names to his friends; however, documents do reveal a great deal of detail as to exactly who he was working with in the fall of 1963. Given his responsibility for operations, he was closely associated with JMWAVE missions, as well as maritime operations (including both the TILT mission and Commando Mambises activities) led by individuals such as Rip Robertson and Grayston Lynch. Beyond that, his role included training support for the new AMWORLD project, as well as operational support for the Cuban Intelligence Group (AMOTs) in its activities both inside Cuba and in Mexico. In 1963 that group was led by a close personal friend of David Morales, Tony Sforza – both men had previously operated under cover inside Cuba.

While those connections are documented and understandable, what seems inexplicable is the fact that career CIA officer David Morales was also personally connected to anti-Castro activist John Martino. That connection cannot be strictly explained by Martino's participation in the TILT mission during the summer of 1963. While Rip Robertson led the CIA element of that effort and other officers participated, there is no indication that Morales would have met Martino as part of that project.

In fact, security protocols should have restricted Robertson himself from any contact with Martino other than on the actual boat mission itself. Yet we know from Martino's family that Robertson himself developed a bond with Martino – so much so that they recalled ongoing visits to Martino's family home by "Rip." While the TILT mission provides at least some justification for a social connection between Robertson and Martino, Martino's knowledge about Morales goes back well before the summer of 1963 – revealed in the personal and confidential information in Chapter 4 of Martino's own book, *I Was Castro's Prisoner*.

In that book, Martino identified Morales by name as a CIA officer – something which the CIA itself would never confirm. In fact, the

CIA refused to either identify or even acknowledge Morales as a CIA employee, or as associated with JMWAVE, in response to specific inquiries from the HSCA. In later years, work by researchers including Robert Dorff and the author, as well as by the ARRB, revealed the extent of Morales's CIA career and his various covers within the Army, State Department and USAID.[186]

Martino also wrote of Morales as being under cover in Cuba as a State Department attaché in the American embassy in Havana, and described Morales' repeated warnings to the CIA about Castro going communist. Martino's information on CIA activities in Havana was so detailed that he was able to write about Morales' predecessor in Havana and provide considerable detail as to infighting among the embassy staff.

The fact that Martino was able to identify both Earl Wilson and David Morales as CIA officers working undercover while assigned to the American Embassy in Havana, something which should have driven CIA security officers mad – this certainly was not something Martino would have picked up while working in the Havana casinos. Beyond that, there are also indications that the personal connection between Morales and Martino continued in the years following the assassination of JFK. Both men became involved in Latin American business activities, with Morales making personal introductions for Martino in Guatemala.[187]

Gene Wheaton

In support of the JFK Records Act of 1992, an independent agency – the Assassination Records Review Board – was formed, with the charter of locating and bringing into the National Archives materials pertinent to the assassination of President John Kennedy. The Board and its staff began work in October 1994 and operated for four years. Due to media visibility over the JFK Records Act and the Board's public meetings and work, a number of individuals privately contacted the Board with information they felt to be relevant to the Kennedy assassination.[188]

One of those individuals, Genc Whcaton, approachcd thc ARRB with a fax to its chairman John Tunheim on October 20, 1995. Wheaton indicated that he felt he might have information relevant to the Board's work. As part of that contact, Wheaton provided a four-page biography of himself, as well as a letter of commendation from President Richard Nixon for Wheaton's earlier anti-drug work during an assignment in Iran.

Wheaton's career experience was in law enforcement and security operations, initially with police work and then service with both the Air Force Office of Special (criminal) Investigations and with the Army Counter Intelligence Division (criminal and narcotics investigations). Following military service he had obtained his Bachelor's Degree in law enforcement, and a Master's Degree in Public Administration. After obtaining his Masters he had moved into security consulting in the Middle East, working in Saudi Arabia, in Egypt (security design for the Cairo Airport) and as an advisor on security, police practices and anti-terrorism to the pre-revolutionary government of Iran. His work on counter-drug activities with Iranian law enforcement resulted in a special commendation from President Richard Nixon.

While in Iran he also worked as Director of Security for Rockwell International on its IBEX program, a project involving both photographic and communications intelligence surveillance and intelligence collections.[189] Following his IBEX assignment, Wheaton did security consulting work with Iran, Egypt, Pakistan and Saudi Arabia; his assignments included working for Bechtel Corporation in the development of the huge Jeddah airport project. Wheaton's biographical data – which has been confirmed – was impressive, not only in respect to law enforcement, but in terms of his experience in intelligence and security practices.

Wheaton followed up his introduction by stating that he wished to refer a potential source of information on the assassination. He noted that the individual in question had worked for him in the mid-1980s, and had been a close personal friend at that time. The individual had an earlier career as a senior CIA paramilitary officer (his wife was also a high-level CIA employee). He had worked as an operations officer on the CIA's Cuba project as well as in follow-on anti-Castro activities – his work had involved infiltrations, sabotage and assassination. While working for Wheaton in air transportation/logistics sales related to the Nicaraguan Contra effort, the individual had introduced Wheaton to Cuban and American veterans of the CIA's anti-Castro operations.

The individual Wheaton named to the ARRB as having knowledge related to the Kennedy assassination was CIA paramilitary officer Carl Jenkins. In addition to Jenkin's name, Wheaton offered a very limited amount of information, which he had heard in private conversations among anti-Castro military personnel who had worked with Jenkins in earlier years. The men had trained under Jenkins and conducted a variety of missions against Castro's regime, including maritime operations into Cuba.

The conversations had occurred during the period when Jenkins was working as a sales manager for Wheaton, soliciting air transportation contracts for the Reagan-era Contra support aimed at ousting the governing regime of Nicaragua.[190] Known participants in the conversation were CIA military trainer Carl Jenkins and Rafael Quintero, a participant in the original Cuba Project. Quintero had been a member of a special paramilitary leadership cadre trained for Cuba Project maritime infiltration under CIA officer Carl Jenkins. Later Quintero became a CIA asset, and ultimately the second in command of the AMWORLD project which began under Manuel Artime in 1963. Quintero was personally associated with several of the most active anti-Communist exile figures, including long-time CIA covert operator Felix Rodriquez.

Only recently have we come to understand the full operational importance of the names associated with Carl Jenkins.[191] That context is especially important, given that Wheaton related few details other than the fact that Cuban exiles trained by Jenkins and known to Quintero had participated in the conspiracy which killed President Kennedy.

Due to the document work of David Boylan and Bill Simpich, as well as their related work in identifying the individuals associated with CIA crypts, it is possible to present a full and documented picture of the individuals who worked under Jenkins during the Cuba Project, and later with JMWAVE officers such as Rip Robertson in anti-Castro operations, including missions and activities against Cuba from 1960-1963.

We now can also verify that certain of these same individuals were involved with infiltration missions intended to assassinate Fidel Castro, via well-planned sniper attacks. That becomes especially interesting given that it is an exact match for John Roselli's remarks that CIA-trained Cuban exiles – who had been targeted on Castro – were the individuals who were directly involved in the assassination of President Kennedy.[192]

Beyond the lead to Carl Jenkins, Wheaton provided one other insight, something he had heard from the CIA operations veterans during their "war story sessions":

"The street level people Cubans felt JFK was a traitor and wanted to kill him....people above the Cubans wanted him killed for other reasons" [193]

Rafael Quintero

Quintero had been an early volunteer for the initial CIA Cuba Project, going through special training and participating in infiltration missions into Cuba prior to the failed landing of the Cuban Expeditionary Force. He had operated covertly inside Cuba, as had others of the special infiltration cadre including Tony Izquierdo and Felix Rodriquez. All three had managed to evade and escape during the Bay of Pigs landings and the following massive roundup of suspected insurgents. Following his return to the United States, he had drafted plans for a new covert operations initiative and presented them to Special Group leaders Robert Kennedy and

Maxwell Taylor, who in turn offered the plans to CIA Deputy Director Richard Helms.

Quintero was well respected, both within the CIA community and by senior members of the Kennedy administration, who thought highly of him. Helms was favorably impressed and forwarded Quintero's plans on to the president's military representatives.[194] As the Artime project evolved into AMWORLD, Quintero was appointed second in command of the new project, working along with Carl Jenkins for some two years.

Quintero is of interest as a source for two reasons, the first being his corroboration that he was personally close to Gene Wheaton, as was Carl Jenkins. Quintero also verified that Wheaton had indeed heard the types of discussions which he described, from long time anti-Castro Cuban paramilitary operators. He refused to comment further, much less elaborate, only cautioning that Wheaton might have "misunderstood" some of the comments which were made during the conversations.

The second reason Quintero remains of interest is literally for what he apparently knew, but did not say – as noted in a quote from his obituary:

"If I were ever granted immunity, and compelled to testify about past actions, about Dallas and the Bay of Pigs, it would be the biggest scandal ever to rock the United States." [195]

Felipe Vidal Santiago

Felipe Vidal was an independent, but much respected, activist within the Cuban exile community. He had also been an officer in the Cuban Navy. Vidal had no affiliation with the CIA or with JMWAVE; however he was known to be personally close to John Martino (confirmed by Martino in interviews with the FBI) and Roy Hargraves, as well as in routine contact with Frank Sturgis. He and Hargraves had organized several independent missions into Cuba –

both men were almost killed by an unexplained boat explosion and fire following the Kennedy assassination.

Vidal's reputation within the exile community is revealed in a March 1963 CIA intelligence report by Frank Sturgis (as reported to CIA case officer Bernard Barker). Sturgis provided details on a major maritime mission to be led by Vidal. The plan was highly ambitious, involving a 185-foot mother ship and several other vessels. It was to involve a diversionary attack at sea as cover for landing two separate fighting groups on the island. Vidal had been chosen to lead the mission because of his maritime experience and commitment to action against Castro.

Funding for the mission was to come from old line Cuban business sources in New York City via Julio Lobo, and both MDC and Unidad groups were to provide personnel.[196] Yet as with many such missions organized during 1963, the plan was uncovered and the project was interdicted by government agencies. One of the consequences was that Vidal was among those placed under a local area travel restriction by the INS. His previously-noted trips to Dallas in the fall of 1963 were a violation of that restriction.

Following the assassination, Vidal continued to be both independent and active in action against Castro. Ultimately, he was captured during an extremely risky attempt to enter Cuba in early 1964 – and executed. Cuban forces were waiting as he came on shore and immediately took him into custody following a fire fight in which he was wounded.

As with Quintero, Vidal did not speak directly about the assassination; however, he had remarked that he was one of those in the exile community that was passed the word that President Kennedy had abandoned the exiles and was going to negotiate some sort of relationship between the United States and the Castro regime. Vidal described that information as having a dramatic impact on the activist anti-Castro exiles – "it was almost like a bomb." [197]

Roy Hargraves

Hargraves had been one of the earliest American volunteers to work inside the exile community in Miami, involved early on in training anti-Castro group fighters from some of the smaller, most independent groups. He was deeply embedded inside that community well before his association with Gerry Hemming, or the short lived INTERPEN group.[198]

Hargraves was an independent anti-Castro activist, not associated with the CIA.[199] He operated on the periphery, finding limited funds via schemes (and scams) with individuals such as Sam Benton, and old line ultra-conservative Cuban donors. Yet he stands out as one of the only independent Americans to actually organize and conduct military missions into Cuba. In 1963 he obtained the money and support required to carry out a successful (and highly publicized) boat mission in which he captured Cuban fishing vessels. Following the capture, he and his team fought a running battle with Cuban patrol boats and ultimately took the Cuban boats to Bermuda – triggering a minor international incident with the British.

The fact that Hargraves had knowledge of and should be considered an actual suspect in the Kennedy assassination was reported to the FBI early in the Warren Commission's inquiry. [200] That report came from an individual in Miami who had known Hargraves personally, a neighbor of Hargraves. William Blanton Acker stated that he had come to know an individual named "Roy" who lived with his girlfriend in the same trailer park as Acker. Acker had seen rifles, scoped weapons, grenades and dynamite in Roy's possession.

Acker stated that "Roy" lived at the trailer park with a girlfriend only known to Acker as Silvia. Prior to the Kennedy assassination Silvia had told Acker that Roy could get him into the exile fight against Castro and that "*somebody is going to die…somebody who hasn't hurt anybody…he doesn't know it but he is going to die.*" She also told him that "*Roy is in something big, the biggest thing this country has ever seen.*" [201]

Following the assassination, Acker had attended a party where Hargraves bitterly blamed JFK as being personally responsible for the death of Roy's friends at the Bay of Pigs. Acker took Hargraves seriously, because his friends were discussing the fact that Roy had been to Dallas in late 1963 and had Secret Service credentials in his possession.

As with a number of similar reports offered to the FBI, Blanton's information was investigated in a very superficial fashion. The FBI officially claimed that it could not confirm "Roy" was Roy Hargraves. Beyond that, they discounted the report because Acker had been in a veteran's hospital, describing him as having a "diseased mind."

Decades later independent research by both Noel Twyman and this author established that Roy Hargraves was indeed "Roy," that he had been a neighbor to Blanton in the same trailer park and that his girlfriend had been accurately described by Blanton.[202]

Later, in 2001, Noel Twyman personally interviewed Roy Hargraves – Hargraves privately admitted that both he and Felipe Vidal had been in Dallas, Texas on November 22, 1963 in support of the assault on the president.[203] Hargraves stated that he had been brought into the action to prepare an explosive device – which did not have to be used because of the successful shooting attack on the president. It is a matter of record that Hargraves did specialize in explosive devices, and circa 1968 had been investigated by the FBI for building and detonating bombs targeting political targets (anti-Vietnam war and Black Panther offices) in Los Angeles.

Rolondo Otero

Otero was a source for House Select Committee on Assassinations investigator Gaeton Fonzi, expressing to Fonzi his personal knowledge that a CIA officer had been circulating among certain Cuban exiles in the late summer/early fall of 1963 – talking of treasonous activities of JFK in regard to a secret diplomatic outreach to Cuba and Castro. Otero himself was a personal friend of Nestor (Tony) Izquierdo.

Otero also claimed to have heard a similar story to that related in the conversations described by Gene Wheaton – that Cuban exiles had been involved in the attack on JFK, in revenge for his failure to support the Cuban landings with air cover and for his ongoing treachery. Otero provided Fonzi with the name of a local Cuban exile who purportedly had a broader knowledge of those involved – Bernardo De Torres. De Torres was a Bay of Pigs veteran whose brother operated a well-established detective agency in Miami. In 1963, De Torres had been the intelligence officer for the reorganized Brigade 2506 group in Miami. Later De Torres would play a major role in exposing and attempting to divert the Garrison investigation of the Kennedy assassination.

Otero's remarks in regard to a secret JFK/Castro outreach have been confirmed in a variety of sources.[204] The fact that new Kennedy/Castro secret contacts had begun in the fall 1963 was indeed very real and held extremely closely by the president and select State Department officers. The contacts were being made with deniable State Department assets – entirely outside the purview of the CIA, and even the National Security Council. The first actual meeting between American and Cuban representatives was being scheduled for late November 1963.

Otero provided no details about the assassination or the conspiracy other than in regard to the motives of those involved:

Cuban exiles were provoked by CIA officers into an action against President Kennedy with information that JFK was acting against their efforts to oust Castro and betraying them in his policies towards Cuba.[205]

Wayne January

Wayne January operated an aircraft servicing and sales company at Red Bird airport in Dallas.[206] Following the assassination, he contacted the FBI and reported a suspicious incident with unidentified individuals who had tried to rent an aircraft for a long-distance flight just before the assassination. The FBI showed little interest in that lead, instead questioning January primarily about the fact that he had on occasion visited Jack Ruby's club in Dallas. In later years, English researcher Matthew Smith contacted January, and over a number of years developed a significant amount of information about a separate incident that had occurred during the same week of the assassination.

During 1963, January was partnered in the sale of a small number of multi-engine transport aircraft which were being sold to a third-party company with offices at the Houston Air Center. January was responsible for servicing, checking and making any fixes required by the buyers who were accepting the aircraft. The last aircraft being sold was actually a WWII troop carrier which had been heavily modified, having all the seats removed and reconfigured as a cargo carrier. Early in the week of the November 22 assassination, two individuals arrived to take receipt of the last aircraft. One, an American, left immediately after a brief introduction to January. The second was Latino; he essentially accepted the aircraft, overseeing any corrective maintenance work which was required. The Cuban spent the week working alongside January.

While the aircraft was being accepted, the pilot/aircraft mechanic conducting the acceptance identified himself as a Cuban (he spoke English with no particular accent) who had previously flown similar aircraft in Cuba. He had joined the Cuban Expeditionary Force as a pilot and had flown at the Bay of Pigs (both B-26 fighter bombers and parachute troop transports were involved in support of the landings). The Cuban told January that he was familiar with the type of aircraft which was being accepted and had flown similar planes as an officer in the Cuban Air Force.

Later he mentioned that the American who had arrived with him to take possession of the aircraft was a Colonel in the U.S. Air Force. Recent research suggests that the aircraft was being obtained for the AMWORLD project and that the Cuban was a pilot involved in covert CIA air operations; the American Colonel may have been a JMWAVE officer assigned to the project for logistics and security purposes. The American spent no time at the Red Bird airport, and did not appear again until around mid-day on November 22.[207]

The Cuban became comfortable after talking with January over several days but was outspoken in relating that his friends had died during the Bay of Pigs landings – because JFK had not delivered the promised air cover for them. January felt the man to be quite sincere but that he was simply exaggerating about revenge against President Kennedy. No more was said about the subject until the afternoon of November 22. January talked to the Cuban for a few moments after the assassination, and was told that things were happening just as he had been told. In the excitement of that afternoon January did not actually observe the aircraft depart or see who was in it.

Nothing about the pilot's remarks indicates he was directly involved in the Dallas attack; he had been there working on the aircraft's checking and acceptance since Nov. 18. However, they are quite consistent with other sources on the motive and the individuals actually involved in the attack in Dallas.

My friends lost relatives and comrades who died because your President Kennedy failed to send the planes that were promised for the landings at the Bay of Pigs – they are going to kill Kennedy for that - "They are going to kill your president." [208]

Jack Ruby

Jack Ruby had been directly involved in Cuban affairs since 1959. He was personally associated with the Havana casino crowd through several people including Louis McWillie and Norman Rothman. Ruby also appears to have played a key role as a courier and liaison in a deal that freed Santo Trafficante from a Cuban jail. He was known as a ready and willing volunteer for any deal that came along, especially if it might improve his standing with the sorts of people he respected as successful, people who had made it in the club and gambling circuit.

An examination of his contacts, travels and behavior both before and after the assassination strongly suggests his involvement in a peripheral role – a role which changed dramatically after the original plan came apart with Lee Oswald being taken into custody. Ruby attempted to disclose information to the Warren Commission, however he was denied the protection required to make such disclosures. Still, he offered corroboration of a conspiracy, and of the fact that his role changed to the extent that both he and his family were at risk.[209]

"I have been used for a purpose"; You can get more out of me", "Unless you take me to Washington you can't get a fair shake out of me....I want to tell the truth...my life is in danger here....my whole family is in jeopardy...would you rather delete what I said and pretend nothing is going on?"

At several points during his polygraph examination in Dallas, Ruby repeatedly expressed to Earl Warren and others that he did not feel comfortable with his testimony being taken in Dallas and requested to be taken to Washington D.C. where he would be able to make his remarks directly to "the people of the highest authority" in regard to why he had acted as he did.

Mr. RUBY. From the moment I started my testimony, have I sounded as though, with the exception of becoming emotional, have I sounded as though I made sense, what I was speaking about?

Chief Justice WARREN. You have indeed. I understood everything you have said. If I haven't, it is my fault.

Mr. RUBY. Then I follow this up. I may not live tomorrow to give any further testimony. The reason why I add this to this, since you assure me that I have been speaking sense by then, I might be speaking sense by following what I have said, and the only thing I want to get out to the public, and I can't say it here, is with authenticity, with sincerity of the truth of everything and why my act was committed, but it can't be said here. It can be said, it's got to be said amongst people of the highest authority that would give me the benefit of doubt. And following that, immediately give me the lie detector test after I do make the statement.[210]

William Patterson

Secret Service Agent Patterson affirmed in an official report that FBI Agent James Hosty – the morning following the assassination – had stated to him that *"Oswald had contacted two known subversives about two weeks before the assassination."* [211] That remark appears to confirm that Oswald was under some level of FBI surveillance in Dallas, beyond the routine FBI contacts acknowledged by the Bureau. Hosty made a similar remark to Dallas Police detective Jack Revill, stating that Oswald had been under observation but that information on him had been restricted, since it was an espionage/security matter.[212]

Oswald had been monitored by the FBI following his return from the Soviet Union, mail watches were routinely maintained on him, he had been on the FBI's internal security watch list (mandated as an apparent officer in an officially designated subversive organization such as the FPCC), his employment was checked (a "pretext call" confirmed his employment at the Texas School Book Depository), and his travel was also monitored (according to William Kline, chief of U.S. customs in Laredo Texas).[213]

One possibility is that Oswald might indeed have been in touch with anti-Castro Cuban activists connected to a house on Harlandale Street, a repeat of his efforts to approach DRE activists in New Orleans. We do know that the FBI had an active sting in play against efforts to buy weapons by Cuban exiles in Dallas. Surveillance of the Harlandale residence might well have been in play along with that sting. Unfortunately, we have no information from the Dallas FBI files on what subversive investigations Hosty might have referred to in his remarks. Still, it is now possible to confirm that the FBI was actively monitoring "subversives" in Dallas.

We have a record of the Dallas FBI office being actively involved in at least one suspected Cuban agent investigation, an investigation that had begun in Miami and moved to Dallas. As of November 1963, the FBI was some months into an extended investigation of Osvaldo Pino Pino. Pino Pino was suspected of being a possible Castro agent, and FBI documents show that Pino Pino was known to keep company with individuals who frequented the house on Harlandale Street. The Dallas inquiry into Pino Pinio was being carried out by FBI Special Agent Walter Heitman.[214] However up to this point we have been able to locate no subversive files from the Dallas office other than Heitman's work on the Pino Pino investigation, which only concluded in 1964.

Hosty himself became personally interested in Oswald's associations, including the report of his visit to the Odio family in Dallas. His ultimate conclusion on that incident was that Sylvia Odio had been visited by Cubans associated with William Pawley and opposed to JURE, suggesting a DRE affiliation by her visitors.

William Kent

CIA psychological operations specialist William officer Kent served at JMWAVE through several of the Cuba projects of the early 1960s; he signed off on George Joannides' reports and reviewed his DRE case officer work in 1963. Kent was quite familiar with the activities of the DRE.

He offered no official remarks on the Kennedy assassination. But later, in private remarks to family members, Kent provided two key insights.

When asked about Lee Oswald he simply responded:

"Lee Oswald was a useful idiot." In professional intelligence usage, that term describes a person acting under the influence of others, without fully comprehending the goals and agenda of those manipulating them.

When asked about the Kennedy assassination by a family member, he also gave a simple response:

"It's better you don't know." [215]

A Witches' Brew – Fall 1963

By October 1963, the talk against President Kennedy within segments of the anti-Castro community had become harsh enough, and common enough, that the FBI reportedly advised the Secret Service office in Chicago that individuals traveling there might pose a threat to the president. Very real threats of hostile demonstrations – and worse – also circulated within the Miami Cuban community, threats which seriously worried the Secret Service about JFK's safety in his scheduled November travel to Florida. We know that worry was justified, as there were active threats during his visit to Miami.[216]

But what was the actual genesis of the conspiracy known to the sources we have cited, a conspiracy which would have drawn individuals who considered themselves to be American and Cuban patriots into an act of treason, the planned murder of an elected president?

Certainly by the early fall of 1963, CIA personnel at JMWAVE were increasingly frustrated with Kennedy administration policies towards Cuba, and by the new Cuban Committee programs such as AMWORLD and AMTRUNK. They had been upset to see the CIA assigned to a strictly support role in the campaign against Castro – first in the interdepartmental MONGOOSE effort under Lansdale and the Special Group Augmented, and then in the new programs being developed under the interdepartmental Cuban Coordinating Committee (with strategy nominally being a responsibility of the State Department).

At CIA headquarters, the new head of Cuban activities (the Special Affairs Staff), Desmond Fitzgerald, appeared positive about the new programs being developed. But the view at JMWAVE was far more negative – neither Shackley nor Morales were personally impressed and made little effort to conceal their attitudes. Chief of Station Shackley was vocal in his opposition to both the new strategies.[217] He was also extremely skeptical about Manual Artime, designated to play the leading role in the new, highly deniable, autonomous anti-Castro effort. The fact that Artime's selection was largely influenced by Robert Kennedy appears to have been especially annoying to the senior officers in Miami.

Of course, under President Kennedy the CIA had not retained the preeminent position that it had held during the Eisenhower administration. That had been a unique situation with Secretary of State John Foster Dulles driving American policy, and Eisenhower turning to John's brother Allen Dulles whenever covert action was needed to enforce the policies. There is no doubt that the failure of the 1960/61 Cuba Project had lessened the strategic influence of the Agency, and of its Director. It had lost its position as a driving force in national policy, and the single resource for clandestine and covert action. The inquiries which followed the disaster at the Bay of Pigs had produced recommendations that the CIA's covert operations be restricted in both scope and size, with the Department of Defense assigned a formal role in clandestine military activities.

JFK had allowed the CIA to continue to share (along with the State Department and the Army, with its White Star personnel) the responsibility for covert paramilitary operations in Laos, as well as to continue small scale military activities in Tibet, and in the Congo. While Laos had been a crisis for the new administration as Kennedy came into office, the military situation had stabilized to some extent during 1962, and Kennedy had authorized additional weapons for the CIA's surrogate forces in the north (the Hmong) – equipping them with 75 mm heavy rifles as well as standard infantry weapons.

During 1963 JFK also agreed to provide the Hmong with heavier artillery (mortars and howitzers), support aircraft and approved increased funding for military activities in Laos (NSAM 256). But in doing so he also expanded the DOD role, authorizing a buildup of covert military support for Laos via the deployment of Air Force units to Thailand and heavy lift helicopters to be used inside Laos (NSAM 249). Kennedy also moved to deploy a similar mix of CIA surrogate forces and American military units to the Congo.

The CIA was allowed to expand and arm a Cuban volunteer unit (the Makasi force) which had been first deployed to the Congo in 1962. With twelve ground attack aircraft and seven B-26 bombers it was proving an effective force, increasingly deployed in strikes against various rebel groups. But that move was also accompanied by the deployment of regular Air Force transports and support troops in a visible display for the Congolese central government.

In a more dramatic shift, with strong support from Secretary of Defense McNamara, President Kennedy had assigned the Department of Defense (through the Army and Navy) to take charge of covert action against North Vietnam. By the summer of 1963 he had also authorized the Joint Chiefs to develop a new proposal for accelerating covert military action against Cuba. Clearly the DOD and the military services were becoming much more involved in covert and clandestine military missions. JFK himself had personally expressed his enthusiasm for Special Forces (such as the Army Green Berets) and covert military action in contrast to large scale conventional combat.[218]

While JFK was increasingly involving the military in covert operations following the Bay of Pigs, he had quickly moved to turn strategic planning for covert projects to interdepartmental groups. Increasingly he had allowed the State Department a major role in decision making – while initiating moves involving operational elements of covert action over to the Department of Defense.

Despite their new covert taskings, conventional military action remained the mantra at the level of the Joint Chiefs of Staff. The Chiefs had continually taken the position that conventional action was the only option to oust Castro – in their view the CIA's Cuba Project had only reinforced that attitude. They had maintained that position through the Cuban Missile Crisis, and to some extent JFK himself had left open a conventional military option – supporting a major 1962 military exercise under CINCLANT discussed previously. That exercise was clearly designed as nothing less than a conventional invasion of Cuba, intended to put an American supported regime in place.

As of 1963 additional plans and proposals were being developed by the SACSA Joint Chiefs staff, anticipated an expanding series of DOD covert actions against Cuba, actions designed to trigger a revolt that could be supported by conventional American forces.

In the context of global military action (covert, clandestine and conventional), during 1963 JFK continued to demonstrate his fundamental pragmatism – holding all options open. It was a practice that gave him maximum options; his earlier plan for blocking a Soviet advance through Berlin – "Poodle Blanket/Pony Blanket" – was similar, with options from passively but directly blocking Soviet Forces with American units, escalating through divisional combat, all the way to the selective use of tactical nuclear weapons.[219] Kennedy had pursued the same approach during the Cuban Missile Crisis, holding all options open even in the face of virtually unanimous military opposition. It had proved to be an effective practice, but one which created serious frustration and tension among the various groups under his command.

That tension tended to be exacerbated by conflicting views even among the services. That had become clear to JFK in the earliest months of his time in office, when the Joint Chiefs generally supported major conventional action in Laos, and potentially across all SE Asia. However, the more questions the president asked, the more the individual Chiefs' proposals shifted – with a unified plan from the Joint Chiefs never emerging. Following the fiasco at the Bay of Pigs, JFK had become much more pointed in his questioning about military options and, in regard to Laos, simply failed to get answers and proposals that were agreed on by all parties (or even all the services).

President Kennedy did authorize preparations to deploy a variety of military assets to SE Asia in response to events in Laos, but he failed to get substantive answers to his questions about the logistics of a major conventional military operation inside Laos. He also received no specific operational plans or recommendations which would have involved both Laos and Vietnam – conflicting and changing views even within the Joint Chiefs made reading a decision on conventional military intervention even more challenging. Conflicting views among the Joint Chiefs would remain a problem even in regard to Cuba. By the summer of 1963 the Air Force was objecting to a DOD plan that would have assigned primary responsibility for new covert military operations against Cuba to Commander in Chief Atlantic (a Navy Admiral).

During the course of 1963, there would also be constant conflict in assessments of progress in Vietnam. During the first quarter of the year Admiral Harry Felt, Commander of U.S. forces in the Pacific, was optimistic, stating that the defeat of the Vietcong was inevitable. In contrast Secretary of State Rusk called the situation difficult and dangerous, with no quick victory in sight. JFK struggled to determine which assessments were accurate, forced to weigh the realities between positive military reports from MACV (Military Assistance Command / Vietnam) and the much more negative reports from other sources within the State Department and from the American ambassador to Vietnam in Saigon.

During 1963, even some senior Army staff were beginning to lose faith in the ability of the South Vietnamese Army (ARVN) to confront anti-government military units in battle. That concern began to solidify after the failed ARVN assault at Ap Bac in January, 1963. President Kennedy faced such a disconnect in opinions about Vietnam that he responded by sending a special fact-finding mission, with one representative (General Victor Krulak) from the Joint Chiefs staff and the other from the State Department (career diplomat Joseph Mendenhall). Krulak met with MACV commanders who were still speaking of impressive progress by the ARVN. Mendenhall focused on his own long-time contacts in Hanoi and other urban areas. Upon their return, Krulak assured JFK that the U.S. was winning in Vietnam. Mendenhall described hearing of a reign of terror by the Diem regime – with a ground swell of support for the Viet Cong in cities such as Hue and Danang, simply to remove Diem from power. After hearing from both men the president's response reflected his frustration: *"Did you two gentlemen even visit the same country?"* [220]

As 1963 progressed, there was a growing feeling that ARNV's failures were largely ones of leadership, of command – and that the Diem government's selection and control of its officer corps was a fundamental problem. It was increasingly obvious that Diem selected and promoted ARVN officers based on political reliability and personal loyalty – rather than military skill. [221] Yet neither JFK nor his senior advisors showed any sign of moving away from the position that the struggle was one the South Vietnamese themselves had to win.

To give them more time to do that, to pressure North Vietnam not to escalate its involvement in the south, and to allow the Diem regime's much-touted counter insurgency projects time to prove themselves, both JFK and Secretary McNamara endorsed a significantly increased program of military covert action against Ho Chi Minh's regime in the north. The move towards a Department of Defense takeover of action against the North had been set in motion during 1962, with the implementation of the office of Special Assistant for Counterinsurgency and Special Activities (SACSA) in the Joint Chiefs staff. In January 1963, the Joint Chiefs sent a high-ranking fact-finding team to Vietnam, and their report (Military Operations in North Vietnam) proposed a series of ground actions against the north, carried out by South Vietnamese – under overall control of the Commander in Chief Pacific (CINCPAC).[222] Further plans were developed and presented in June – they were enthusiastically approved by both Secretary of Defense McNamara and President Kennedy.[223]

Covert action against North Vietnam was viewed as complementary to counter-insurgency in the South Vietnam; up to 1963 the North had been "relatively immune" to any economic or military penalties for aiding and abetting the Viet Cong insurgency. Covert action would send the message that reprisals were available and there would be a price to pay.[224] Plans for the new effort included military action with hit and run attacks, psychological warfare operations, propaganda warfare, long-term agent insertions, and the destruction of key military assets.

The plans for expanding covert action against North Vietnam continued to be an integral part of strategic planning up to the time of President Kennedy's assassination. McGeorge Bundy's draft of what would become NSAM 273 emphasized the use of South Vietnamese forces in the effort:

"Paragraph 7. With respect to action against North Vietnam, there should be a detailed plan for the development of additional Government of Vietnam resources, especially for sea-going activity, and such planning should indicate the time and investment necessary to achieve a wholly new level of effectiveness in this field of action."

However, expanding the program and switching from the CIA to the American military was going to take time. As of early fall 1963, even the best-case estimate assumed escalated operations would not begin until February 1964. The Army and Navy eventually did proceed with the covert operations tasking, and by early spring 1964 began launching successful maritime missions against the North, damaging or destroying a limited number of both military and economic targets. It would be those covert maritime missions which ultimately triggered North Vietnamese retaliation against an American destroyer in the Gulf of Tonkin. The destroyer was viewed as supporting the increasingly destructive attacks along the North Vietnamese coast (among other tasks the destroyers had indeed been tasked with ELINT / electronics intelligence collection to support the coastal attacks).[225]

Still, as of September 1963, the focus on, and faith in counter-insurgency, was largely the only point of agreement among all those involved with the conflict in Vietnam – the Military Assistance Command / Vietnam (MACV), President Kennedy and even the State Department. Certainly, JFK was frustrated with the Diem regime's efforts to deal with the Viet Cong insurgency; his comment in a CBS interview that September made that point extremely clear: *"It's their war, they are the ones that have to win it or lose it."* ARVN would have to win its own war against the Viet Cong, and hopefully the expanded covert action program against the North would discourage Ho Chi Minh from escalating the conflict into conventional force warfare.

Yet the most fundamental issue – whether the Army of Vietnam could ever really be effective, under the type of political command and control that the Diem regime had imposed on it, remained the "elephant in the room" during Kennedy administration strategy discussions on Vietnam. In earlier years, ARVN and its generals had demonstrated the will to fight, and fight both brutally and effectively. At the beginning of the Diem regime, those generals had soundly crushed the powerful Binh Xuyen anti-government (gangster) faction in house-to-house fighting across Saigon. Following that vicious series of battles, Diem's military had shown themselves capable of taking terrible punishment and grinding their opponents down while themselves taking heavy losses.[226]

During 1954-55, Diem had ordered the ARVN to follow the victory in Saigon by moving into the Mekong Delta, against the major guerilla force opposing the central government – the anti-communist, nationalist movement under Ba Cut. Once again the ARVN proved itself, overwhelming the guerillas and capturing Ba Cut, who was ordered guillotined by Diem. Yet in later years under Diem's ongoing rule, the ARVN appeared to have become increasingly a political tool rather than a combat force. Diem had made ARVN promotions a matter of good reports – reports which would keep American political support and American aid.

One of the justifications for American encouragement of an ARVN general's coup against Diem in November 1963 was the hope that with the military in control, they might break from Diem's political micromanagement and show the tenacity and skill they had demonstrated in earlier years. Robert Kennedy later described the basic issue with Diem, in both his policies and his military command:

"Well, I just think he was just, Diem wouldn't make even the slightest concessions. He was difficult to reason with...., but the important thing was to try to get somebody who could replace him and somebody who could keep, continue the war and keep the country united, and that was far more difficult. So that was what was of great concern to all of us during this period of time. Nobody liked Diem particularly, but how to get rid of him and get somebody that would continue the war, not split the country in two, and therefore lose not only the war but the country. That was the great problem." [227]

The November coup did place the generals in control. They held the power and might well have reasserted effective military control, possibly even organizing an effective campaign against the Viet Cong guerrillas without consideration of political interference (or concern for Diem family priorities). As of November 5, 1963 Ambassador Lodge was still hopeful, "*I believe the prospects of victory are much improved if the generals stay united.*" [228] The open question of November remained whether or not the new military leaders would be able to stay focused on counter-insurgency military efforts.

Among the various American political and military voices, the preference for counter-insurgency and opposition to conventional military solutions continued in some circles well into 1964, even following President Kennedy's assassination. When President Johnson assigned General Westmoreland to take command in South Vietnam, the commander of the Army Special Warfare Center advised Westmoreland that "the entire conflict in Southeast Asia was 80 percent in the realm of ideas, and only 20 percent in the field of physical conflict."

He elaborated by saying that there were no circumstances which could "twist" the American strategy into any deployment that would require sending U.S. combat divisions.[229] Major General William Yarbrough went even further, assuring Westmoreland that there were no military targets which would warrant division-sized attacks and that "nothing would be more futile than a large-scale sweep though Viet Cong country." [230]

As of September 1963 – the point in time in which the conspiracy to assassinate President Kennedy appears to have jelled – the nature of the American military commitment to Vietnam simply remained in flux. Without doubt, JFK remained skeptical of using American forces in conventional military action in SE Asia, increasingly cautious about maintaining large numbers of "advisors." Eisenhower had deployed some 700 American military personnel to Vietnam; in May 1961 JFK had approved sending in 500 Special Forces personnel strictly in an advisory role. However, in 1962 he had agreed to a request to surge in some 9,000 more personnel (at the end of that year there were something on the order of 11,000 Americans in country and 53 military personnel had been killed).

More personnel were sent in during 1963, hitting a total deployment of over 16,000. But in October, the president reviewed and ultimately accepted proposals to actually reduce the uniformed military presence in-country, with the first phase to be accomplished by the end of the year.[231] As that was being done, he also directed an escalation in covert military action against the north – using South Vietnamese forces.[232]

As with the other areas of Cold War confrontation, JFK was acting pragmatically in the fall of 1963. Across Southeast Asia, in Africa, and in regard to Cuba, he continued to pursue multiple approaches and solutions – a practice which allowed him to keep his options as open as possible. Objectively, it is clear that he always treated conventional warfare as the last option, to be avoided if at all possible. We know that both from the record of his actions, and directly from his brother.[233]

One of the things that distinguished President Kennedy was his understanding of the geopolitical realities of anti-colonialism and of nationalism – as well as acceptance of the concept of neutrality as a working tool to block communist advances. He had achieved considerable success with that approach with India and in Indonesia. However, neutrality was not a concept which the old-line CIA establishment (built around the policies of the Dulles brothers) accepted, nor one which the American military endorsed.

John Kenneth Galbraith gives us the best synopsis of the boldness (and daring) of JFK's emerging geopolitical strategy. He characterized that approach (which might best be described as "deconfliction") as first becoming visible in Laos and Berlin during 1961. It became even more visible in the resolution and non-invasion pledge regarding Cuba in 1962, and finally in the Nuclear Test Ban Treaty in 1963. It was an approach to securing global peace and avoiding nuclear war laid out in a highly public fashion by Kennedy at his American University commencement speech of June 10, 1963.

Kennedy was the first American president with the global experience to appreciate that the forces of nationalism and anti-colonialism were as much of a factor in the contemporary geopolitics as the ideology of communism. And he had demonstrated that he was willing to at least attempt to advance American interest though neutrality, successfully in improved relations with India and with negotiation initiatives ranging from Indonesia to Yugoslavia.[234]

As Galbraith described it, JFK's goal was to resolve conflicts through negotiations (even including the option of settlements including neutrality agreements) in order to diminish the chance of nuclear Armageddon. But that was neither a goal nor a strategy which could be pursued without increasing domestic political tensions. These tensions revealed themselves throughout the entire year of 1963, in rampant conservative political opposition to Kennedy's initiatives on issues ranging from civil rights and school integration, to the nuclear test ban treaty, and even American wheat sales to Russia.

As the nation entered the fall of 1963, the president faced a variety of domestic political tensions as well as ongoing geopolitical challenges – from Berlin, to the Congo, and across Southeast Asia. The same domestic and international challenges had been in play for years, and JFK continued to wrestle with all of them. None of them offered any easy or quick path to resolution. And all of them left certain individuals, in both Washington D.C. and Miami, bitterly questioning the president's priorities and decision-making. Some even questioned his loyalties.

Tipping Point

By October 1963, some of those individuals moved beyond questioning to action. For them the tipping point, the single issue which demanded immediate action, was not some future decision but a dramatic commitment that Kennedy appeared to be the process of making – a commitment to a negotiated compromise which would have restored American relations with Fidel Castro's Cuba.

To recap, that possibility had been initially raised in January 1963, following an outreach from Fidel Castro via the American negotiator, William Donovan, who had been involved with negotiating the release of the Bay of Pigs prisoners and other Americans who were being held prisoner in Cuba.[235] That outreach has been mentioned earlier in this work; however, it deserves review considering that the timing of its events may well have been critical in the initiation of a conspiracy against President Kennedy.

While the full story of the contacts between Fidel Castro, the Kennedy administration and specifically JFK have only emerged over several decades, we now have a reasonably comprehensive history of that process, supported by documents and even taped conversations. That research is available courtesy of the National Security Archive, and the various articles on the contacts by historian Peter Kornbluh.[236]

During his final prisoner release follow-up trip to Cuba, Donovan was approached by Castro's personal physician and friend Rene Vallejo. Vallejo expressed Castro's thoughts that some level of diplomatic relations with the United States would be desirable, and invited Donovan back to discuss the idea directly with Castro. Upon his return to the U.S., Donovan advised both the State Department (Dean Rusk) and the CIA (John McCone) of Castro's outreach. In March, JFK expressed his own interest and stressed that it was time to begin thinking along more "flexible lines." He also stressed that no conditions should be imposed on the opening of contacts with Castro.

The following month, Gordon Chase, the Latin American specialist on the National Security Council, prepared a detailed options study, recommending a serious look at the Castro approach. CIA Director McCone weighed in with a note to President Kennedy stating that Castro had to know opening relationships would be to Cuba's benefit, and was likely serious about the matter. McCone and Kennedy talked, with McCone offering to send Donovan back to Cuba.

Based on an earlier request of November 1962 a journalist, Lisa Howard, managed to obtain a personal interview with Castro in late April 1963. In that interview, Castro expressed his interest in improving relations with the United States, confirming the private views that Vallejo had earlier expressed to William Donovan. Howard was privately interviewed by the CIA upon her return to the United States, and before her program could air, Richard Helms wrote a detailed CIA Briefing Paper on her contacts and insights. That paper was forwarded to Director McCone, the National Intelligence Board, the DIA, the National Security Advisor, the Attorney General and others.[237]

For her part, Howard had written directly to the president, endorsing the outreach and offering her services.[238] In his memorandum, Helms took the opportunity to offer negative comments on Howard's potential role as an intermediary. Helms and others would continue to frustrate Howard's efforts, even into the Johnson administration, when Castro attempted to extend an even more interesting offer to LBJ. In later years, Helms attempted to minimize JFK's interest in any dialogue with Castro. In 1987 he told historian Michael Beschloss that the president was really only interested in covert action, and that any talk of negotiations was at most a "feint".[239]

The CIA's own internal reaction to any such dialogue with Castro was aggressively negative. Its senior officers pushed back against the idea of any response to either the Donovan or Howard approach. In response to Helm's debriefing report on Howard, Director McCone cautioned that her information should be "handled in a most limited and sensitive manner" and that "no active steps be taken on the rapprochement matter." Beyond that, McCone strongly urged only the "most limited Washington discussions" on the idea of any type of accommodation with Castro.

It should also be noted that McCone and Helms were not the only aggressive opponents to any negotiations with Castro. McGeorge Bundy also appears to have been active in blocking the outreach – so much so that in 1964, when Castro made a second and even more dramatic effort to open communications with President Johnson, Bundy directly acted to block Castro's offer from even reaching the president.[240]

Even Robert Kennedy had cautioned JFK on the potential political repercussions if Congress were to find out that any sort of contacts with Castro were underway. Those early concerns appear to have undermined any further response from the president, although a May Special Group discussion raised the concern that it might be impossible to get rid of Castro. In that meeting, the Secretary of Defense raised the possible necessity of bargaining an end to the American trade embargo in exchange for a break between Castro and the Soviet Union. But with the surge of new anti-Castro projects which began during the summer, any sign of interest in the possibility diplomatic contacts with Cuba appears to have faded away, very likely reassuring Helms and many of those who had been copied on his earlier report of Howard's contact with Castro.

It also has to be noted that any new consideration of negotiations with Cuba would have elevated ongoing concerns about JFK's approach to neutrality in Laos. While the military situation had stabilized there during 1963, there was still widespread skepticism about political dealings with any communist faction – the concepts of neutrality and non-alignment solutions remained nothing less than anathema to the hard-line cadre of CIA cold warriors such as Allen Dulles, Richard Helms, and James Angleton – individuals who had been covertly fighting communism since 1947. Beyond that, there would have been a highly personal element to many in the CIA. Any diplomatic solution of the Cuba problem which recognized the Castro regime would effectively have repudiated all the work done by the CIA's Plans (Operations) Directorate over the proceeding five years – in particular the work of J.C. King's Western Hemisphere directorate and even the new Special Affairs Staff (SAS) under Desmond Fitzgerald.

As our assassination sources related, the motive for the shooters in Dallas was revenge, an act against perceived betrayal. Those above the shooters had a higher agenda. Perhaps it was simply to ensure there was no accommodation with Castro, perhaps it was an even broader concern than that. Certainly any successful negotiation which moved Cuba out of the Soviet orbit would have encouraged President Kennedy to further break from the Truman/Eisenhower Cold War geopolitics of choosing sides. Those practices had been based on the view that nations were either with the Western Bloc or the Eastern Bloc; there could be no neutrality. Neutral nations were perceived as potential adversaries and constantly designated as targets for CIA political action and regime change. JFK had begun to demonstrate that he was willing to move outside that "box," something quite uncomfortable to the establishment "cold warriors."

Trickle Down

There is no doubt that both Cuban volunteers and some CIA operations officers had come to mistrust JFK, to blame him for the loss of friends and family, and for the failure to free Cuba from Castro. As individuals, some of them had actually come to hate him. Those feelings only became stronger during 1963, as the Kennedy administration publicly moved to shut down independent anti-Castro military action, to actually interdict the few missions which groups managed to fund and organize, and to move all of its own anti-Castro efforts under a cloak of secrecy – giving the appearance of having given up any effort to unseat the Castro regime.

Although CIA Director McCone had initially tried to dampen discussions of any accommodation over Cuba, Helm's original briefing paper on Lisa Howard's visit had raised the subject across much of the national intelligence community as well as the State Department, not to mention other agencies. Combined with the airing of Howard's Castro interviews on television, during April and May the possibility of new approaches to Castro was an obvious topic of discussion (and concern) among virtually any group involved with Cuban affairs. The Secretary of Defense even raised the idea of the possibility of negotiating some sort of deal with Castro in the May meeting of the Special Group. All things considered, by early summer the possibility of a change in approach to the Cuba problem very likely had begun to "trickle down" from Washington to those most actively involved in the front lines of the bringing down the Castro regime.

One obvious conduit to JMWAVE for gossip about the Castro outreach and JFK's interest may very well have been William Harvey. In the ZRRIFLE assassination effort, assigned to Harvey by Helms, Harvey had been involved with JMWAVE, specifically with William Shackley, and very likely with both DCS chief Moore and Operations Chief Morales – as well as Johnny Roselli. According to Roselli's testimony to the Church Committee that project had involved both rifle attacks and poison efforts.[241] Apparently when poison failed once again in 1962/63, the effort had turned to infiltrating rifle teams. It was one of those teams which Roselli maintained had been turned on JFK, killing him in Dallas (with the misdirection that the Dallas attack had been directed by Castro).[242]

In April 1963, William Harvey traveled to Miami between April 13 and April 21, staying for three days at a hotel in Plantation Key, Florida. The trip was officially expensed as part of the ZRIFLE project.[243] At that time and through the summer, Harvey was still directly involved with Staff D, which itself continued to be involved in intelligence collections activities targeting Cuba – in particular its embassy and consulates in Mexico. Harvey also retained sole management of the ZRIFLE assassination project, which itself was hidden within Staff D, both as a cover for its expenses (personally approved by Richard Helms), and its ongoing use of contract employees for illegal activities both domestically and overseas.

While in Miami, Harvey met with and entertained at least two other individuals at hotels in Miami (the Eden Rock and Fontainebleau), one almost certainly being John Roselli, and the other a senior officer from JMWAVE, either Moore or Morales. In addition to the hotel meetings and entertainment in Miami, Harvey and Roselli traveled to the Florida Keys, staying in a Plantation Key motel for at least three days; from there calls were made and a private boat was chartered for travel to Islamorada, further out in the island chain. Islamorada housed a CIA facility which supported maritime missions into Cuban waters.[244]

Given the paucity of information on Phase II of the Castro assassination activities under Harvey and Roselli, the Florida trip, and in particular the travel out to a CIA maritime operations base in the Florida Keys, remains largely a mystery. Harvey's expense report designated his Florida trip as "operational" in nature and all we can really say is that Helms had assigned ZRRIFLE funding documents for the entire year. It should also be noted that beyond ZRRIFLE, assassinations remained an element of almost all the ongoing CIA projects targeting Cuba, including those involving both SAS and AMWORLD.

The idea of assassinating Castro was most definitely not taken off the table within the CIA during 1963. Desmond Fitzgerald pursued the subject of assassination with Rolondo Cubela, as part of his new SAS initiative to trigger a domestic coup inside Cuba. A variety of project memoranda discuss Castro's assassination as being mandatory if the AMTRUNK project were to succeed. And assassination was discussed at length in memoranda and proposals related to the Artime AMWORLD project. Rafael Quintero specifically proposed the idea in writing, and Castro assassination missions were among the very first organized and launched once Artime actually got his new group operational in 1964.

Harvey in Miami, meeting with Roselli and an undocumented third party. A week in Florida, travel to a paramilitary operations facility in the Keys, and spending some three days in and around that location – it all seems significant and remains unexplained. Any idea that the April trip to Florida was actually in regard to the project's termination is also refuted by documents which show that ZRRIFLE "operational phone calls" were still being made as of May 15, 1963.[245]

This leaves us with reason to question any explanation that Helms had suddenly terminated Castro assassination efforts in April, or whether the Harvey/Roselli trip to the Keys was actually "operational" for some unstated purpose.

As Bill Simpich notes in *State Secret*, Harvey remained extremely bitter towards RFK following his experience with Task Force W and Mongoose, and only moderately less vitriolic against President Kennedy. Harvey certainly never forgave Robert Kennedy's chastisement during the Cuban Missile Crisis, when RFK had berated him for continuing to send covert boat missions into Cuba.[246] He also appears to have been no fan of Richard Helms, feeling Helms had sacrificed him to political concerns and was sending him to Italy simply to keep him out of sight and out of mind – clearly closing out his career.

In later years Harvey admitted that he had detested the Kennedys and strongly resented Richard Helms. There is no doubt that the events of the past months had left Harvey personally infuriated with the Kennedy brothers at the time of his trip to Florida in April 1963. Whatever the nature of the Florida trip, it's easy to imagine that any conversations with those he met with there would have only fueled existing frustration and skepticism in regard to President Kennedy and his policies – especially given the likelihood of Harvey's knowledge of the spring outreach from Castro and JFK's positive response to it.

Of course, there were other channels for "trickle down" from CIA headquarters to JMWAVE as well, channels involving individuals who had worked together for years against Castro and his regime. A number of individuals who had worked at Miami station during the initial Cuba Project had been reassigned to headquarters in 1963, as part of the new SAS effort under Fitzgerald. Several of their co-workers from 1960/61 remained in Miami, and given that JMWAVE personnel provided intelligence, political action and operational support for SAS, there was ample reason for ongoing communications.

For example, Alfonso Rodriquez had been transferred from Miami to the SAS team at CIA headquarters. In the spring of 1963, Rodriquez and others at SAS were beginning new projects such as AMTRUNK (an effort to bring about a coup against Castro inside Cuba), and working to establish contacts inside Cuba to support such a coup (Rolando Cubela / AMLASH).[247] Several JMWAVE staff including DCS Moore and political action officer Emilio Rodriquez were directly involved in the projects intended to fragment and undermine the Castro regime.

SAS had begun its new regime fragmentation effort ("Split the Regime" including the AMTRUNK project) in February, and routinely communicated with JMWAVE in search of intelligence and as needed for operational support. David Morales attended one of their first project meetings and served as a liaison to JMWAVE.[248] Alfonso Rodriquez and David Morales were involved in a variety of Cuban activities; the two were among the first CIA personnel to be contacted by Manuel Artime upon his return from Cuba, and Morales was the first CIA officer to receive Artime's new proposal to begin working again with the CIA.[249]

It is certainly reasonable to expect that individuals like Rodriquez would have shared news and issues related to Cuban affairs in their contacts with their counterparts at JMWAVE. In fact, we have documents that such conversations did happen (and were security concerns). The nature of the conversations also illustrated the internal discord over the new SAS projects which had begun during 1963.[250]

In short, during 1963 there was a strong social network in place between CIA Headquarters staff, the SAS team, and JMWAVE staff (several of whom worked for SAS but were resident in Miami). And while those in Washington discussed strategy and launched new projects, Mongoose was cancelled, Task Force W disbanded, and military missions against Cuba put on hold. At JMWAVE in Miami frustration, dissatisfaction – and a certain air of malaise – had become the order of the day.

Still, during the first half of the year, there were signs things might improve. JFK had chosen not to follow up on the Castro advance, and discussions about that faded away in Washington. JMWAVE initiated, organized and began to prepare new Commando Mambises attacks on Cuba. There were even ongoing discussions and proposals for a new round of sabotage mission planning against Cuba – an effort encouraged and approved by the president. At that point it appeared that any chance for a change in the hostile relationship between the United States and Cuba had faded away.

But in September, within a matter of weeks, a dramatically new, and seemingly imminent option, suddenly came into play. It began within the State Department, when Lisa Howard's friend William Attwood (a special advisor to the U.S. Delegation at the United Nations) broached the idea of establishing a back channel to Castro via contacts at the United Nations. The idea was endorsed by Averill Harriman, Undersecretary of State for Political Affairs and Adlai Stevenson, the U.S. Ambassador to the United Nations. The initial Cuban contact would be made through Carlos Lechuga, a Cuban UN delegate, with the outreach itself socially facilitated by Lisa Howard.

Attwood and Harriman's concept was to work towards the departure from Cuba of Soviet military personnel and gain a commitment from Castro to cease subversive activities across Latin America. The overall goal was to move Cuba to non-aligned status, and establish its neutrality in geopolitical affairs – rather than have it acting as a Soviet client state. It was a heady idea, and one clearly consistent with JFK's own neutrality strategy in Laos.

Within weeks, by September 24, Attwood had met personally with President Kennedy and was given the authority to proceed; he had also met socially with Lechuga at a party hosted by Howard, and Lechuga had been quite receptive, inviting him to Cuba. The initiative was to be kept totally confidential, known to only those parties named above, with Lechuga and Rene Vallejo acting as the conduits to Castro. There was to be no initial notification to the CIA or other agencies. Contacts were to be made at the UN and via Howard's apartment, using her personal telephone.

The contacts moved forward swiftly during October, and by November 11, Vallejo was on the phone to Howard, informing her that Castro himself had agreed to be present at talks in Cuba, and that no one else (specifically Che Guevera) would be involved. He stressed Castro's interest but warned Howard of the need for absolute security in private communications.

At this point, it must again be noted that all telephone and telegraphic communications into and out of Cuba were monitored by the NSA, and reports submitted to the CIA and other agencies according to specific targeting instructions. We also know that the CIA Office of Security had made arrangements to wiretap selected foreign representatives at the United Nations and at other locations in New York City, including at the diplomat's homes.[251] Beyond that, Cuban diplomats at the U.N., including Lechuga, were specifically being targeted by the CIA in counter intelligence and political action operations.

Research by Bill Simpich has fully documented the fact that during 1963 both Carlos Lechuga and his wife were of special interest to

CIA staff, who were working on a regime-splitting project which William Harvey had proposed during his Task Force W assignment. The regime splitting activity was continued as an element of AMTRUNK when Desmond Fitzgerald and SAS replaced William Harvey's Task Force W.[252] One element of the effort targeted specific Castro regime figures within the Cuban diplomatic service, either recruiting them as sources or double agents. If that failed, the tactic was to plant information which would raise doubts about their loyalty, increasing security measures and fueling discontent (this project involved some of the dirtiest elements of political action in the CIA's playbook, including the use of sexual blackmail).

During 1963 the Cuban diplomatic sexual blackmail targets included UN Ambassador Carlos Lechuga and his wife.[253] Counter intelligence offices at CIA headquarters had become aware that he had carried out an extended affair with Sylvia Duran (his former secretary).[254] While Lechuga had moved to New York City and a diplomatic role at the United Nations, Duran remained at the Cuban consulate in Mexico City. The SAS counter intelligence goal was to leverage that affair with Mrs. Lechuga, hopefully obtaining her as an informant while also forcing Mr. Lechuga and the family back inside Cuba – where the wife could potentially become an especially valuable CIA source. In pursuit of that goal, the CIA focused intelligence collection on both Lechuga at the United Nations, and Duran at the Cuban embassy in Mexico City.[255]

Given the routine NSA monitoring of both private and commercial communications with Cuba, and the fact that Lechuga would have certainly have been on the watch list not only as a Cuban diplomat, but also as a special CIA counter intelligence target, it seems very likely conversations relating to the Kennedy/Castro outreach would have been captured – both those made by Lechuga, and the calls made from Howard's apartment. Certainly there is every reason to suspect that individuals within CIA intelligence operations were aware of the highly confidential restart of the rapprochement initially proposed by Castro.

That suspicion is reinforced by the fact that Rene Vallejo suddenly became an object of considerable CIA intelligence interest in the fall of 1963. There is no record that he had been the subject of any particular interest prior to that date, but in October CIA headquarters began communicating with both JMWAVE and its sub office in Mexico City in regard to Vallejo.

Documents reveal that the CIA Director's office was seeking background information on him, soliciting details to be obtained by the Cuban Intelligence Service (the AMOTS, initially organized under David Morales and in 1963 managed by Morales' very close personal friend Tony Sforza). Based on the available documents, there appear to have been ongoing communications (beginning as early as October 9) between Mexico City and the CIA Directors' office, in regard to Vallejo. There was also a special interest in using AMOT contacts to collect information on him.[256]

The Attwood/Howard contacts with Vallejo continued into November, working towards sending a personal representative of JFK to meet with Castro inside Cuba. As an example, Attwood and Howard called Vallejo in Cuba from her apartment on November 13. When they were unable to reach him, they sent a telegram instead (telegraphic traffic to and from Cuba was also monitored by the NSA). Arrangements were in progress which would have had the American representative traveling to Mexico, picked up there by a private plane and then flown to Cuba for a personal meeting with Castro at his Veradero Beach retreat.

Matters had moved so far by early November that the outreach was finally shared in certain very limited circles. By November 5, the Special Group was briefed and gave its endorsement to a contact via the UN. However the CIA, via Richard Helms, continued to oppose the effort, moving to delay matters by demanding that "all possible angles" be explored before continuing.

Helms proposed "war gaming" the possible consequences of any such talks, something that would no doubt have frozen the matter in place. Instead, JFK decided to act at his own initiative and removed the CIA from further discussion, quickly and personally moving the effort forwards.[257] He demonstrated his seriousness in discussions with a French journalist, Jean Daniel, whom he asked to deliver his interest personally to Fidel Castro in Havana – the message was being discussed with Castro when news of the president's assassination arrived.

In later years, Helms tried to maintain that JFK had never really been serious about the Castro outreach. Unfortunately experience (and Helms' own conviction for perjury) has taught us that it is difficult to accept his word on a great many things, certainly in regard to anything relating to Cuban affairs.[258] Regardless of Helms' attempts at obfuscation, we know just how serious President Kennedy had become, based on both documents and taped conversions. By November he was commenting that Attwood might actually have to leave his position at the U.N. in order to be able to act as a personal representative for Kennedy in the discussions with Castro.

President Kennedy publicly expressed his own interest in changing the nation's relationship with Cuba. He may even have telegraphed his minimal conditions for negotiation in a speech he made on November 18, 1963. In that speech, he stated that if only Castro would drop his present relationship with the Soviet Union and cease subversion in Latin America, "everything is possible". Such remarks were not well received by the Cuban exile community; the exiles depended on the actual ouster of the Castro regime in order for them to return home and establish a totally new government inside Cuba.

Both Kennedy and Castro were obviously serious about opening a dialogue. Castro needed some sort of settlement which would improve trade with the United States. He was also quite unhappy with the Soviet Union's behavior in regard to the recent missile crisis, and was in the process of suppressing the Cuban Communist party, which he felt to be a Soviet tool. In turn, removing the Soviet military from Cuba and establishing Cuba as a non-aligned nation could have been a major political boost for President Kennedy, not only strengthening his position in the 1964 election but providing much needed impetus to his overall global strategy.

Still, those directly involved in the effort (Attwood, Schlesinger and Harriman) realized the extreme political risk if the effort be revealed to the public while only in its early stages – another reason that talks needed to begin and move quickly. Later it would become clear that they had failed to recognize a second major risk.

In interviews with Anthony Summers decades later, Attwood acknowledged that they had neglected to consider two "glaring loopholes" in regard to the secrecy of their communications. He and Schlesinger admitted that with the NSA monitoring of all communications to and from Cuba, the CIA must have known about the new dialogue at an early stage. Those involved had not considered that calls from Howard's apartment would be monitored, or taken into consideration that the CIA and its Office of Security (as well as James Angleton in counter intelligence) routinely wire-tapped the members of the Cuban delegation to the United Nations.[259]

Attwood described an even greater risk, given CIA knowledge of the negotiations in their earliest stages:

"If the CIA did find out what we were doing, this would have trickled down to the lower echelon of activists [anti-Castro Cuban exiles] and the more gung ho CIA people who had been involved in the Bay of Pigs....I can understand why they would have reacted violently...this was the end of their dreams of returning to Cuba and they might have been impelled to take violent action." [260]

Oswald in Play

As a tipping point for a conspiracy to act against President Kennedy (and block any new relationship with Castro and Cuba) emerged, there is every reason to believe that Lee Oswald was not only well known to multiple CIA officers at Miami Station, but that his New Orleans persona as a Castro and Fair Play for Cuba Committee advocate was already in play in CIA-supported propaganda and political action efforts.

When Lee Oswald began to pursue his Cuban interests in New Orleans, he had first reached out to the local anti-Castro Cuban community, with an approach to Carlos Bringuier and the DRE. As it turns out, that approach was not strictly coincidence. Before his approach to Bringuier, Oswald had made contact with the head of a local language school, expressing an interest in learning Spanish.

That school was the Modern Language Institute of New Orleans, headed by Arnesto Rodriguez Jr. Rodriquez Jr. later confirmed that Oswald had contacted him during the last week of July or the first week of August 1963. While the two talked about language training they also talked of other things, and in the end Oswald did not enroll for courses. Although Arnesto Rodriquez minimized his contact with Oswald, there is reason to speculate that Arnesto had become interested in Oswald and his activities in New Orleans. A CIA source in New Orleans later reported that on November 23, 1963 Arnesto's mother-in-law had remarked during a private conversation that Arnesto had been a "friend" of Lee Oswald. She also discussed his tape recording of Oswald's radio appearance.[261]

While Arnesto became increasingly reticent to discuss his conversation with Oswald in detail, what we do know is that one of Arnesto's closest associates in New Orleans was Carlos Bringuier – and both men acted as sources for the FBI (Arnesto aka Ernesto was assigned FBI source number 1213 S). During the Garrison investigation, District Attorney Garrison determined that Oswald had inquired with Arnesto/Ernesto about Castro activists in New Orleans, and was very likely referred to Bringuier.

The father of the Rodriguez family, Arnesto Napoleon Rodriguez Gonzales had his own intelligence connections, having worked for the Office of Naval Intelligence during World War II; he had also served as an on-island source for the CIA before leaving Cuba.[262] Arnesto Senior carried his own CIA crypt as AMJUTE-1. Basically, the entire family was extremely conservative in its political views, strongly anti-Communist, and adamantly anti-Castro.

Arnesto Rodriquez Jr. was himself very much involved in anti-Castro activities, supporting Bringuier and the DRE. It was Arnesto Rodriguez Jr. who on 12/2/63 used a tape of Oswald's radio debate with Bringuier to provide the FBI with both a copy of the broadcast and an English transcript of the debate. The FBI immediately delivered those items to the airport; an Eastern Airlines flight carried them to Washington D.C., where they were received by SAIC Robert Bouck of the Protective Research Section of the Secret Service. Arnesto Jr. also appears to have previously prepared transcripts of the taped interview in Spanish as well as English for use in DRE propaganda activities.[263]

In terms of Lee Oswald's being known to a nascent conspiracy in Miami, an important element is the Rodriquez family connection between New Orleans and CIA SAS staff at JMWAVE. That connection was directly to Emilio Americo Rodriquez Casanova (crypt AMIRE-1). CIA officer Emilio Rodriquez was brother to Arnesto Jr. and Arnesto Senior's son. He was a close friend to both David Morales and Tony Sforza and as well as a number of other SAS and JMWAVE officers. He had also worked with, and appears to have been in contact with, David Phillips in 1963.[264]

Following the Castro revolution, Emilio had been a principal CIA deep cover stay-behind agent inside Cuba. He was multi-lingual and had approached the CIA in 1959, volunteering his services in action against the Castro regime. In fact, his background (as developed in the research of John Newman) was virtually ideal from the CIA's perspective – he had attended high school and Tulane University in New Orleans, obtained his BS and MA in Psychology, worked for the Civil Service as a military records specialist and Foreign Affairs Officer and had been only a year away from completing his PhD when he returned to Cuba with his family.[265] There (under the pseudonym Peter J. Digerveno) he managed a sales office which served six different American manufacturing companies.[266]

By May 1960 he had been cleared and security vetted, employed under contract and assigned to stay in place in Havana. Under the pseudonym Eugenio, he had worked under various business covers as part of CIA officer Tony Sforza's stay-behind network (Sforza operated under cover inside Cuba as gambler Frank Stevens, but with pseudonym Henry Sloman). Emilio's specific case officer inside Cuba was Henry Hecksher, who had been working inside Cuba since 1958, making contacts with anti-Batista revolutionary groups and providing intelligence reports on the rapidly evolving protest and street demonstrations.

John Newman has used a number of documents to place Emilio Rodriguez working inside Cuba during 1960/61. In addition to being a principal agent for a stay-behind network, he appears to also have performed certain of the duties previously carried out by David Phillips (including placing sources inside targeted groups) before Phillips himself had been exposed and forced out of Cuba.[267] During the latter part of his CIA career, Emilio would be given a similar "penetration and spotting" role (focusing on "leftist and extremist" groups) during an assignment in Venezuela.[268]

Ultimately when both Sforza and Rodriguez were themselves taken out of Cuba in the summer of 1961, they were moved into foreign intelligence positions at JMWAVE. Rodriguez's personnel file suggests that there was a special need to protect his identity, because in addition to JMWAVE office access, he also performed covert activities outside the office.[269] Both men received CIA intelligence medals for their work inside Cuba, indicating an outstanding level of performance – especially for Rodriguez, as he was only a contract employee during that period.[270]

Given Emilio's family connections to New Orleans, including to individuals actually having been in personal contact with Lee Oswald, it is virtually certain that he would have heard about Oswald's sudden appearance in New Orleans and Oswald's very public support of the Castro regime. That would mean that by the end of summer 1963, Oswald was not only known to JMWAVE through DRE reporting and to DRE case officers, but very likely to foreign intelligence and Cuban Intelligence Service (AMOT) personnel at JMWAVE.

If certain CIA officers in Miami were ultimately brought to the point of conspiracy to act against President Kennedy, and needed a false flag figure to point an attack on the president towards Fidel Castro and Cuba (a standard practice, noted by William Harvey himself in his notes about setting up the assassination project which would be used against Castro), it seems quite feasible that Lee Oswald's name would have quickly surfaced as a candidate for that role.

Useful Idiot

While it now seems virtually certain that Lee Oswald was known to and of operational interest to a variety of groups within the CIA, over an extended period of time, it is of particular note that those interests appear to have become much complex during 1963. Individuals at Domestic Operations, SAS and JMWAVE were collecting information on Oswald and using his identity for a variety of purposes, including propaganda and intelligence collection.

Although we can identify the CIA interests in Oswald, it is more challenging to specify exactly which officers in the groups were using him or his identity, and to what exact ends. It is also extremely difficult to determine if Oswald was personally aware of his use by the CIA. In contrast he can be shown to have offered to provide information to the FBI on "subversives" and did so on one and possibly more occasions.

The following is the author's best effort to lay out the extent of at least certain of the activities in which Oswald (and his identity) crossed the path of actual CIA operations in 1963.

Officers at SAS / JMWAVE involved in standard and sanctioned intelligence activities ("dangles", counter intelligence collections, propaganda, and exile group penetrations) used personal information on Lee Oswald, and leveraged the public image that he had established in New Orleans. At a deeper level, it is likely that individuals stationed in Miami, and ultimately associated with the conspiracy targeting JFK, would have realized that linking Oswald to an action against the president would drive the CIA to distance itself from any subsequent investigation.

During 1963, JMWAVE in Miami, and its subsidiary station in Mexico City, remained deeply involved in intelligence collections and counter intelligence against Cuba. In doing so, Miami Station continued as the primary operational tool of the new anti-Castro CIA initiative being carried out by Desmond Fitzgerald's Special Affairs Staff. SAS itself was the major project being carried out by the Western Hemisphere Division under J.C. King. King had remained in place since the original Cuba Project under Eisenhower.

In terms of overall anti-Castro strategies and activities, SAS served as an arm of the Cuban Coordinating Committee (an interdepartmental group, ostensibly led by the State Department, which replaced the interdepartmental Mongoose initiative). JMWAVE functioned as an asset for SAS, and its operational intelligence and military missions against Cuba were under the oversight of the Special Group, which was charged with monitoring all American covert action programs. While there was a SAS staff group, it generally turned to JMWAVE for personnel and logistics when field work was needed. JMWAVE officers supported a broad range of activities targeting Cuba and the Castro regime – including intelligence collections, propaganda efforts, counter intelligence and maritime operations. Both JMWAVE and SAS staff stationed in Miami were under the oversight of Station Chief Shackley and Deputy Chief Moore; Moore signed off on performance reviews for the SAS staff, had oversight over all activities, and personally involved himself with both maritime and political action projects.

The base's major intelligence and counter intelligence assets were its foreign intelligence officers, and its Cuban Intelligence Group (AMOTs), managed by Tony Sforza in 1963. Sforza supported projects not only involving intelligence collection, but also a range of aggressive counter intelligence activities, focused on either compromising or "turning" Cuban diplomatic personnel at the

United Nations in New York and in the Cuban consulate and embassy in Mexico City.

One of the foreign intelligence officers assigned to Miami and the SAS anti-Castro effort was the previously mentioned Emilio Rodriquez, a veteran of covert intelligence work in Cuba. His history was similar to that of several other Cuba Project officers who had been working against Castro for some three to four years – several of whom had initially operated under various covers inside Cuba. JMWAVE's Chief of Operations (David Morales) had been stationed in Havana, under U.S. Embassy State Department cover. Officers such as Henry Hecksher, David Phillips and Tony Sforza had all operated more deeply inside Cuba under personal, commercial covers. Hecksher himself had personally recruited SAS foreign intelligence officer Emilio Rodriquez as a deep indigenous agent inside Cuba, and served as his original case officer.

While Morales and Phillips had both been outed by Cuban intelligence and forced to leave (lucky to do so), Emilio Rodriquez and Anthony Sforza become part of an extremely high risk "stay behind" network inside Cuba following the revolution. Ultimately both were exposed, and David Morales managed to organize their exfiltration from the island.

All those Cuba veterans continued to work together for years, still involved in anti-Castro CIA projects and activities during 1963. In regard to using Lee Oswald as a "useful idiot," Emilio Rodriquez may have been one of the first officers at JMWAVE to learn of Oswald, through his own family contacts in New Orleans. Certainly it is significant that a veteran foreign intelligence officer was the brother of the first individual in New Orleans whom Lee Oswald approached about his interest in both Spanish and in Cuban affairs – and who referred Oswald to the DRE and Carlos Bringuier. The question remains as to whether other intelligence officers inside the CIA, particularly those tasked with propaganda involving the FPCC, would have been separately involved with Oswald via the "Hidell identity" at an earlier date.[271]

Rodriquez was himself active in counter intelligence field work. He was authorized to establish a residential cover in New York City and traveled there frequently during 1962 and 1963, in support of efforts against the Cuban staff at the United Nations.[272] He was given a cover as a consultant in electronics and electrical systems, and due to the nature of his work was granted a Top Secret security clearance. While speculative, it is also possible that he traveled to New Orleans to build a dossier on Oswald and evaluate him from a counter intelligence perspective.

One of the primary tasks for both the FBI and the CIA was monitoring staff at the U.N. in New York – with the FBI acting directly under its domestic intelligence charter, and the CIA acting unilaterally as part of its efforts against the Castro regime, by 1963 particularly as part of the ongoing SAS effort to fragment the Cuban regime. For its part, the CIA was also aggressively conducting such efforts against a variety of regime members, including diplomatic staff.[273]

Which leads to the speculation that the knowledge of Oswald, as a highly visible Fair Play for Cuba advocate and self-proclaimed head of an FPCC chapter, might well have played directly into the intelligence activities of SAS/JMWAVE in the fall of 1963. Specifically, Oswald himself (or simply his "identity") held potential value for tasks being undertaken by Tony Sforza (AMRYE-1), who led the Cuban intelligence effort at JMWAVE, Emilio Rodriquez (AMIRE-1), the foreign intelligence officer assigned to counter intelligence work targeting Cuban diplomats, and David Phillips, newly assigned to SAS and tasked with propaganda and counter intelligence activities in Mexico City. All three individuals can be shown to be connected to activities targeting Cuban diplomatic staff associated with Mexico City, and Phillips himself made a still-unexplained visit to Miami base in the fall of 1963.

Emilio Rodriquez's activities are particularly interesting given that he was targeting U.N. diplomatic staff and might have been one of the earliest CIA officers to gain knowledge of the backchannel exchanges between JFK and Castro. Also, as noted earlier, his personal notebook of that period contains an entry for David Phillips. It appears that a variety of counter intelligence and propaganda activities could have brought Oswald/Hidell to the attention of all three men during 1963.

The CIA's use of Oswald in anti-Castro and anti-FPCC propaganda likely began under John Tilton, later supported by propaganda specialists such as Alan Kent, and possibly handed off to Phillips in early fall, when he was tasked to support SAS and Fitzgerald as well as the Mexico City station. Planned propaganda activities very possibly extended to the targeted distribution of the Spanish language propaganda record prepared by INCA. INCA, the Information Council of the Americas, was busily preparing the Oswald record, which used Oswald's radio appearances and related materials – the record used tape recordings of Oswald and transcriptions provided by Emilio Rodriquez's brother.

But along with his new SAS propaganda role, Phillips also retained his former assignment in Mexico City – which involved counter intelligence against both the Cuban and Russian embassies. Phillips himself described that role *"Each intelligence service in Mexico City plays the cat-and-mouse game of trying to infiltrate the other's organization."* [274]

In 1963, JMWAVE, Tony Sforza and the AMOTS were given an expanded role in supporting Phillip's "cat and mouse" game. Based on extensive document research by Bill Simpich, we now know that beginning that summer Mexico City CIA Station Chief Winston Scott was directly pressuring SAS to use its resources – including Sforza and the AMOTS – to get a Cuban Embassy figure, Eusebio Azcue, to "turn".[275] Based on that request, Jose Casas (AMOT-106), a source on a number of Cuban regime figures, was approached and dispatched to Mexico City and the Cuban embassy. Casas managed to talk directly with Azcue directly for an extended period of time.[276]

As part of his report on the visit, Casas noted the particularly friendly remarks to visa applicants that were being made by a secretary at the consulate, Sylvia Duran – as well as a somewhat negative remark from her regarding Cuba. Such observations were always given attention due to the interest in recruiting any and all staff as unwitting sources, if not actual assets. In this instance, they were especially relevant given that Duran was known to have been the mistress of a Cuban U.N. official (Lechuga) whose family was a major target for compromise.

Given that Azcue was also a recruiting target, Casas' observation that Duran was also quite comfortable with him, enough so to tease him in public, was important – as was other information that Duran had been recommended for the job by Theresa Proenza (another known CIA target) and that Duran was working at the consulate at Azcue's request, filling in for her cousin who had died in a car accident.

Quality research into a number of such "spy games" going on around the Cuban consulate and embassy in Mexico City – as well as with Cuban United Nations diplomats – has become extensive, going far beyond the focus of this work. Of particular interest are a number of anti-FPCC intelligence and propaganda activities including a joint FBI/CIA project (AMSANTA) which was built around using actual FPCC members to collect regime intelligence from inside Cuba.[277] The FPCC members were to be inserted via visas and travel through Mexico City. FPCC membership and recommendation was a key element in the effort, and its first agent insertion in the summer of 1963 proved to be exceptionally productive – yet it appears to have been canceled for no particular reason in the fall of that year.

In regard to the possible CIA use of Lee Oswald (either in person or simply using his identity) for sanctioned CIA operations, the AMSANTA project, the SAS propaganda initiative against the FPCC, and the counter intelligence effort to recruit (or compromise) Cuban diplomatic staff all have to be considered. With that in mind, it's no wonder that even the most basic facts about the official story of Oswald's trip to Mexico City in October 1963 have come into question.

Issues relating to Lee Oswald's trip to Mexico City have become a constant point of discussion in recent years, especially as new documents have revealed extensive disconnects in both FBI and CIA communications about his presence there in September 1963. With those documents in hand, there is little doubt that the positions of both agencies in regard to his reported visit there changed during the hours and days immediately following the assassination.

In recent years researchers such as John Newman, Bill Simpich and David Josephs have written extensively about issues regarding Oswald's presence in Mexico City. Their research and works are widely available and serve as recommended reading. The author has summarized a few of those issues, most particularly the disconnects in communications and questionable information coming out of the CIA station in Mexico City following the assassination.[278]

Unfortunately, even after extensive research, a host of questions in regard to Oswald in Mexico City remain open. The following is offered as a possible scenario in which Oswald (or simply his identity) may have been used by SAS and JMWAVE in pursuit of political action projects which we now know they were pursuing in the fall of 1963.

According to the Warren Commission, Lee Oswald appeared at the Cuban consulate, and applied for a travel visa to Cuba with the goal of traveling on to the Soviet Union. "Oswald" presented documents at the Cuban consulate in Mexico City – offering materials related to the FPCC, the Communist Party USA, his marriage certificate.[279] The FBI later verified that Oswald could not have had actual documents such as a Communist Party card (the CPUSA did not issue them) of that nature, but might have used copies of his own correspondence with the FPCC and CPUSA.[280] Copies of FPCC communications also confirmed that Lee Oswald had not been officially sanctioned as a group leader nor given credentials by the FPCC.

During his appearance at the consulate "Oswald" interacted at some length – in a friendly manner – with both Sylvia Duran and then in a more offensive manner with counsel Azcue when he was told no transit visa could be issued without appropriate documents from the Soviet Union. Following a single visit, telephone calls were purportedly made from the Cuban to the Soviet embassy, including a call ostensibly involving Duran and Oswald – a call that Duran denied and which we now know was almost certainly an impersonation of Oswald as well as Duran.

Given the suppression of information and inconsistencies in the official record, there remains extended debate in regard to Oswald and Mexico City, as regards to both the Cuban and Soviet diplomatic facilities.[281] What appears most probable is the Oswald "persona," originally created around Oswald's FPCC activities as well as in various letters to the Communist Party and the Socialist Workers Party, was used as a "dangle" to Cuban consulate staff. Duran and Azcue, both targets of a broader CIA counter intelligence project involving Carlos Lechuga, would have been particularly interesting targets for just such an approach.

Such a project would have involved or been known to JMWAVE/SAS staff such as Tony Sforza and Emilio Rodriquez; it would also likely have been known to David Phillips, serving in Mexico City but with new SAS responsibilities. Journalist Jefferson Morley uncovered anecdotal evidence of such a SAS operation when he managed to locate Jane Roman, a former senior CIA counter intelligence officer. In reviewing documents relating to Oswald and Mexico City she remarked to Morley that the phrasing of the cable indicated "a keen interest in Oswald held very closely on the need to know basis" (i.e., within the Special Affairs Staff, the unit within CIA operations tasked with anti-Castro activities).[282] Such an operation would certainly support JMWAVE officer William Kent's private remark that Oswald was simply a "useful idiot" as far as the CIA was concerned.

It is impossible to reverse engineer exactly what such a dangle was specifically meant to accomplish. Most likely, as with any such activity, the outcomes were largely situational; a variety of Cuban responses could have occurred and over time would have been pursued as opportunities presented themselves. At a minimum it would have been a standard "dangle" (much like putting Casas into the Cuban Consulate earlier) with the possibility of both collecting more information for compromise and potentially as a recruiting contact. Depending on the consulate's response it might have generated a story to be used in anti-FPCC propaganda, along the lines of what was already in the process of being developed around Oswald's FPCC activities in New Orleans.

At the time it would have been just one of many such moves in the ongoing intelligence games, relatively minor, but something which would have connected the CIA to Lee Oswald in a sensational fashion following the attack in Dallas. If any such use was made of the Oswald identity, and the fact became known to members of the conspiracy, it would have been clear that the CIA had been "contaminated" in terms of conducting any open, in-depth investigation of the assassination of the president.

We know that the FBI was so concerned by its own contacts with Oswald that it destroyed and altered evidence of those contacts. There is also good reason to believe that an FBI subversive source file did exist on Oswald and was never offered into evidence. If the FBI was that concerned over simply having received communications from Oswald, the CIA's use of the Oswald/Hidell persona would have surely generated a far more extreme response within the CIA. That view is strengthened by the fact that Richard Helms went to great lengths to ensure that the Mexico City story was managed, even to the extent of replacing the original staff officer assigned to the assassination inquiry as to Oswald in Mexico City with James Angleton, the director of CIA counter intelligence.

While such actions may have successfully obfuscated matters for the Warren Commission, it appears likely that, in the end, the matters may have become clearer to FBI Director Hoover. If so, it would certainly explain the remark he annotated to internal FBI memorandum proposing joint activities with the CIA:

"OK, but I hope you are not being taken in…I can't forget the CIA withholding the French espionage activities in the U.S. or *the false story re. Oswald's trip to Mexico, only to mention two cases of their double dealing!*" [283]

The Conspiracy

Assets

All of which brings us back to a conspiracy of CIA officers turning assets assembled to kill Fidel Castro against President Kennedy. From what we can now see of that conspiracy, it appears to have been constructed around standard CIA practices – CIA officers plan covert actions and provide support, but surrogates always carry out the operation and make the actual attack – combined with William Harvey's criteria for executive action. According to Harvey's own notes, those practices meant that nothing would ever be put on paper, the word assassination would never be used in conversation, all related documents would be forged and backdated, the action itself should be coordinated by officers who were working counter espionage/counter intelligence (not case officers), and there should always be provisions for blaming the action on the communists.[284]

If we credit private remarks from our sources, including the remarks by John Roselli, certain of the same personnel used in earlier Castro assassination efforts were secured for Dallas, recruited from the highly trained Cuban volunteers who had been among the earliest to join the Cuba Project. Volunteers trained under Carl Jenkins first in Panama, then were sent to the camps in Guatemala. From there they were moved first to specialty training at Belle Chase in Louisiana, and finally into safe houses in Florida – where they waited to be assigned to maritime infiltration missions into Cuba.

We now know a good deal about several of those individuals, some of whom show up even in their CIA records as superior marksmen. We can also identify at least some of the individuals who were actually assigned to Castro assassination missions. David Boylan and I have covered their training and activities in our "Wheaton Lead Exploration" research paper.[285] What we cannot know for certain is exactly who volunteered to go to Dallas. There are suggestions and rumors, but they are simply that – no more, no less.

Given a mission to kill the president of the United States, absolute trust was the first criteria in recruiting the shooters. In that regard, only an individual such as Rip Robertson would have both the trust and paramilitary skills to have been involved in both recruiting and organizing tactical elements of the attack. As for the shooters, they would have to be experienced, proficient, highly trusted, and totally committed. Another assumption which seems reasonable is that they were personally known and trusted by the recruiting officer, individuals who had served under his command or even on his missions.

Given his 1963 activities, it is highly probable that Robertson provided operational support for the 1962/63 Castro assassination efforts supported by JMWAVE. Given his history in anti-Castro operations, it would be difficult to find someone more trusted, and more likely to be recruited into a project to stop any possible move which would have left Castro in power in Cuba. Robertson would have been in an ideal position to recruit, prepare and equip the shooters – just as he had for the Castro missions. As detailed previously, Robertson's teams trusted him and asked no questions about his orders.

Given their passion and commitment, risk would not have been an issue. Even if they were captured in the act, it would have provided them an opportunity for public exposure of the secret Kennedy/Castro contacts, effectively bringing that effort to an end and damaging Kennedy politically in the process. If successful, they would have their revenge – and possibly bring about direct American retaliation action against Castro if he could be linked to the attack. As to Robertson, given his own history with their missions, there would be no surprise even if they found him in Dallas with them. They would have expected no less.

John Roselli's role in a conspiracy would have been quite similar to that which he had played in the Castro assassination programs – that of locating local contacts in Dallas, making introductions and providing access to a local asset capable of supporting the operation. That was especially easy as far as Dallas was concerned. Jack Ruby had already been involved in Cuban affairs, and had served effectively as a courier (and not bragged about it) into Cuba. Ruby would have been easily persuaded by figures whom he admired and wished to emulate, men like Louis McWillie, Norman Rothman and of course Roselli himself.

As discussed previously, Ruby's role (as that of any local asset) was to be limited, highly compartmentalized, and well within his known personal limitations. As a field asset, Ruby could easily provide information on the motorcade planning and security preparations simply by chatting up his friends and patrons on the force. If requested, he was also in a position to identify individuals who could be used for minor tasks, ranging from planting evidence against Oswald to performing peripheral roles involving "shielding" security and overwatch on the day of the president's visit. All of which could have been done without disclosing the actual intent to kill JFK.

Beyond recruiting shooters and making arrangements for local support, there was also a need for a very limited number of other individuals, surrogates who could not be linked to Miami base or to the CIA – some would support the actual attack on the president, others would perform logistics and communications duties. Ideally they would be American, have at least some minimal cover to explain their presence in Dallas, and have demonstrated a high level of commitment to actions against Castro, regardless of risk.

Unfortunately, while we have insights from our sources on the motive and origins of the conspiracy, we have virtually no detail on its tactical execution other than that two anti-Castro shooters, rather than Lee Oswald, shot and killed the president. Beyond David Morales and John Roselli, those who either admitted to or were specifically named as being involved were in minor roles: John Martino as a courier, carrying messages and money between Miami, New Orleans and Dallas. Felipe Vidal also acting as a courier, and both Vidal and Roy Hargraves as support personnel, performing field communications and overwatch – and with Hargraves having built an explosive device that was not actually needed in the attack.[286] Another name, Bernardo De Torres, has surfaced as someone having information about the attack, but not necessarily participating himself. His name certainly does enter into the conspiracy record, but only after the fact, in a role to obfuscate and block inquiries about Cuban exile involvement as well as in exposing the Garrison investigation.[287]

In terms of the conspiracy, Lee Oswald's role remains the most nebulous of all – submerged due to his murder by Jack Ruby, and in the extensive effort made after the assassination to conceal evidence of conspiracy and manipulate evidence to position Oswald as the only person involved.[288] Matters are further clouded by the official necessity of ensuring that Oswald was portrayed in the media and the record as a "lone nut." That step was required partly to suppress any investigation of a broader conspiracy, but also to obscure the fact that Oswald had no motive for shooting President Kennedy, and publicly denied any involvement at all with the president's murder.[289]

Oswald himself demonstrated no signs of guilt immediately following the shooting; not only did he not claim responsibility as a political act (after supposedly having left his own rifle to implicate himself), but his own actions show no evidence of any plan for fleeing the crime scene – escape by local transit bus or even by taxi seems an unlikely part of a premeditated plan to murder a president.

What is obvious is that a live Oswald posed a huge risk to the conspiracy, one sufficient to require a total change in Jack Ruby's role. Such a change was in itself a huge exposure given Ruby's own lack of motive. Later remarks by Ruby's first lawyer noted that the original alibi given – that Ruby wanted to ensure Jackie Kennedy would not have to suffer through Oswald's trial – was his own creation since Ruby had no other obvious motive. Whatever the plan had been, having Oswald go to public trial certainly could not have been part of it, especially given how little had been done to firmly establish Oswald as a shooter – or even on the sixth floor at the time of the shooting.

At most a rifle was hidden underneath boxes on the sixth floor, and three hulls which matched the rifle caliber were placed by a window.[290] One unexpended round was found in the rifle itself. Research has revealed no crime scene evidence or witnesses to positively demonstrate that Oswald had taken a gun to the TSBD; the only item offered to that point was a very large paper sack which was not photographed at the scene nor definitively connected to Oswald.

The evidentiary issues in regard to that sack were actually far worse than was initially apparent, a fact that was only exposed decades later, when a document was recovered describing the fact that the one witness to Oswald taking a paper sack to work was shown the actual sack in evidence during a polygraph examination the evening of the assassination. At that point he (Buell Frazier) flatly declared (confirmed as a true polygraph statement) that the bag in evidence was not the one he had seen Oswald carry to work that very morning.[291]

The lack of forensics evidence is also striking in that there were no fingerprints on the rifle barrel, trigger guard, ammunition clip or the stock. The only print entered into evidence was one produced by the FBI, from underneath the gun stock.[292]

In a larger sense, Oswald's behavior of record, both before noon and beyond the time of the shooting at twelve thirty, provides little evidence of his personal involvement or even his consciousness that he was directly implicated as the assassin. For context on that point, readers are encouraged to consider the full suite of Oswald's remarks as compiled by Mae Brussell.[293] While elements of the police interrogations remain in question – since no tape recordings nor real time transcriptions were made – several of Oswald's personal comments to press and other individuals are a matter of record.

Tactics and Tools

One of the conspiracy sources previously noted, John Roselli, privately admitted his involvement in the Kennedy conspiracy. Years before that admission, as DA Garrison's investigation began to gain momentum but had not yet gained public attention, Roselli had taken the extremely risky move of communicating knowledge of an assassination conspiracy to very senior government officials in Washington D.C. In doing so he disclosed a key piece of information – the actual shooters in Dallas had been individuals previously used in the attempted assassination of Fidel Castro. His story served to test Washington's interest in reexamining the Kennedy assassination, as well as attempting once again to point a conspiracy towards Cuba and Fidel Castro.

Roselli's description of the conspiracy revolved around the involvement of a CIA-organized Castro assassination team. That is particularly interesting, because we have come to learn a great deal about the people who were sent into Cuba to carry out shooting attacks on Castro, how they were trained, inserted and even who organized their efforts.[294] One of the lessons learned from that research (even though we have only limited details) is that the Castro attack efforts were indeed carefully developed and planned, with the collection of considerable information on the points of attack obtained from both local intelligence and information on the target's movement and security practices.

While those efforts were structured with the classic infantry elements – shooters, and local support personnel for intelligence collection on the target – the number of personnel involved was quite limited. In practice the attacks were planned more as guerrilla actions rather than infantry classic assaults. They were to employ only one or two shooters, and an overall team of perhaps four to six individuals. The individuals involved were extremely well trained in basic infantry skills, advanced covert operations skills, especially in infiltration and exfiltration.

They constituted a very special cadre within the Cuba Project trainees and practiced the highest operational security. Their skill level can be seen in individuals such as Felix Rodriquez, Carlos Hernandez, Nestor Izquierdo, and Segundo Borgas, all of whom managed to make multiple missions in and out of Cuba, even successfully getting off island following the Bay of Pigs landings, when the entire island was under the tightest security possible.

In addition, they were able to rely on the local population for intelligence, to melt back into it as necessary and to benefit from reconnaissance performed by individuals not at all associated with the attack itself. Those local connections allowed them to move unnoticed, even in areas that were personally unfamiliar to them. Given that they were using well-established guerrilla tactics, they may well have arranged for their weapons to have been stashed for pick up by individuals completely separated from the attack itself.[295]

Given this insight into elements of the paramilitary efforts against Fidel Castro, it is reasonable to posit that any team involved in the Dallas attack would have been small – Martino's remark about only two shooters is quite consistent – and would have involved perhaps only five to six individuals total, performing the actual shooting, providing security functions to shield the shooters, and monitoring of the target into the designated kill zone.

Martino remarked that the individuals involved arrived on the ground in Dallas some days in advance – while he offered no details and was only repeating second hand information (there is no indication he knew details of the attack itself), it is most likely they were there confirming the route of the motorcade, finalizing the positioning of personnel, and scouting infiltration routes and exfiltration routes. Such activities would be quite consistent with what we know of actual practices. Such tasks would be familiar to the well-trained paramilitary operators involved in actions inside Cuba.

CIA officers at JMWAVE had access to the right personnel for an assault on the president, with the skills to infiltrate and operate covertly. They had knowledge of Lee Oswald, a figure who could be used to point the assassination towards Castro and Cuba. But one final element was critical to carrying out an operation in Dallas.

Successful covert action is often impossible without having local intelligence, and if at all possible, local resources. The CIA paramilitary operatives who had been able to work effectively inside Cuba were the ones who had friends, family, social networks and access to key information about the location of Castro security and police forces – including their routines and how to best move and function without being detected. Those who had reliable local assets infiltrated, were able to circulate and ultimately to move back off-island. Those who did not failed, generally being captured and executed. Success required skill – and connections.

Certainly, some of the individuals previously discussed had anti-Castro social connections and group affiliations which would have provided covers in regard to travel to Dallas, as well as in circulating within the Dallas anti-Castro community.

John Martino was able to travel to both New Orleans and Dallas in promotional activities for his new book, *I Was Castro's Prisoner*. His travel and the subject of his book allowed him to visit and communicate with Cuban exiles and anti-Castro activists in both cities. It was an ideal cover for someone who ultimately admitted to acting as a courier for the conspiracy; it was only compromised by the fact that his last and most extended visit to Dallas – in late October, only weeks before the assassination – was unrelated to any book promotion activities.

Martino's close friend Felipe Vidal also traveled to Dallas repeatedly in the fall. Vidal admitted being active in spreading the word in Miami about JFK betraying the anti-Castro effort – what he might actually have done in Dallas is simply not known – and his trips to Dallas would have passed through New Orleans. Even though Vidal was under INS restriction not to leave the Miami area, that had as little effect on his travel as it did on his efforts to conduct boat missions into Cuba.

Vidal was monitored by the FBI in his travels, which he later explained as efforts to raise funds from right wing Dallas figures. While such fundraising was not uncommon for anti-Castro activists, it was normally done by figures such as Gerry Patrick Hemming. There is no confirmation that Vidal's visits to Dallas actually involved fundraising. There had been lots of talk about support coming out of Dallas, but very little of that effort translated to actual money. Still, it did provide a type of cover for Vidal when questioned as to why he had spent so much energy and time in Dallas.

As we have seen, there was other travel from Miami to Dallas as well. DRE leaders and members were in motion, traveling to Chicago and Dallas – being monitored by the FBI in both locations. While we know the names of some of those individuals such as Manuel Salvat and Juan Blanco; there were others who are unnamed and who were new faces in Dallas. Making speeches and trying to raise money, and speaking heatedly about JFK, so much so that on at least one occasion one of them had to make threats to recover a tape of his remarks.

If we had the names of those "subversives" FBI Agent Hosty described as meeting with Lee Oswald, it might clear up the picture. At this point in time, all we can know for sure is that some unknown Cuban exiles did appear in Dallas, and they were able to freely circulate within the anti-Castro community there. The same thing had occurred earlier in New Orleans; Carlos Bringuier himself observed that Oswald – who was under some sort of watch by DRE members there after his becoming known as a Castro supporter – had been seen meeting with unknown Cubans, strangers to the New Orleans community who certainly stayed no longer than Oswald himself.

There were newcomers circulating in both New Orleans and Dallas, but there were also a variety of anti-Castro Cubans associated with groups, particularly the DRE, traveling out of Miami. Fundraising, recruiting and weapons buying provided a type of cover, and if any of the visitors were also engaged in becoming familiar with the city, the routes of the anticipated presidential motorcade and potential venues for the president's appearances (JFK's travel to Dallas had become public knowledge as early as September 13), it would have drawn little special notice.

Still, becoming familiar with the target geography does not imply "support," and local support is especially critical in regard to being successful in small-group, clandestine operations – especially key in actions against "secured" targets. Given the amount of public hostility towards JFK in Dallas, it was a given that both the Secret Service and the Dallas Police would be alert to the possibility of protests, and disturbances during the president's visit. The level of precautions to be anticipated were evident in the president's fall travel – an appearance in Chicago had been cancelled at the last moment, and extreme security was deployed on his Florida trips, in both Miami and Tampa. Having local intelligence on police practices and plans would have been invaluable. The possibility of compromising that local security would even have been more attractive.

Jack Ruby

All of which leads to Jack Ruby, an individual who was almost certainly brought into the Dallas conspiracy in a support role – as he himself stated, "*I have been used for a purpose*." Ruby's interest and history in Cuban affairs, his early contacts with Robert McKeown and the facts pointing to his serving as a courier and cut-out in a deal to free Santo Trafficante from prison in Cuba, suggest that he would have responded to an outreach from the people who had been involved in revolutionary era Cuba. Such individuals would certainly include his longtime friend Lewis McWillie, as well as any other figures who had been involved with brokering or funding the Trafficante release.

Lewis McWillie (aka Joe Martin) and Ruby had been associated for years, as friends and in a variety of shady business deals; both show up in Dallas CID (Criminal Investigation Division) records as of 1957.[296] Elaine Mynier, a friend of both men, spoke of their many joint business trips during 1952-1958. Mynier worked at a car rental agency and was in a position to note their comings and goings; she told investigators that in 1959 she herself traveled to Havana, carrying McWillie a short note from Jack Ruby. Mynier was found quite credible by the HSCA, which concluded that Ruby had indeed been "serving as a courier to the gambling interests" in Havana.[297]

In Havana, McWillie first worked at the Tropicana resort, later at the Sans Souci – both were controlled by Meyer Lansky. John Roselli (mentored by Lansky) later served as a troubleshooter and cleanup manager for both casinos.[298] McWillie also worked at the Deuville along with Norman Rothman (another old time Dallas acquaintance of Jack Ruby). The Deuville was managed by Mike McLaney – and John Martino worked there, supplying his electronics gaming expertise.

Both McWillie and Rothman stayed in the gambling industry after returning to the United States, although McWillie appears to have had the more successful career, moving on first to the Cal Neva Lodge in Lake Tahoe and to Las Vegas – in later years he would end up working in Caribbean casinos for Mike McLaney. Jack Ruby maintained contact with his friend McWillie, even making a series of telephone calls to him in May and June 1963. Interestingly, Ruby's own movements in June proved something of a puzzle to investigators. He was supposedly in New Orleans, but there were three days when no one saw or heard from him – much as during his second trip to New Orleans in mid-October.[299]

As for Rothman, he fared less well after leaving Cuba and moving back to Florida, incarcerated in Federal penitentiaries for a variety of charges including weapons trafficking, for which he was arrested in 1960. Interestingly enough, one of the individuals named in that activity was Frank Sturgis – the weapons violations in question had actually dated back to 1958. It appears that Ruby at least followed some of Rothman's movements (Rothman spent time in various institutions between 1961 to 1963); Ruby apparently knew where to start looking for him and on October 3, 1963 began making a series of calls to Rothman's wife in Shreveport Louisiana, trying to get in touch with him.

On November 12/13, Ralph Gruber, an old acquaintance from Ruby's Chicago days, then living in Los Angeles, visited Jack Ruby in Dallas. That was the first recorded contact between the two men in at least ten years, and Gruber would offer no explanation for the visit other than saying he had business in Arkansas and decided just to drop in on Jack. In addition to that personal visit, on the afternoon of President Kennedy's assassination Ruby visited his club and ordered it closed, made only one telephone call and went to visit his sister – his single telephone call was to Alex Gruber in Los Angeles. Gruber himself offered no reason for his sudden visit to Dallas or for the spurt of contacts with Ruby. The Warren Commission's investigation of Gruber and the Ruby contacts was – in the House Select Committee on Assassination's own characterization – "at best cursory and without any focus." [300]

Three days later (November 18/19), Jack Ruby was observed by two separate sources in Las Vegas. One source made a report to the Las Vegas sheriff's office, the other to the FBI. At the time one of the sources verified that it was Ruby by checking hotel room and telephone records.[301] Ruby was reported specifically as having been at the Tropicana, where his friend McWillie had worked. The FBI was unable to determine McWillie's exact location at the time; he would state only that he had been spending some time at the Tahoe Cal Neva Lodge.

The Tropicana was also a favorite venue for Johnny Roselli during his visits to Las Vegas. Roselli had not only been a member of the group which founded the Tropicana, he ran concessions, owned the parking franchise, owned the gift shop and was in charge of booking entertainment – which earned him ten percent of the fees paid to the headline acts, the stage shows and the band, an annual revenue estimated to be in the neighborhood of a million dollars a year.[302]

Ruby was also reported as having been seen at the Stardust, cashing a check and using McWillie's name as a reference. While the sources were quite clear on Ruby's identification and presence in Las Vegas, the Warren Commission refused to add his appearance there to Ruby's officially recorded activities. Interestingly, it was on November 19 that Ruby informed his lawyer that he had the money to settle his long-standing tax problems with the IRS.

There is little doubt that there was access to Ruby, through his old Dallas friends who had made it in the high-class gambling circuit in Havana, Miami, and Las Vegas. Ruby admired them and was eager to help them; it is hard to challenge his role as a courier and liaison in helping McWillie put together a deal to release Santo Trafficante from a Cuban jail. And it had been Trafficante himself who put together the 1960/61 casino contacts to help Roselli move poison into Havana for a Castro assassination effort.

Certainly Ruby's activities both before and following JFK's murder are more than a little suspicious; however, the common mantra has been that Ruby would never have been brought into any actual conspiracy to murder the president. Reasons cited for that view are that he had too many friends and contacts on the police force (which would actually have made him a potential asset to a conspiracy rather than liability), he was rightfully rumored to be a snitch to the police (especially on the practices of his club's competitors), and he had even been a source for the FBI on criminal activities.

J. Edgar Hoover was forced to admit to the Warren Commission that Ruby had been used as a source, offering no details but simply stating that Ruby had offered information on criminal activities but had proved to be of little value. Hoover provided no records or substantiation – any actual criminal activities of Jack Ruby were studiously avoided by both the FBI and the Warren Commission. The commission's own investigators in Dallas, Leon Hubert and Burt Griffin,[303] faced a variety of obstacles, including charges by the Dallas Police that they were being disruptive. They appear to have received little encouragement in their inquiries and essentially dropped out of the investigation. Although Hubert and Griffin had done the most background work on Jack Ruby, when the Warren Commission made its sole trip to Dallas, to conduct their sole interview with Ruby, they did not take along these investigators.

We only know that Ruby did have FBI source interviews some nine times in 1959, the same year he was most definitely involved in travel to Cuba and other associated activities, as well as in contact with Castro weapons dealer Robert McKeown. Officially the response was simply that Ruby ended up offering no viable criminal information and was dropped as a source – the agent of record, Charles Flynn, who met with Ruby responded only that he recalled nothing of substance about his dealings during the nine meetings over the course of a year.

One of the arguments most often encountered against any "use" of Jack Ruby is that he knew police by the dozens, from patrol officers and motorcycle patrolmen to detectives. Beyond that, Ruby also knew sheriff's officers and was well acquainted with the Dallas Assistant District Attorney. Of course, all of that was simply part of Jack's club business in Dallas, he wanted to be a friend to the police. He wanted them in his club, and he wanted to be able to be on everyone's good side if there was a dispute at his club or a problem with one of his performers, or any consequences of Jack personally taking care of a troublesome customer – either by escorting them out or pitching them onto the street.

Ruby may not have been a success like some of his friends, but he was a hustler by trade and inclination, a tireless promoter of his club and its talent – all of which operated under union rules including all his dancers (who were under AGVA performers' union contracts, a constant annoyance to Jack since it meant he had to meet his competitors' wage scales). The Carousel had a full-time band; its trumpeter had been with Stan Kenton's orchestra and performers included ventriloquists, magicians, and vocalists as well as the dancers that came out on the runways later in the evening. Magician Harry Blackstone Jr. performed at the Carousel on occasion and went on to become one of the premier stage magicians in the country.

The club itself was also routinely open in the afternoon as sort of a gathering place for reporters and other downtown workers; the Carousel itself was located directly across the street from the prestigious Adolphus hotel. Even without Jack's police contacts, the Carousel was a place to pick up Dallas political gossip and news about the upcoming appearance of the president and Jackie Kennedy.

A great deal has been written about Ruby and his clubs, however the years of work by English research Ian Griggs give us the most in-depth and objective view not only of Ruby's personality, but the true nature of the Carousel Club and its place in Dallas – including both the nature of its customers and Ruby's relationship with Dallas law enforcement. Individuals such as the manager of the Adolphus Hotel, Dallas District Attorney Harry Wade, and a variety of other media and business persons all held Carousel Club permanent guest passes.[304] Griggs, who did a massive amount of research on the Dallas Police, estimates that while great pains were taken to minimize Ruby's contacts with local law enforcement, somewhere between 200 and 400 of the entire force of approximately 1,000 personnel were known to and familiar with Jack Ruby.[305]

While it might be a stretch to call DPD officers "friends" of Ruby, a number of them had ongoing contacts with his club, with his dancers and with Ruby himself. DPD Patrolman Harry Olsen provides a practical example of such relationships.[306] Olsen himself described dropping in at the Carousel Club over some three years, making routine checks at least once or twice a week. He described his involvement in calming Ruby down on occasions when Ruby got into disputes with his help or his customers.

Olsen had considerable insight into such things, as he had begun dating one of Ruby's entertainers, Kathy Kay, and would, in December of 1963, marry her. Apparently Ruby thought enough of Olsen to ask advice on handling his girls, especially when they wanted to quit. In turn he gave Kathy Kay time off on occasions when Olsen asked. Olsen also confirmed for the Warren Commission that Ruby was friendly with a good many Dallas police officers, enough so that on occasion Ruby would socialize with some of them. Olsen stated that he had injured his leg and was on medical leave at the time of the assassination – his injury occurred when ice skating. However, in his testimony Olsen failed to mention that he had been ice skating along with Jack Ruby at the time the injury occurred.[307] Other officers including Detective Joe Cody also described ice skating outings with Ruby.

In addition to his contacts with regular Dallas police officers, Ruby also had ongoing contacts with the District Attorney's office. Some dealt with legal actions pertaining to his club, others are still a bit mysterious. As an example, Ruby was in Assistant District Attorney Alexander's office on November 21, the same day he visited a bail bondsman and made a telephone call to the lawyer acting for John Thomas Masen, a name now familiar to us from the convoluted DRE weapons buying efforts in Dallas, the sting run against Masen by Army Intelligence and the FBI, and a weapons theft from the Terrell, Texas National Guard Armory (a theft in which Ruby himself may have acted as a cut-out).[308]

There is little doubt that Jack Ruby would have been an ideal source of exactly the type of "ground level" information a tactical team would need to know to operate in Dallas; he knew the city like the back of his hand, especially downtown Dallas. He knew the routines of its law enforcement officers, the police patrols, where they went and where they didn't (the relative lack of information on details of his own minor, but still illegal activities illustrate that point). Ruby could talk to anyone without arousing suspicions. He would continually do so at police headquarters in the aftermath of the assassination, to an amazing extent. Everybody knew Jack; he did various favors for them; they tolerated him. He could answer questions about security and police assignments and he could find out who was scheduled to work where on November 22 (including details of the motorcade). Success in covert infiltration and exfiltration is based on field intelligence and "connections," and Ruby had them.

Beyond that, Ruby was in a position to bring in actual DPD officers who could be used for minor tasks such as providing notice of any unanticipated last-minute changes in the motorcade, conduct surveillance (referred to as "overwatch") to provide real time warning of potential security threats to the tactical team, or even facilitate the planting of material pointing towards Lee Oswald as a shooter. The advantages of co-opting local security personnel are basic to successful covert operations. It can be done through bribes, or though blackmail, and in such a manner to largely distance the assets themselves from any potential consequences. To that point, it should be noted that Jack Ruby himself appears not to have been at all aware that the minor tasks he was performing were of any real risk or consequence.

What Ruby might have been told will never be fully known. It may have been simply that people like McWillie or even Roselli needed a couple of favors – some information about police activities, perhaps the names of cops who could be trusted for a bit of work on the side. Ruby appears not to have been hesitant to talk about coming into money, about his plans for travel and a new apartment or even to take any actions to conceal his communications with Gruber – or his likely appearance in Las Vegas immediately before the assassination.

He was comfortable enough to invite a friend (unknown to him an IRS informant) downtown to watch JFK and Jackie and see the "fireworks." Did he expect a demonstration, some sort of protest – we have no idea, but a detailed examination of his subsequent behavior (including his actually becoming physically ill) after learning of the president's murder reveals a great deal.

Of course, after the assassination, Ruby's proclivities were also cited as the reason as to why nobody could have possibly considered involving him in murdering the president. Nobody would have trusted Jack with a secret – "he talked too much." A plausible argument, but one that does not apply to simply using him as a source for information, under any type of cover story. It is also a point disproven by Ruby's own history.

Ruby never talked about his business dealings over a number of years in which he was traveling with Lewis McWillie, and he didn't brag about his true activities during his trips to Havana in 1959. He didn't talk or brag about his various activities in relatively minor illegal activities over the years, whether it was trafficking in slot machines out of New Mexico or as a cut out in weapons deals. Even after shooting Lee Oswald, he didn't talk about any of that, even though while in jail he bitterly complained to a friend that it would all come out – "*Cuba, the Guns, New Orleans, Everything*!" [309] Clearly Jack could indeed keep his mouth shut when it was necessary.

Many of the objections in regard to any involvement of Ruby in the Kennedy assassination have to do with Ruby's somewhat volatile temperament, and with the fact that his police contacts in Dallas meant that he was viewed by some as a "snitch." In reality it appears that most of Ruby's "snitching" had to do with his competitors in the club business, and certainly not with local crime figures. One of the leading local syndicate figures (Joe Campesi) visited him in jail, after his shooting of Lee Oswald. The visit was a personal show of support, but also a reminder of that Ruby was expected to offer no information about vice or other criminal activities in the city.

More importantly, what those objections miss is that Ruby's actual behavior indicates no substantative role in the assassination, and most likely no knowledge that JFK was going to be actually attacked, much less killed. That premise is supported by a careful, hour by hour study of the dramatic change in Ruby's behavior on November 23-24 (as well as by his personal contacts and communications). That detail is best documented in Seth Kantor's excellent work on Jack Ruby (*The Ruby Cover-Up,* November 1980). The following summarizes material from Kantor and details presented in *Someone Would Have Talked* 2010 (Chapter 18, pages 278-282):

As of Friday morning, November 22, Ruby appears to have been largely pleased with having come into some unexpected (and unexplained) cash. He had gone so far as to invite a friend (unknown to him an IRS informant) to watch the motorcade downtown. At that point his friend described Ruby as "happy, jovial and joking." After seeing JFK and Jackie's car pass on Main Street, Ruby had hurried off to the Dallas Morning News Office – he appears to have been there earlier to place his routine weekly club advertisement, just going down the street to meet his friend for the parade.

But by 12:40, back at the news office he had gone pale upon hearing of the shooting. He quickly became subdued, leaving the newspaper office at around 1:10. Based on Kantor and other witnesses, Ruby appears to have gone directly to Parkland Hospital to try and find out about the president's condition – and possibly what rumors might already be in play. Kantor observed him to be "miserable, grim and pale." There is every sign that what had happened was a total shock to Ruby (just as when Oswald had heard about the attack on the president and his death).

He was next reported at the Carousel Club, calmer but closing the club for the evening. Then came the call to Al Gruber in Los Angeles, claimed by both men to simply be about sending Gruber a pet dog. After that conversation Ruby's mood dramatically shifted once again – after arriving at his sisters' he said nothing, went into the bathroom and threw up.

Ruby's world had clearly changed over the course of a few hours. One of his employees at the Carousel Club (Larry Crafard) related that a series of calls had come into the club for Ruby, but what other calls Ruby may have made or received from public phones is totally a matter of speculation. Crafard himself began hitchhiking out of Dallas the following morning.

Ruby's next moves suggest what had been a very limited and safe "use" up to the time of the assassination had become something else entirely following Lee Oswald's arrest. For the next two days Ruby became a man with a mission, first to monitor the police handling of Oswald, then to get close to him, and ultimately to kill him. By 7 PM Friday evening Ruby was back at the police station – something he would later deny since it suggested that by Friday evening he had already become focused on Lee Oswald and monitoring his movements (certainly evidence of pre-meditation). The Warren Commission refused to accept numerous reports of Ruby at the police station and essentially stalking Oswald over the next two days; it was all far too suggestive of something other than an impulsive, emotional act of murder.

Beginning early Saturday and all that day, Ruby circulated among the media, among the police, among the crowds, constantly shaking hands and asking questions. To all appearances he was being his usual self, promoting his club even during a tragedy. However, his movements took him around his police contacts and even to the door of the room where Oswald was being held for interrogation. And his remarks to a television crew revealed that he was keeping current on the police handling of Oswald, with very timely news from sources within the DPD – aware first that Oswald was to be moved, and then that the move had been cancelled.

By that evening Ruby was still there, circulating among officers he knew, mixing in as if he were assisting foreign press persons, with a notebook and glasses posing as a reporter, and in the late-night press showing of Oswald, standing out by correcting District Attorney Harry Wade when he named Oswald as belonging to the "Free Cuba Committee" (an anti-Castro group). It may have been that Carousel Club owner Jack Ruby was the only one in the audience that knew that Oswald's affiliation was actually with the pro-Castro "Fair Play for Cuba Committee."

The following morning, Jack would be with the press again during Oswald's transfer, lunging forward through the basement crowd to kill Lee Oswald.

Beyond that, it's unlikely that Ruby knew all that much, or for that matter had initially been asked to do all that much. If someone had contacted him using McWillie's name, or even more significantly, Roselli's, nothing more would have been needed. Even a reference to the "Boys in Vegas" would have been enough if he had just been asked to pass on certain information about what the police were doing for Kennedy's visit, who was assigned where, anything that would have enhanced his reputation about knowing what was going on in Dallas. Perhaps even the name of a police officer who might be available for some minor task on November 22.[310] He had worked as a cut out for those people before – surely he would be eager to do that again. And for that matter, even afterwards he never really said more than implying something big had been in play and that he himself had simply been "used."

Jack Ruby stated that he had been "used" in regard to the assassination of the president. With his history in Cuban affairs and his former role as a cut out and courier, it is easy enough to see how he could once again have been brought into a minor role, even to the point of tracing when and who might have done so. As to what he was "used" to do, a review of some of his contacts on the police force and of the anomalous and mysterious actions of certain officers on November 22, 1963 may well provide us with some idea of what Ruby might have first been used for, beyond providing the basic field intelligence so critical to any covert paramilitary action.

Harry Olsen

Harry Olsen, Ruby's patrol officer acquaintance and skating partner, was off active police duty on November 22, working as a security guard at an estate in Oak Cliff. Later Olsen was unable or unwilling to provide the name of the "estate's" owner, the individual who paid for his services or the name of the individual who referred him to the job. Still, Olsen's rather vague description of the estate's location, as related to Eighth Street, describes the particular area of Oak Cliff containing Oswald's residence, Ruby's residence, Officer Tippit's shooting, and the Texas Theatre – all quite relevant to the assassination.

Later, in 1977, Olsen described the place as a dilapidated little house on an estate of someone deceased (yet he had told the Warren Commission he heard about the assassination in a telephone call from someone calling the owner of the "estate").[311] Olsen was consistent in saying that the place was also being guarded by a DPD motorcycle officer, who relieved him at the end of Olsen's shift. One candidate for the motorcade officer has been identified by researchers as Bobby Joe Dale (he rode at the rear of the JFK motorcade on November 22), and Olsen was sharing Dale's apartment in the fall of 1963. Dale normally had a patrol route in Oak Cliff, but had been pulled from his regular schedule for the motorcade. Dale was also reported as being a frequent visitor to Ruby's Carousel night club.

Olsen was not asked any questions about whether the "security" at the "estate" was ongoing or simply for that one day. There is certainly reason to question whether or not something special was going on at the location in order for it to be guarded day and night – whether it was high stakes gambling or something more temporary is open to question. Olsen could not provide the name of his employer or the location of the estate. He also did not explain why, with a broken knee cap and his leg in a cast, he would walk over four blocks from there to his girlfriend's home that afternoon rather than have her pick him up. There was also no explanation of how he had gotten to the location earlier in the day.

Certainly Harry Olsen's activities on November 22 are interesting, particularly when considering that the location of his "security" job was within a four block walk to his girlfriend Kathy's apartment (a walk which he said he had done, on crutches with a broken kneecap, that afternoon). Kathy Kay lived a half block off East Eighth Street, on Ewing – a location in proximity to a great many points of interest and in the vicinity of Oswald's apartment house. As Penn Jones pointed out decades ago, Olsen's likely location and the local geography suggests that from Olsen's position, Lee Oswald would even have been visible crossing Eighth Street – on his way to the Texas Theatre. As for Olsen and Kathy Kay, the couple described encountering Ruby at a downtown car park very late on the night of the assassination, chatting for some time (in reality the time they spent together appears to have been at least a full hour and perhaps longer).

Little is known about what the two did on Saturday, but on Sunday – the day Ruby shot Lee Oswald – they later stated they had driven from Dallas to Wichita Falls, Texas, only returning late that evening (neither mentioned the trip in their official testimony). But within two days Kathy Kay had left the Carousel Club and shortly afterwards left Dallas for good. The AGVA union manager in Dallas told the Warren Commission Kay had been frightened and wanted to get out of town as soon as possible. In later testimony, Olsen told the FBI that Kathy Kay was indeed quite scared – by something Ruby had told her. Olsen and Kathy Kay were married shortly after the assassination and moved to California within two months.[312]

Harry Olsen's own activities on November 22 appear more than a little mysterious, and leave a number of open questions. Kathy Kay's fear over something Jack Ruby told her is equally interesting and perhaps more significant. In that same vein, the activities of another Dallas Police officer also leave us with open questions – and may reveal the reach of a conspiracy which reached into the Dallas Police Department.

J.D. Tippit

On the afternoon of the assassination, Oswald's purported deviation from a direct path to the Texas Theatre may – or may not – have led directly to officer J.D. Tippit. In the official story of the Kennedy assassination, that encounter led to Oswald fatally shooting Tippit. Later research has raised numerous questions about that encounter and Tippit's murder.

Yet apart from that encounter, Tippit's own activities earlier on that day pose a number of questions which suggest his possible involvement in the conspiracy, at least in a minor role. One of the best detailed summaries of the anomalies in Tippit's behavior on November 22 can be found in the writing of English researcher Chris

Scally.[313] As Scally details, there are conflicts and "holes" in Officer Tippit's activities that day which begin even prior to his reported dispatch to Oak Cliff following the assassination.

As early as 12:17, when Tippit notified the police dispatcher that he would be out of his patrol car for a moment, the conflicts begin. Around that time, Tippit is variously described as having stopped due to a complaint about a reported house break-in (that complaint is not noted in the dispatcher's log, the police dispatch recordings or Tippit's own log book), or of a shoplifting suspect at Hodges Supermarket – or for some other reason. If it was to respond to a shoplifting complaint, no record of the complaint or Tippit's response entered into the record. What is known for certain is that he exited his patrol car for approximately three minutes and the most obvious reason (in the opinion of one of the police dispatchers) was that he had stopped to make a short, personal land line telephone call, as he would again later that afternoon.

After the shooting in Dealey Plaza, at 12:46 Tippit was ordered to move north from his location in Cedar Crest and into Oak Cliff.[314] His response indicates that he had remained in the same Bonnie View area as noted in his "out of car" transmission. Although he had cleared back in action, he appears not to actually have moved away from Bonnie View Road in the interim.

At 12:54, the dispatcher asked him for a location check, and he replied that he was at Lancaster and Eight Street. The problem is that at that approximate time five independent witnesses (all of whom knew Tippit personally) reported seeing Officer Tippit parked at the GLOCOL gas station on Zang's Boulevard, watching traffic come across the Houston Street Viaduct Bridge from downtown Dallas into Oak Cliff. The witnesses, three of whom worked at the station, reported waving to Tippit at approximately 12:45 and watching as he remained parked there for some ten minutes. At that point he left the station at speed and proceeded down Lancaster Street. While the details and timing of the gas station incident remain less than totally clear, it does indeed seem that Tippit was in Oak Cliff and performing some type of watch on traffic coming out of Dallas following the assassination.

A police dispatcher call to Tippit for a location check at 1:03 drew no response – at the approximate time another witness (James A. Andrews) driving west on Tenth Street reported being overtaken and forced to stop by a patrol car cutting in front of him. The officer in the car ran back to Andrews, said nothing to him, surveyed the back seat area of the car and immediately ran back to the patrol car and moved off at high speed. Andrews did get a clear look at the officer's uniform name plate and it read "Tippit."

Shortly after the reported time of that car stop, a clerk at the Top Ten Records Shop (located around a minute away from the Andrews traffic stop and a short way west of the Texas Theatre) observed Tippit park his car on Bishop Street and come into the shop, asking to use the telephone. Tippit was in an obvious hurry, asking people in an aisle to step aside. The clerk (Louis Cortinas) said that Tippit dialed a number, said nothing while holding the phone, and waited for a period of time equivalent to seven or eight rings before hurrying out the door, apparently upset. In driving away, he actually ran a stop sign as he turned onto Sunset Street. The owner of the Top Ten Record Shop (Dub Stark) fully confirmed the incident as described by Cortinas; both men were well acquainted with Tippit and noted that he spoke to neither of them as he rushed out of the store. Stark noted that Tippit had been a customer of the store while on duty and in uniform, and had used the store phone on previous occasions.

The route reported by Cortinas and Stark would have taken Tippit to East Tenth, where he would shortly be killed, after exiting his patrol car. According to Cortinas, he actually heard a radio broadcast of an officer shooting not long after Tippit had left the shop – KLIF carried that broadcast at 1:33 in the afternoon. While the exact timing for the Record Shop stop remains in doubt, the sequence of events (as an alternative to the official record of Tippit's movements) appears to be clear. Upon moving into Oak Cliff, he had taken up a station to watch traffic coming from downtown

Dallas into Oak Cliff; he had then stopped and visually searched a car for someone hiding in the back seat, and had gone on to the Record Shop to make a call, not talking but only listening. From there he appears to have proceeded to East Tenth Street, and changed from his formerly hurried movements to simply cruising the street slowly until the encounter which led to his death.

While that encounter has been discussed and analyzed in immense detail, noteworthy points are that the first officer on the scene after Tippit's death found that Tippit's patrol car's driver side door was open and the car engine was still running. Photos show that the passenger side window was also rolled down, suggesting Tippit had first approached someone and talked to them through the window rather than stopping the car and exiting to confront a potentially dangerous suspect. The dispatcher tapes also show no sign that Tippit attempted to call the dispatcher to report such a stop, which would have been standard patrol practice. Beyond that, both the nature of a shot into the side of Tippit's head and eyewitness testimony suggest that he was shot after falling to the ground on his side, very intentionally and certainly fatally.

The anomalies in Tippit's behavior include his apparent monitoring of traffic over the bridge from downtown Dallas, making an unexplained land line call from the Record Shop, and stopping cars, searching for someone hiding in them. His stops, high speed movements, telephone call, and his appearance of concern at the Record Shop suggest that Tippit might have had a special assignment that day – perhaps an assignment that involved nothing more than watching and reporting on Lee Oswald's return to Oak Cliff. It that return had not gone according to plan, or if Tippit had not been fully aware of all that was to occur, his increasingly erratic behavior would certainly make more sense than the official story of his simply being ordered to move from his normal patrol zone and await further instructions. Along with that speculation, it also has to be noted that there are indications that Tippit may have had his own connections into the Cuban community in Dallas, possibly even with individuals connected to the house on Harlandale Street.[315]

Yet there were individuals whose behavior is even more mysterious, and far more suggestive than either Officers Olsen or Tippit. Perhaps the most dramatic example of truly conspiratorial behavior is that related to unnamed and unidentified individuals behind the fence line on the grassy knoll immediately following the shooting.

DPD Officer Joe Smith approached a man in the parking lot behind the fence. He drew his service weapon and approached him; however, the man showed credentials which appeared to Smith to be Federal. Thinking him to be a Secret Service agent, Smith asked no further questions and moved on. Later Smith would recall he had been surprised because the man was not dressed as an agent; he had on casual clothing and appeared more like an auto mechanic – he was especially surprised by how dirty the man's fingernails appeared to be when showing his credentials.

Other local law enforcement personnel who entered the area behind the fence also encountered individuals who later research has shown to be suspicious. W.W. Mabra (Deputy Sheriff) and Orville Smith (County Baliff) moved behind into the area of the parking lot directly behind the fence – where multiple witnesses had felt shots had originated – and approached a uniformed DPD officer, who immediately turned them away and told them that no search in that area was necessary.

W.W. Mabra later stated that the officer had told them *"I was stationed in the rail yards and had this whole area in view. Nobody came this way."* [316] He reinforced that by telling them *"Fellas, I've been here for an hour and there hasn't been a thing here, not even a stray dog."*

At that point, Mabra and Smith gave up their search of the area. If they had continued behind the fence line, they might well have discovered the evidence (later documented) that someone had indeed been behind the fence for a considerable time, smoking in a small area between a parked car and the fence, and leaving muddy foot prints there and on the car bumper (which suggested they were standing up to watch over the fence). Apparently the individual had been watching and waiting in that relatively concealed area for some time, in advance of the motorcade's arrival. The individual might also have gotten their hands dirty picking up any suspicious evidence which would have remained – explaining the dirty fingernails Smith had noticed during his encounter.

Later research in the Dallas Police reports on security preparations for President Kennedy's visit revealed that no DPD officers were assigned to that rail yard or behind the fence in the parking area – or anywhere along the Elm Street extension in front of the Texas School Book Depository. When questioned about the incident by researchers, Mabra initially stated he had recognized the man behind the fence but would not give his name. He refused to talk further about the incident when referred to records of officer assignments which clearly showed no DPD personnel were indeed stationed in that area.

While speculative, it is also possible that DPD officers could actually have been brought far enough into the conspiracy to actually plant evidence pointing towards Lee Oswald. What is certain is that many of the key items of crime scene evidence have extremely poor chains of possession, and would likely have never survived admission into any objective jury trial. The majority of those issues relate to evidence at the scene of the shooting – including the paper bag ostensibly used by Oswald to carry a rifle to the Texas School Depository, and the three hulls associated with the Mannlicher–Carcano recovered in the building.

The whole question of planted evidence is further obscured by the almost incredibly poor record keeping related to areas of the crime scene and the DPD forensics investigations, including items which are now known to have disappeared from the official record. The missing materials (all documented as existing at some point in time) include a list of vehicle tags made as the cars in the TSBD parking lot were released, a list of the witnesses in the Texas Theatre, a polygraph of the man (Frazier) who drove Oswald to work on the day of the assassination (in which he stated the bag taken into evidence by the Dallas Police did not appear to him to be similar to the sack he had seen Oswald carry to work that morning)[317], and a record of a crime scene unit investigation of a bullet strike on the south side of Elm Street. We have independent evidence that all those things occurred, yet none of them made it into the official DPD records.

Perhaps the most outstanding mystery in terms of police evidence handling is the "three wallet" problem. One wallet was recovered from the Paine residence, where Lee Oswald had left it with his wife Marina. A second wallet was reported over Dallas Police radio as being recovered from Oswald's pocket while he was being transported by police car following his arrest. Yet police records actually show three wallets associated with Oswald being taken into evidence. And statements from officers at the Tippit shooting scene, as well as video evidence, confirm that a wallet (not Tippit's) was recovered at the scene of Officer Tippit's murder.[318]

The issue of the wallet from the Tippit murder scene is particularly important as it relates to which wallet contained the identification card linking Lee Oswald to the Hidell alias – which in turn connected him to the Fair Play for Cuba Committee which was so important to his pro-Cuba, pro-Castro image. And the wallet clearly recovered at the Tippit crime scene is mentioned nowhere in Dallas police reports or officer statements. Which means that even with the most lenient interpretation – that the official story of the wallet with the Hidell ID was taken from Oswald inside the police patrol car after his arrest is true – there remains the fact that a wallet from the Tippit crime scene went undocumented and remains a total mystery! Given the scope of such evidentiary issues, it becomes challenging to separate the possibility of Dallas Police involvement in evidence manipulation from simply sloppy professional practices.

Oswald in Dallas

An additional mystery related to DPD evidence handling raises speculation that Lee Oswald might have been in contact with individuals associated with the new Artime AMWORLD project. While the idea of covert contact with Oswald has been mentioned previously, there is a possibility that when Oswald was ultimately taken into custody on November 22, he was found to be in the possession of a torn dollar bill. If such a bill had been recorded, it could be seen as a sign of actual "tradecraft" being used by people in touch with Oswald – we know that exactly that same contact mechanism was being used inside the AMWORLD project, specifically as a personal recognition signal.[319]

Unfortunately, the torn bill remains strictly a matter of controversy and debate, as nothing of that nature does exist in the extant official record. Researcher John Armstrong did locate Dallas Police materials (which he copied and has made available) that documents the existence of two torn bill halves existing within the DPD records at some point in time. However, nothing connecting them to Oswald exists, and the annotation that confirms the torn bill existed, and was related to Oswald, had disappeared from the record by the time the relevant document reached the National Archives.

Which leaves the idea and implication of a torn bill in the same intensely gray area as that of multiple wallets, and questions about which wallet contained exactly what pieces of personal identification. Of course by this point in time, given decades of research as well as the work of the ARRB, the possibility of missing or even altered records (especially if they might connect Oswald to the intelligence community) has been well established.[320] If the torn bill had indeed been recovered by police and documented as Armstrong describes, it would not only suggest that Oswald was being covertly contacted, but also indicate an effort to eliminate a very suggestive piece of evidence. If a torn bill can ever be proven to have existed, and connected to Oswald, it would be no great shock to find it had gone missing from the records.

Beyond the question of covert contacts with Oswald, it remains unclear when he was selected as a patsy specifically for the Dallas attack. It is virtually impossible to resolve specific sponsors for his activities while in New Orleans, including his letters to the

Communist Party USA and Socialist Workers Party. The question remains whether that letter-writing might have been suggested to Oswald by the FBI, or possibly carried out as part of a propaganda project for the CIA.

Regardless of any such influence on Oswald, one thing is clear. After the events of the summer of 1963 in New Orleans, any anti-Castro Cuban exiles Oswald might have later approached would almost certainly have known or quickly learned of his highly public Castro support. That suggests that at some point, individuals contacting Oswald in order to gain his interest and further manipulate him as a "pointer" towards Cuba and Castro, might have represented themselves as actual Castro agents. That would have been consistent with the very first test of Oswald in New Orleans, when a DRE associate, earlier rumored to have been a Castro supporter, assumed that role in his contacts with Oswald.

It is also possible that an association between Oswald and suspected Cuban agents in Dallas might have occurred as part of an ongoing FBI subversive investigation being conducted there. Special Agent Walter Heitman had been carrying out an active investigation of one and possibly more Cubans in Dallas reported to be Castro double agents – one of the individuals was directly associated with the group frequenting the previously mentioned house on Harlandale – reportedly visited by Lee Oswald.

One of Heitman's subversive targets in 1963 had been Osvaldo Aurelio Pino Pino. Pino had been reported in Miami as being a Cuban intelligence informant, and Heitman followed the inquiry when Pino moved to Dallas. The Harlandale house was rented by a friend of Pino's, Jose Salazar. Heitman also investigated Pino as possibly being involved with incidents related to Sylvia Odio.[321] Pino himself admitted to Heitman that he had joined a variety of exile groups in Dallas – this was confirmed by a series of FBI informants. Heitman ostensibly was forced to suspend the Pino Pino inquiry for several months, due to being assigned to the FBI's JFK assassination investigation; he only completed his report on Pino

Pino in the fall of 1964.[322] Unfortunately we have no other subversive files related to Heitman's work in Dallas.

The Attack

The attack involved the deployment and support of a small tactical team, two shooters with two to three others to monitor news and progress of the motorcade as well as provide low profile shielding for the infiltration and exfiltration of the shooters. It very likely included diversions to focus attention away from the team as its members entered and exited the plaza. We certainly find indications of distractions and diversions in Dealey Plaza – a pickup stalled under the overpass on Elm Street, drawing police attention in the hour before the motorcade arrived, and an ambulance blocking the intersection at Elm and Houston also drawing crowd and police attention (the ambulance can be seen departing just as the motorcade turns onto Houston).[323]

Then there was a puff of the smoke behind the knoll fence at the time of the shooting. The smoke was quite visible to a number of the observers watching the motorcade from the railroad overpass. From their view it was lit by the sun and quite visible. Along with the noise of the shooting it led them to believe shots had been fired from behind the fence line – and to rush to that location. One witness, Sam Holland, reported it as an obvious puff of smoke, coming over the fence and through the trees about six to eight feet off the ground – "like someone had thrown a firecracker," an impression based on the smoke and the sound that accompanied it.[324] That smoke certainly drew the attention of onlookers and helped ensure that several of the first police to approach the scene were directed to the fence line – only to be turned away by an unidentified, uniformed police officer. And as noted earlier, any remains of a firecracker, black powder squib or even shells, could have been quickly dug out of the dirt and pocketed, resulting in the dirty fingernails observed by Officer Smith.

All the standard elements of a successful guerrilla ambush appear to have been in play; the only thing missing was someone to pick up the weapons as the shooters exfiltrated. However, given that the police did virtually no searching other than inside the Texas School Book Depository, concealment at points around the plaza could have been quickly done. The weapons used could have been picked up hours or even days after the attack.

What remains uncertain, especially given the fact that Oswald himself appears to have behaved in an "uncontrolled" manner – before, during, and after the shooting – is to what level was he actively involved? Or was he simply framed? Martino tells us Oswald was supposed to meet a contact at the Texas Theatre that day, but offered nothing more, including when the meeting was to occur. It certainly appears that Martino himself did not know all the operational details (as a whole, the information he did relate was quite limited). And a number of Oswald's remarks and activities suggest that he was not aware that President Kennedy would be attacked, much less killed. In that respect, his behavior is quite similar to Jack Ruby's; tracing his changes in behavior that afternoon suggests Oswald was simply reacting to events, following no well-orchestrated course of action.[325]

From a tactical standpoint, what little insight was offered by our sources on the attack itself leaves us with a straightforward scenario, something very similar to the plans that had been in play in putting Castro assassination missions into Cuba. The difference being that in Dallas, unlike Cuba, the advantage was all with the attackers. After numerous incidents involving a variety of attempted attacks on Castro, including medium range attacks with weapons including a bazooka, his security had become extensive – prepared for all types of attacks, from any distance and from virtually any location.

Castro did make public appearances, but with a type of wide area security entirely unlike the protective service arrangements which were standard for American leaders – security which focused largely on close-in threats to the president. That approach was based on the history of presidential attacks; the Secret Service emphasized body protection, implemented to protect the president when in contact with crowds and as a defense against pistol attacks, and expanded security at the sites of extended public appearances, such as speeches (extended area security had been in place for the president's speech in Fort Worth that morning, and was also in place for the president's scheduled luncheon that day).

It must also be noted that the Secret Service had developed a practice of relating threats to specific geographies. In the fall of 1963, a credible threat of rifle attack from a tall building had come out of Miami, but since the threat referenced Washington D.C., it was investigated in that context and filed with the Washington office. Concerns about demonstrations or even violence during President Kennedy's fall trip to Florida resulted in elaborate security precautions, focused on the Cuban communities in Miami and Tampa. In Miami the Secret Service even solicited CIA assistance from the JMWAVE station. However, when planning was being done for the Texas trip, the protective service threat file checks focused specifically on the cities being visited in that state.

There were anticipated threats (primarily seen as related to demonstrations) in Dallas; warnings were expressed by local business leaders and politicians. Dallas was developing a reputation for violent protests. Earlier, Vice President Johnson and his wife had literally been chased through downtown Dallas by an ultra-right mob led by women protesters. That fall the American UN Ambassador had been actually pummeled by sign-wielding protestors during his visit to the city. The primary security concern for President Kennedy's visit was political protests, demonstrations going out of control and becoming violent. Texas Congressmen and prominent local citizens actually called and wrote to Washington, warning that Dallas might not be safe for the president.

Exceptional precautions were taken for the anticipated political violence during the president's public appearance at the Trade Mart. They included creating photo books of local protestors and briefing security, to block or otherwise detain them if they appeared at the Trade Center where JFK was to speak. Some demonstrators at the

Trade Center were challenged while the motorcade was still proceeding through Dallas. The major Dallas police physical security effort was focused on the Trade Center; the DPD officers in charge of security preparations were there waiting for the president's arrival. Beyond that, the Dallas Council had passed a special new law against violent political protests, the Chief of Police went on television and there was a general appeal to citizens to actually intervene to prevent any demonstrations or violent protests during the president's appearance.

In contrast, the president's motorcade was treated more as a traffic control challenge, with special precautions to ensure the route did not become blocked – allowing a street protest to develop around the president or vice president. DPD Traffic Control sent a scout car in advance to look for such problems, officers were stationed at major intersections on the route, and that morning's DPD briefing was all about making the "parade" go smoothly.

Secret Service personnel had done their best at the airport to keep JFK back from the crowds – that was always difficult. They had come on and off the president's limo and the security car at different points as the car slowed several times on the long route through the city. But there was simply no wide area protective security in play on the long route down Main Street, onto Houston and out to the freeway via Elm Street. That was the traditional route for political parades in Dallas, one that had been first described and later illustrated in the paper earlier that week.[326] With the information available and the DPD focused on traffic control, paramilitary operatives trained to go after Fidel Castro in heavily defended venues inside Cuba faced little in the way of protective challenge in their assault on the American president.

And it is at that point which the scenario for the actual attack on the president encounters the limitations of the information from our sources – a rifle attack by well trained, skilled, experienced, CIA-trained Cuban exiles. Men who were veterans of the training in the Cuba Project, of operations for the Miami CIA station. Individuals motivated by revenge and their own national patriotism, dedicated to the fight against communism in Cuba and to ousting the Castro regime. A conspiracy not just to kill JFK but to frame Lee Oswald for the shooting, and to leverage his known Fair Play for Cuba media visibility to link the assassination to Cuba, to Fidel Castro.

An attack which killed President Kennedy (and ended any possibly of any new American relationship with a neutral, non-aligned Cuba), but failed to point the blame towards Castro – that effort was defeated by the "lone nut" damage control out of Washington D.C. which immediately swung into play during the first 48 hours following the president's murder.

A Visible Conspiracy

There is simply no indication that any effort was made to restrict or structure the attack on President Kennedy to create the perception of a lone shooter – that was strictly an artifact of the "lone nut" messaging that emerged during the 48 hours following President Kennedy's murder. Certainly, the first day reports out of Dallas provided ample suggestion of an organized attack by multiple participants and of a well-planned conspiracy at work. Smoke from the fence line on Elm Street, mysterious individuals behind the fence line (one a uniformed Dallas patrolman), suspicious out of state cars circulating through a restricted/fenced parking area behind the fence line, the blocking of the motorcade intersection at Elm and Houston by an ambulance at the scheduled time of arrival of the motorcade, a stalled pick-up blocking one line under the railroad underpass which was towed away only at the last moment, more bullet impacts and actual recovered bullets than match the supposed three shots fired by Oswald, the list goes on and on.

FBI Director Hoover was upset that the Dallas Police were talking to the press far too much about indications of anyone other than Oswald being involved. A prime example was Dallas Police Chief Curry's televised statements that the police had witnesses who had seen Oswald picked up after the shooting by a Negro driving a station wagon (a point later confirmed by at least three independent witnesses).[327]

Some of the leads suggesting multiple participants and indications of conspiracy were investigated, but very quietly and with a number of the related reports simply disappearing over time – much like the polygraph of Buell Frazier rejecting the "sack" as Oswald's, the list of license plates for cars parked behind the fence line, the possibility of an unaccounted-for bullet impacting on the south side of Elm Street, or the list of witnesses at the Texas School Book depository. Leads and evidence which did not fit the "lone nut" story line literally faded away during the early days of the official inquiry.

Other leads towards conspiracy were more actively suppressed, beginning as early as the evening of the assassination. A number of such incidents are anecdotal, but supported in remarks by various individuals in law enforcement. The suppression included calls from the White House to Dallas police and other Texas law enforcement officials, in Dallas and elsewhere, which included direct orders not to bring charges of conspiracy against Lee Oswald or otherwise make any mention of others being involved in the attack.[328]

Interviews conducted by the ARRB revealed that, over the weekend following the assassination, the original photographic study of the Zapruder film (taken in the Plaza at the time of the shooting) may well have suggested multiple shooters. A set of photographic storyboards from the film was prepared Saturday evening at the National Photographic Interpretation Center (NPIC). Those storyboards were used to brief CIA Director McCone and possibly other senior national security personnel on Sunday. Following that briefing, a second set of storyboards were prepared (without the knowledge of the individuals involved in the construction of the first set; one of whom told the ARRB that he had clearly seen evidence of shots from multiple locations). The second set of storyboards came to represent the official illustration of the shooting. The original set were apparently left stored at NPIC, only to be quickly destroyed when it was discovered some years later.[329]

Other first day suggestions of conspiracy have been obscured and are now only evident in a variety of issues with the Bethesda autopsy materials – illustrated by the loss or destruction of autopsy notes from all three doctors, the destruction and revision of multiple versions of the official autopsy report (the ARRB was unable to specifically determine how many versions had existed), missing autopsy photographs described both by the Bethesda photographers and the autopsy doctors, the fact that – in violation of all normal protocols – the professional medical illustrator was not allowed to view the autopsy photos or X-rays in developing the official sketches documenting shots and wounds, and the fact that the doctors apparently did not mark or annotate the autopsy photographs according to required evidentiary protocols.

Problems with the Bethesda autopsy evidence only add to the numerous issues of chains of evidence within both the Dallas Police and the FBI. Beyond that, certain of the evidence collected by the Secret Service exhibits similar issues. Those problems are well illustrated by the Secret Service handling of the key piece of evidence (Commission Exhibit 399) connecting the wounds of both President Kennedy and Governor John Connolly to the rifle found in the Texas School Book Depository – CE399 being the bullet which purportedly struck both men, essential to the three-shot shooting sequence offered in the Warren Commission Report and to linking Oswald's rifle to the shooting.

Surprisingly, the bullet officially in evidence as CE399 could not be positively identified by the Secret Service agent who had taken it into evidence at Parkland Hospital in Dallas. The recipient of the bullet in Washington, Secret Service Chief James Rowley, also stated that he could not verify the bullet given to him by that agent as being CE399. Yet a third Secret Service Agent did verify CE399 as the bullet that had given to him by Chief Rowley. Based on those statements CE 399 came from Chief Rowley, but could not be linked to Dallas or the wounding of Kennedy and Connally. Yet it would have been only one of many evidentiary problems if Lee Harvey Oswald had actually come to trial.[330]

Beyond questions of evidence manipulation, the suppression of initial concerns over the possibility of conspiracy is now well documented. As noted in the introduction to this work, we now have records and sources which confirm that even while the Oswald "lone nut" story was being created with the media and in the initial FBI report, the Directors of both the FBI and CIA were still very much concerned that a conspiracy had been in play, and that even if Lee Oswald had done all the shooting, he had not acted on his own. In the introduction to this work, it was noted that a similar view was also very privately held by some of JFK's closest friends, by individuals in his administration – and by both his brother and his wife. Years later, one of Jackie Kennedy's close personal friends, William Walton, related that Mrs. Kennedy had actually used him in a backchannel communication to the Soviet leadership. Knowing that he was scheduled to go to Moscow, she asked that he ask his friend Georgi Bolshakov, an associate of Soviet leader Nikita Khrushchev, to pass on the message that President Kennedy had been killed by a conspiracy, not simply by a lone gunman.[331]

Yet regardless of those suspicions – as well as many highly suggestive leads and pieces of evidence – the public position of a "lone nut" assassin was essentially forced into place within the first 72 hours. But that effort was so disconnected and uncoordinated, that dozens if not hundreds of issues and loose ends have emerged over the years. Those loose ends were called out in the early work done by citizen researchers, inquiries during the Garrison investigation, by the House Select Committee on Assassinations, and ultimately by the work of the Assassinations Records Review Board and its staff.

The evidentiary problems, the missing materials, even the original issues, objections and dissension among members of the Warren Commission – all argue against any well-planned or coordinated "cover up" after the fact. Instead, we find a series of knee-jerk responses by the Johnson administration to establish and sustain the image of Oswald as the sole assassin. In addition, as noted in the Senate Select Intelligence Committee (Church Committee) report, there is the definite "possibility that senior officials of both FBI and CIA may have made conscious decisions not to disclose potentially important information" relating to the assassination[332] – decisions most likely based in their own prior knowledge and activities related to Lee Harvey Oswald.

While there is ample evidence of post-assassination information suppression coming into play at the highest levels of the national government – as well as within both the FBI and the CIA – there is no proof that a specific protocol was invoked by Johnson to suppress the investigation of a conspiracy. But we do know that the experience of the Cuban Missile Crisis had sensitized both John and Robert Kennedy to how quickly a national security crisis could spiral out of control, and that there was concern over possible Cuban retaliation against the United States.

That concern was voiced early in 1963, following the Cuban Missile Crisis, and it led to the creation of an inter-departmental committee charged with monitoring potential Cuban actions about American diplomats or political leaders.[333] The individual initially tasked with that planning was none other than William Harvey, most recently head of the CIA's Task Force W – which had been conducting its own assassination efforts against Fidel Castro.

And as of the fall of 1963, there was a new concern – the possibility that Cuban retaliation against the United States might be provoked by unilateral action by anti-Castro activists. That concern is supported by information found in AMWORLD project documents. That project's military leader, Rafael Quintero, was proposing the kidnapping of Cuban United Nations diplomats, and AMWORLD plans also included ongoing efforts by the group to assassinate Castro and other senior regime figures.

Based on the possibility of some action by Cuba, contingency planning had been initiated to establish protocols which would control any immediate government response to incidents involving American officials, including accidents and deaths. By fall, the effort had moved on to actual planning for protocols to control and contain any government response should an attack on American diplomats or government officials occur, or even be suspected.

The Cuban Coordinating Committee had picked up the issue of possible retaliation against American politicians or diplomats, and a planning session for such protocols had actually occurred on November 12, 1963.[334] The protocols addressed keeping details from the press and controlling investigations in such a matter as to avert a crisis over something which had simply been either an accident or a random criminal act.

Our information on this contingency planning is extremely limited, and there is no evidence Johnson as vice president was aware of them. However, it is possible that certain Kennedy administration staff actions immediately following the assassination might have been based in the discussions and concerns raised during the contingency planning.

The Castro linkage?

The sources cited in this work almost unanimously suggest that the attack on President Kennedy was supposed to point to sponsorship by Cuba and Fidel Castro. Certainly the early headlines did take full measure of Lee Oswald as a pro-Castro figure, an activist supporting the Fair Play for Cuba Committee. His activities in New Orleans had generated sufficient grist for that. But several factors also helped ensure that aspect of Oswald's past quickly made it into the national media coverage.

Information from Oswald's time in Soviet Russia, his support of Castro, and his involvement in the FPCC was quickly offered to the press by the DRE, based on files in its Miami office. Beyond that, DRE associates in New Orleans had materials including leaflets used by Oswald, and even a tape of Oswald's radio appearance with Carlos Bringuier and Ed Butler of the Information Council of the Americas (INCA). Oswald had been identified as an official representative of the FPCC in that debate (even though that was not true). The Information Council of the Americas (INCA) distributed the interview as part of a record album "Self Portrait in Red." Other "vanity" special interest record albums utilizing segments of Oswald's interviews were being published by a variety of anti-Communist groups.[335]

As the national media began its coverage of Lee Oswald being the man that killed the president, reporters began to be referred to Hal Hendrix of the Scripts-Howard News Service. We now know that Hendrix was a long-time media contact for the CIA, for its Miami Station and for David Phillips. In fact, Hendrix's Pulitzer award-winning reporting on the Cuban Missile Crisis was based on confidential information provided by the CIA.

Hendrix's insider relationship with the CIA continued for years, with his reporting of a coup in the Dominican Republic a day before it actually occurred (Phillips had been the CIA lead in the Dominican affair), and into the early 1970's during the CIA's anti-Allende project in Chile (led by David Phillips). Hendrix was identified as having provided International Telephone and Telegraph with highly confidential information on the Allende government. When questioned on the matter by a Congressional committee, Hendrix was later shown to have lied in order to cover his CIA source.[336]

On November 22, reporters seeking information from the Scripps Howard service on Cuban affairs and on Lee Oswald were referred to Hal Hendrix in Miami. Hendrix was apparently well prepared with details on Oswald, from Oswald's time in the Soviet Union to the past summer's activities in New Orleans – even though New Orleans was not part of his regular news beat.

Seth Kantor, a reporter calling from Dallas the day of the president's assassination, found Hendrix to have a wealth of information on Oswald and the Soviet Union, on his connection to the Fair Play for Cuba Committee, and his support of the Castro regime. As it turned out, Hendrix himself had quickly taken the initiative to contact

Scripts Howard and offer his services as a source on Oswald's background.

It certainly appears that Hendrix had been given extensive details on Oswald. Perhaps that had been in preparation for Phillip's new anti-FPCC propaganda effort. In support of AMWORLD, Phillips was assigned to target the FPCC across the U.S. and into Central America. In any event, details supplied by Hendrix allowed Oswald to be quickly tagged as a suspect communist, and most definitely a Castro supporter – if not an outright Castro operative.

Yet Hendrix actually had nothing new to offer; it was the same material that had come into play months earlier in New Orleans, aired in multiple radio broadcasts. There was nothing new connecting Oswald to Castro or Cuban agents. There were no names, no leads, and no details on suspicious meetings – nothing to establish Oswald as being directly instigated, encouraged, or even paid to attack President Kennedy.

In other words, nothing from Hendrix, nothing leaked from the investigations, and none of the leads pointing towards Cuba and Castro we would expect from a professionally organized plan – a plan not just to kill JFK, but to absolutely tie his death to Castro. If the plotters were following the guidelines in Harvey's executive action notes, something had happened to the "pointers" which should have been produced to associate the assassination with the communists.

Instead, what we find is a patchwork collection of anecdotal stories, all contrived to bring Cuba into the assassination, but with no credible material to support them beyond the simplest examination. One of the first, and ostensibly the most authoritative, came out of Mexico City, with the promotion of a story from a purported first-hand witness to Oswald receiving money and direction (while in a public area of the Cuban embassy) to kill President Kennedy.

That bizarre story and the witness, Gilberto Alvarado, was endorsed by David Phillips, Mexico City CIA station chief Winston Scott and Ambassador Thomas Mann.[337] The endorsements described the "wealth of detail" from Alvarado, and identified him as a "well known Nicaraguan communist underground member." Even when elements of his story, such as the date of the incident, came under scrutiny, the Mexico City team continued to support his story – "*Alvarado is telling the truth in general outline but mixed up on the dates.*" [338]

Given Phillips's vaunted reputation for disinformation, if he were personally involved with creating the Alvarado story it was an extremely poor effort.[339] Certainly nothing about the Alvarado story suggests that it had been well-crafted or supported with the sort of material found in professional propaganda operations. However, given that Phillips was himself deeply committed to ousting Fidel Castro, it may simply have represented a spontaneous effort to tie Castro to the assassination and prompt action against Cuba. The only element which appeared to corroborate the lead was that the government of Nicaragua verified that Alvarado was an active agent/informant for the Nicaraguan security sources, giving him some initial level of credibility.

The obvious questions of why a Nicaraguan security agent on a penetration mission against the Cubans would not have immediately reported such an incident to Nicaraguan intelligence, or why that would not have been then passed to the CIA, were not raised. In the end, as soon as the Alvarado story came under detailed scrutiny, the lead quickly collapsed – along with the thought that Cuba agents would have ordered and agreed to the assassination of an American president in a public area of their own diplomatic facility.

A second and even more patently false effort to link Oswald to Castro came in a letter which was sent to Lee Oswald's post office box in Dallas (two related letters were sent, to Lyndon Johnson and Robert Kennedy, respectively). All the letters identified someone named as Pedro Charles, and all described a contact between Charles and Oswald in Miami, positioning Charles as a Castro agent and implicating Oswald as working for Castro in the assassination. However, all the letters had been typed on the same typewriter, mailed as a batch, and postmarked in Havana – and all arrived several days after the assassination, even the one congratulating Oswald on what he was ostensibly "about" to do. In short, the Pedro Charles letters were easily exposed as an after-the-fact effort to implicate Castro via Oswald.

One attempt to float actual sources to connect Oswald to Castro came to the FBI from John Martino. And at first Hoover was very interested in Martino's information.[340] Martino was claiming to offer details and sources who could purportedly verify that Oswald had visited Cuba before the assassination and had acted as an agent for Castro in the murder.[341] Martino kept promising the actual sources and evidence, pleading that his sources were inside Cuba and out of communication for a time, or even on the way back to the United States.[342] The FBI also referred Martino to the Secret Service, who filed a report on his assertions – but by that time Martino was no longer citing his personal contacts as sources for his claims.[343] In the end, his lack of any actual concrete confirmation exceeded the FBI's patience and their interest simply faded away.[344]

Other versions of Martino's basic story were also taken to the news media, and anyone else who would listen.[345] The stories came from Carlos Bringuier in New Orleans, Frank Sturgis and his friends the anti-Castro activist Buchanan brothers in Miami, and from Nathanial Weyl.[346] Weyl was Martino's ghost writer and was also working on a book with William Pawley.

Paul Bethel, David Phillip's close friend – who had worked for a time in 1961 at JMWAVE – also brought similar stories to the media. Like Martino he offered sources, and actually named one, attributing his information to the purported confession of Pascual Enrique Gongora, the self-admitted member of a Castro sponsored hit team sent into the United States. A brief investigation turned up the information that Gongora had actually been in a mental institution for some time before the assassination – and nothing that would substantiate his story.

The versions of the "Oswald/Castro" story coming from Martino, Sturgis and Bringuier all referenced unnamed sources, inside Cuba or on covert missions involving Cuba. In some instances, Ruby was added to the mix as a Castro agent.[347] Yet the FBI did have access to one source who had actually been in contact with Oswald, at the time representing himself as a pro-Castro activist. In fact, that individual – Carlos Quiroga – may well have provided Oswald with the first FPCC leaflets used in New Orleans. Quiroga had admitted contact with Oswald, presenting himself as another Castro supporter.

Quiroga himself had actually been suspected of being a Castro agent at one point in time, but after the assassination he had actively promoted an Oswald/Cuba linkage to the media. Surprisingly, even after being quoted and named in a national news on that story, the FBI failed to even interview Quiroga – the one individual who was known to have approached Oswald as a Castro sympathizer.[348]

Still, there are some signs that the conspiracy might have at least made some effort to come up with something concrete to tie Oswald to Castro and Cuba. The most obvious effort may have been to connect him to someone very visibly tied to Castro himself, a friend Castro had taken the trouble to actual visit after the Cuban revolution, a friend who lived in Texas.

President Kennedy's fall trip to Texas was publicly announced on September 13, and in late September John Martino traveled to both New Orleans and Dallas.[349] At approximately that same time, Robert McKeown was approached at his home near Houston. The approach was by two men, one Anglo and one Latino. Only the Anglo offered his name – Lee Oswald – and did the talking, introducing his companion only as Hernandez.[350]

Oswald initially expressing a desire to buy machine guns and bazookas, military class weapons. As previously discussed, McKeown had been charged and convicted of weapons sales to Cuba and was still reporting to a parole officer at the time of the visit. He had also received a good bit of unwanted media visibility when he had been personally visited and thanked by Fidel Castro, following the successful ouster of Batista. In media terms he was well associated with both Cuba and personally with Castro himself, who had offered him a place in his regime. Equally importantly, as early as 1959 McKeown had been approached repeatedly by Jack Ruby for business introductions inside Cuba and to the Castro regime.

But in the fall of 1963, McKeown was in no mood to get involved in another round of weapons deals, especially with strangers. Expressing no desire to broker a deal on military weapons, he sent the two men on their way. Yet within some ten minutes they returned, expressing a desire to buy four Savage hunting rifles, with telescopic sights – they were willing to pay $1,000 apiece for the guns.

McKeown rejected that deal as well, at which time Oswald pressed to buy only a single rifle. It would still have been an outrageous price and the offer made McKeown even more suspicious. The whole thing felt wrong, and McKeown later testified that he actually told Oswald that he could go to any gun shop or to Sears and get the same rifle for around $300. Oswald responded that they wanted to buy the rifle from him.[351] The following is excerpted from McKeown's testimony on the incident:

McKeown. Coat and tie. Very nicely dressed. He was driving the car.

Mr. Dodd. Mr. Hernandez was driving the car?

Mr. McKeown. Right.

Mr. Dodd. What time of day was it?

Mr. McKeown. About 10:00 o'clock in the morning. 9:30, 10:00, something like that.

Mr. Dodd. Let us suspend for just one second.

(Pause) Mr. McKeown, at that meeting that you had with Mr. Oswald and Mr. Hernandez, to the best of your recollection, was that a situation where both Mr. Hernandez and Mr. Oswald were transpiring business, or was Mr. Hernandez merely someone who was driving in the car along with him and it was Mr. Oswald principally who was doing the business?

Mr. McKeown. It was Mr. Oswald who was doing all the talking.

Certainly, if McKeown had supplied weapons, or even a single rifle which could have been tied to an attack on President Kennedy, a definite link to Fidel Castro would have been established. For that matter it could easily have linked both Lee Oswald and Jack Ruby to Cuba and Castro. While that did not happen due to McKeown's suspicions, it is certainly suggestive – even more so because, as McKeown would later state, he thought he recognized Mr. Hernandez as one of the men he had worked with in smuggling weapons into Cuba.

While the identity of Hernandez remains unknown, research has revealed that one of the Cubans originally charged along with McKeown and others was operationally connected on Cuba Project maritime missions with Carlos Hernandez.[352] That individual was Jorge Sotus. As with many others from the revolution against Batista, Sotus turned against the new Castro regime and left Cuba. By early 1961, he was among the special group of Cuba Project trainees who had been selected for advanced training and then assigned to covert maritime missions into Cuba. More specifically, he served on a handpicked infiltration team with Carlos Hernandez.

The McKeown incident certainly could have served to link Oswald with Cuba and Castro if McKeown had chosen to supply rifles, even a single rifle – but he did not.

Based strictly on what we can see after the fact, it appears that while the ambush in Dealey Plaza was well designed and sadly effective, the associated efforts to frame Oswald and connect him to Castro were minimal in comparison.

None of the stories about Oswald (and Ruby) that surfaced after the assassination named any actual Cuban intelligence assets (known or suspected), names which would easily have been found in FBI or

CIA counter intelligence files. Credible names of Cuban agents would have added major traction to the claims Oswald had been influenced or enabled by foreign actors. There were no specifics about meetings at actual locations in Miami, no travel records which would show Oswald having been in Cuba, and no credible records of suspicious mail or voice communications prior to the assassination. In short, nothing of any substance that would have substantiated Cuban intelligence contacts with Oswald – and nothing of the nature of "evidence" which we would expect if experienced CIA psychological operations specialists were driving the framing of Lee Oswald as an agent for Cuba and Castro.

Final Words

There you have it. After some 30 years of research that's what I have to offer. Names have been named – other than those of the two actual shooters. Potential candidates for that role have been discussed in this work and in the Wheaton Lead research. Roles have been defined in regard to the attack in Dallas.

As to the precise origin of the conspiracy, that remains a guess at best. Did Richard Helms, or possibly retired Director Allen Dulles express serious concerns about Kennedy's policies being a risk to national security? JFK's move towards negotiations with Fidel Castro could well have been viewed as the next step beyond his efforts towards neutrality in Laos. Moving Cuba out of the Soviet bloc could have led to negotiations and non-alignment in Vietnam – something virtually all of the CIA's Cold War senior cadre would have strongly and adamantly opposed.

Did James Angleton and William Harvey engage in dialogues about the risks being taken by the Kennedy brothers, dialogues which trickled down to Miami Station? We know that virtually all the senior CIA officers in the Operations Directorate were heatedly opposed to negotiations with Castro, as was Western Hemisphere chief J.C. King. King had been the first to propose assassinating Castro, over three years earlier. Did remarks from one or more of those individuals get passed on to people that had worked on the earlier Castro assassination efforts? The sources cited here provide no answer to those questions, only on the Dallas conspiracy and attack.

Everyone is left to make their own call on those who incited the conspiracy, those who enabled it, and those who directly participated, but I suspect that a number of well-placed individuals had well-justified suspicions. Suspicions and leads expressed only in private remarks:

Robert Kennedy – “One of your guys did it” [353]

David Morales – “Well we took care of that Son of a Bitch!”

William Kent – “It’s better you don’t know!”

David Phillips – “My private opinion is that JFK was done in by a conspiracy, likely including American intelligence officers.” [354]

Citations and Commentary

[1] Assassinations Records Review Board, "Final Report", Chapter 8

[2] Daniel Schorr, "Oswald as Avenger", The Washington Post, November 25, 1983

https://www.washingtonpost.com/archive/politics/1983/11/25/oswald-as-avenger/cc9ab63e-8aeb-4ca9-8b41-15be6dc85830/

[3] Rex Bradford, The Fourteen Minute Gap, Mary Ferrell Foundation

https://www.maryferrell.org/pages/The_Fourteen_Minute_Gap.html

[4] Dan Hardway, "Thank You, Phil Shenon," Real Hillbilly Views, October 27, 2015

https://realhillbillyviews.blogspot.com/2015/10/

[5] Katzenbach Memorandum, Mary Ferrell Foundation

https://www.maryferrell.org/pages/Katzenbach_Memo.html

[6] David Robarge, "DCI John McCone and the Assassination of President John F. Kennedy," George Washington University, September 29, 2014

https://nsarchive2.gwu.edu//NSAEBB/NSAEBB493/docs/intell_ebb_026.PDF

[7] Anthony Summers, *Not in Your Lifetime*, 311, quoting his own 1994 Vanity Fair article ("The Ghosts of November"). Summers also says RFK was speaking to Haynes Johnson, and supplies this further description from Johnson: "Kennedy was utterly in control of his emotions when he came on the line.....and was studiedly brisk as he said 'One of your guys did it.' "

[8] While it is far too detailed to be discussed here, we now have a good understanding why McCone would have thought that, and why he likely was briefed (along with President Johnson) over the weekend of the assassination in regard to the likelihood of multiple shooters – this is

discussed in Chapter 15 "If I Told You" of my book *Someone Would Have Talked.* McCone's view would have come from an initial analysis and storyboard presentation related to frames from the Zapruder film. The details of that activity, as well as of other incidents related to the suppression and obfuscation of evidence which occurred during the first 72 hours after the assassination, are contained in Chapter 15 of the 2010 edition, 232-233. Also Douglas Horne, *Inside the Assassinations Records Review Board*, Volume 4, 2009.

[9] Ibid, 233-237 also Douglas Horne, *Inside the Assassinations Records Review Board*, Volume 1-4, 2009

[10] Jim DiEugenio, "Douglas Horne, Inside the ARRB," *Kennedys and King*, October 16, 2010

https://kennedysandking.com/john-f-kennedy-reviews/horne-douglas-inside-the-arrb

[11] Deposition of Dr. James Humes, Assassination Records Review Board, February 13, 1996

https://mcadams.posc.mu.edu/russ/testimony/humesa.htm

[12] George Lardner Jr., "Archive Photos Not of JFK's Brain, Concludes Aide to Review Board," Washington Post, November 10, 1998; Page A03

https://www.washingtonpost.com/wp-srv/national/longterm/jfk/jfk1110.htm

[13] Rex Bradford, "Whispers from the Silent Generation," Rex Bradford, May 2013; from a talk delivered at the 2008 November in Dallas conference

[14] Alexsandr Fursenko and Timothy Naftali, *One Hell of a Gamble*, W.W. Norton, 345

[15] Jack Pfeiffer, *Official History of the Bay of Pigs Operation,* Volume 3, U.S. Governments Anti-Castro Program Central Intelligence Agency, Central Intelligence Agency, Washington D.C., October 13, 2016, Document Number: 5076ddc4993247d4d82b58da

https://www.maryferrell.org/showDoc.html?docId=146518

[16] The Special Group – a high level policy committee created to conduct oversight over covert foreign actions – was tasked with ensuring that the Cuba Project would not be publicly revealed, or if it did become visible,

could at least be plausibly denied. The Special Group had been created and authorized by NSC Directive 5412/2 to conduct policy supervision of all covert foreign activities.

[17] Jack Pfeiffer, Official History of the Bay of Pigs Operation, Volume 3, U.S. Governments Anti-Castro Program Central Intelligence Agency, Central Intelligence Agency, Washington D.C., October 13, 2016, Document Number: 5076ddc4993247d4d82b58da, 16-18

https://www.maryferrell.org/showDoc.html?docId=146518#relPageId=26

[18] Ibid, 6-9

[19] Ibid, 13

[20] Julia E. Sweig, *Inside the Cuban Revolution*, Harvard University Press, 2002, Chapter 10, The Arms Race, 115

[21] Ibid, 118

[22] Ibid, 148

[23] Interview with Robert McKeown, House Select Committee Report, Volume IX, Section 8, 714-718

https://www.maryferrell.org/showDoc.html?docId=955&relPageId=722

[24] FBI Name Correlation document; information regarding activities of Frank Fiorini as related to Cuba

https://www.archives.gov/files/research/jfk/releases/docid-32300010.pdf

[25] By the end of 1959, both Fiorini and Diaz Lanz would abandon Castro and Cuba, based on their belief that Castro was turning to communism. Following their arrival in Miami, both men became involved in a variety of early, independent actions against Castro – the most spectacular being combined bombing and leafleting missions over Havana in October, during a high-profile international travel agents convention in that city.

[26] FBI Memorandum, Accounting and Fraud Investigation Section, June, 1964

https://www.maryferrell.org/showDoc.html?docId=48681&relPageId=24

[27] David Scheim, *Contract on America*, New York: Kensington, 1988, 221:

"In 1958, Ruby wrote a letter to the State Department's Office of Munitions Controls 'requesting permission to negotiate the purchase of firearms and ammunition from an Italian firm.' The name 'Jack Rubenstein' [Ruby's birth name] was listed in a 1959 Army Intelligence report on U.S. arms dealers. Although located by clerks of these two federal agencies in 1963, both documents are today inexplicably missing."

[28] Peter Dale Scott, *Deep Politics and the Death of JFK*, University of California Press, Ltd, 1993, 179

[29] Interview with Robert McKeown, House Select Committee Report, Volume IX, Section 8, 708-709

https://www.maryferrell.org/showDoc.html?docId=955&relPageId=716

[30] House Select Committee on Assassinations, Vol. 5, 365

https://www.maryferrell.org/showDoc.html?docId=956&relPageId=369

[31] Warren Commission Report, Testimony of Nelson Delgado, 687

https://mcadams.posc.mu.edu/russ/testimony/delgado.htm

[32] Ibid, 687

https://www.maryferrell.org/showDoc.html?docId=946&relPageId=711

[33] Hancock, *In Denial: Secret Wars with Tanks and Airstrikes?*, Chapters 5 and 6

[34] Don Bohning, *The Castro Obsession*, 50

[35] We now have a considerable level of detail in regard to the field officers and Cuban volunteers who would have been most influenced by the remarks carried to Miami by Jake Esterline. That detail is explored in *In Denial*, Chapter 3, "Insurgency," and in more detail (as potentially related to the Kennedy assassination) in the Wheaton Lead research paper by David Boylan and Larry Hancock, available online from the Mary Ferrell Foundation at:

https://www.maryferrell.org/pages/Essay_-_The_Wheaton_Lead.html

[36] Grayston Lynch, *Decision for Disaster; Betrayal at the Bay of Pigs*, Brassey's, 1998, 155 and 159

[37] President Kennedy's specific operational orders directed that the Cuban volunteers be inserted in a totally clandestine fashion. His National Security Directive simply authorized the CIA to conduct deniable actions to return the volunteers to Cuba. In order to ensure the clandestine nature of the mission, he directed that all landing operations had to be conducted at night and that all ships had to be out of Cuban territorial waters and in the open sea by daybreak. In addition, no Americans were allowed to participate in the landings nor as pilots or aircrews with the Cuban volunteer group.

JFK specifically directed that if the landing was detected and opposed, the force was to be evacuated and landed elsewhere – volunteers that remained needed to be trained and prepared to operate as guerrillas. Beyond that, he also specifically ordered that the senior officers of the Cuban force were to be briefed that there would be no US military action against Cuban forces. Although the president did not personally participate in operational meetings during the course of the three days of the landing, he was willing to allow a number of variances in his initial directives in order to support the Brigade as it came under continual attack.

U.S. pilots were authorized to fly Cuban Brigade aircraft in ground attacks in support of the lodgment /beachhead on the second and third days of the landings. Cuban pilots were authorized to fly night time bombing missions against Cuban airfields on the first and second nights after landing. The U.S. Air Force was authorized to fly night supply missions directly over the landing area – although due to lack of planning and preparation those missions were not actually executed.

By the third day, with the volunteer force under extreme pressure, the U.S. Navy was authorized to fly an air support mission over the beach, engaging Cuban aircraft and providing cover for American pilots authorized to fly additional missions in of support for the Brigade. That air cover was supposed to allow the implementation of the plan for evacuating the force – as it turned out no preparations had been made for such a contingency and the Cuban force had never been prepared for evacuation.

At the end, the only military action President Kennedy refused to order was to accept repeated Navy requests to conduct direct military intervention against the Cuban military, which would have constituted an act of war given that Cuban forces had not fired upon or engaged American military personnel or facilities.

In Denial / Secret Wars with Air Strikes and Tanks?, Chapters 4-6, 135-222

[38] Larry Hancock, *In Denial; Secret Wars with Tanks and Airstrikes?,* Chapter 6, 232-236

[39] Don Bohning, *The Castro Obsession*, Chapter 1

[40] Ibid, 74-75

[41] Hancock, *In Denial; Secret Wars with Tanks and Airstrikes*, Chapters 5, 6 and 7

[42] Ibid, Chapter 7

[43] Ibid, Chapter 7, "Hidden Measures"

[44] Security File on Frank Sturgis, HSCA Segregated CIA Collection, Memorandum for the Record, NARA Record Number: 1993.08.05.14:42:12:750028

https://www.maryferrell.org/showDoc.html?docId=104139#relPageId=14

[45] Larry Hancock, *Someone Would Have Talked*, Appendix D, "The Way of JMWAVE," 352-359

[46] Ibid, Appendix I, "Echoes from Dallas," 389-391

[47] Bissell's motives and intentions in his effort to divert blame towards President Kennedy remain debatable. Certainly he did go to great lengths to repudiate charges brought against his own decision making and management of the project – enough so to offer a rebuttal to the CIA Inspector General's assessment of the project's conduct failures. It appears that he may also have wished to suppress inquiry into certain hidden measures he was involved with, measures which were not communicated to President Kennedy. To some extent, he may also have been in a psychological state of denial, wishing to project his failure onto someone else, or simply not willing to openly face certain decisions he had made.

[48] Larry Hancock, *Someone Would Have Talked*, 141

[49] Hancock, *NEXUS*, 61

[50] Following the Kennedy assassination, Ted Shackley, Chief of Base at JMWAVE, would testify that he had made no internal inquires, stating that to be under the purview of the Warren Commission. That statement was proved to be false with the revelation that an investigation of Cuban exile involvement in the assassination had been conducted – under the management of Tony Sforza. The investigation had been extensive and was documented in a report which apparently disappeared after it was prepared.

[51] Hancock, *NEXUS*, 61-62

[52] CIA Memorandum to FBI, Subject: Alpha 66 / An Anti-Castro Organization, September 6, 1962

https://www.cia.gov/library/readingroom/docs/DOC_0000386756.pdf

[53] Hancock and Boylan, "The Wheaton Lead: An Exploration"

https://www.maryferrell.org/pages/Essay_-_The_Wheaton_Lead.html

[54] There remains a possibility that certain of the trainees may have also trained at Camp Stanley in Texas. In addition to being a major storage depot for CIA covert military operations, Camp Stanley appears to have been used for certain training activities, in particular radio communications training.

[55] Larry Hancock, *Someone Would Have Talked*, JFK Lancer Publications, 2010, Appendix E, "Student Warrior", 360-363

[56] Cuba Project mission documents relating to Victor Espinoza Hernandez, Carlos Hernandez, and Cuba Project maritime team operations.

https://www.maryferrell.org/showDoc.html?docId=38005#relPageId=2

https://www.maryferrell.org/showDoc.html?docId=21116#relPageId=3

https://www.maryferrell.org/showDoc.html?docId=34298#relPageId=2

https://www.maryferrell.org/showDoc.html?docId=36146&relPageId=2

https://www.maryferrell.org/showDoc.html?docId=40542&relPageId=3

[57] The crypt AMHAZE appears to broadly refer to covert maritime missions and mission personnel related to several types of missions into Cuba. Individual missions carried their own crypts.

https://www.maryferrell.org/php/cryptdb.php?id=AMHAZE

[58] John Prados, *Safe for Democracy*, Ivan R. Dee, Chicago: 2006, 307, also "On March 12, 1962, Team Cobra infiltrated Pinar del Rio province, creating a network active for some time. In June, AMTORRID went into Oriente, but most of it left in a few months. The one remaining agent and a fresh radioman set up in Santiago de Cuba as a spy mission." Also see 124-90139-10130: Cuban headlines of 11/14/62: "Four Hundred Miners Would Have Died if Terrorist Plan Succeeded," if the Batistiano Lieutenant Miguel Orozco had succeeded in the plans to blow up the mines in Matahambre and Nicaro.

https://www.maryferrell.org/php/cryptdb.php?id=AMCOBRA

https://www.maryferrell.org/showDoc.html?docId=121717

[59] Taylor Branch and George Crile III, "The Kennedy Vendetta / The Cowboys of JMWAVE," Harpers Magazine, July 1975, 9-11

https://www.maryferrell.org/showDoc.html?docId=12695&relPageId=10

[60] Ibid

[61] After first working in the FBI, Harvey had moved to the CIA, working in counter intelligence and specialized intelligence collections, involving activities ranging from wire taps though burglaries to assaults on foreign couriers. In 1962 he was assigned to the CIA's support of a larger, interdepartmental effort against Cuba – Mongoose. The CIA's support effort was designated Task Force W, with Harvey having oversight of activities ranging from the Miami Station / JMWAVE maritime missions to the new Castro assassination project.

[62] SSCIA Document, Record Number 157-10014-10102, Miscellaneous Records of the Church Committee, William Harvey

https://www.maryferrell.org/showDoc.html?docId=148871

[63] HSCA Document 180-10188-10069, Antonio De Varona Chronology

https://www.maryferrell.org/showDoc.html?docId=34140

[64] Larry Hancock, *NEXUS*, 65-71 also Bayard Stockton, *Flawed Patriot; The Rise and Fall of CIA Legend William Harvey*

[65] Hancock, *Someone Would Have Talked* 2010, 20

[66] Office of Security Files, Central Intelligence Agency

https://www.maryferrell.org/showDoc.html?docId=147377

[67] Hancock, *In Denial*, Chapter 7

[68] Hancock, *Someone Would Have Talked* 2010, 20

[69] Jim DiEugenio, *The JFK Assassination*, 2010, 174

[70] To say that Quiroga was an unwilling witness would be an understatement – as revealed in his statement to the Grand Jury convened in support of District Attorney Garrison's inquiry. Orleans Parish Grand Jury Special Investigation, May 24, 1967

https://www.aarclibrary.org/publib/jfk/garr/grandjury/pdf/Quiroga.pdf

[71] Hancock, *Someone Would Have Talked* 2010, 141

[72] Dan Hardway, "An Operational Sketch," 2014

https://aarclibrary.org/wp-content/uploads/2014/09/dan_hardway_aarc_9_26_14.pdf

[73] CIA memorandum, Chief of Station JMWAVE to Chief of Task Force W [William Harvey], AMSPELL [DRE] Progress Report for August, 1962

https://www.maryferrell.org/showDoc.html?docId=23849

[74] Taylor Branch and George Crile III, "The Kennedy Vendetta / The Cowboys of JMWAVE," Harpers Magazine, July 1975, 12

[75] Ibid, 9-11

https://www.maryferrell.org/showDoc.html?docId=12695&relPageId=10

[76] Intercontinental Penetration Force, Spartacus Educational

https://cuban-exile.com/doc_076-100/doc0090.html

https://spartacus-educational.com/JFKinterpen.htm

[77] Tangodown 63, The Assassination of President John Fitzgerald Kennedy

https://tangodown63.com/de-joseph-larry/

[78] FBI memorandum, FBI Miami to Director, March 28, 1963 also Cuban Information Archives

https://www.archives.gov/files/research/jfk/releases/docid-32340659.pdf

https://cuban-exile.com/doc_076-100/doc0090.html

[79] FBI Memorandum, Filipe Vidal Santiago, background investigation

https://www.archives.gov/files/research/jfk/releases/104-10221-10222.pdf

[80] House Select Committee on Assassinations, Volume X, Section IX, Overview of the DRE group

https://www.maryferrell.org/showDoc.html?docId=1212#relPageId=85

[81] Hancock, *Someone Would Have Talked* 2010, 141, 85 also

http://wimw-ford.blogspot.com/2006/11/ortsac-philbriglex-62.html

[82] The irony of President Kennedy's support of, and even personal participation in, conventional military exercises is further illustrated in yet another activity of 1962. That activity – designated as SEATO operation Tulungan – was personally observed by the president in March, 1962. The Tulungan exercises were conducted in the Philippines, coming during the final phase of a series of SEATO war games. JFK boarded the USS Oklahoma City to watch an amphibious landing, supported by a vertical envelopment carried out by a helicopter-borne force of U.S. Marines. Additional support for the exercise came from Marines carried in on troop transports from Okinawa, and troops were landed by boat, aircraft and helicopter.

Within two years many of the same American commanders, troops and tactics would come into play, not with orders from President Kennedy, but rather as part of his successor's decision to dramatically increase the deployment of conventional American military forces into Vietnam.

https://www.officialgazette.gov.ph/1962/04/02/official-week-in-review-march-25-march-31-1962/

https://www.navy.gov.au/sites/default/files/documents/Navy_News-May-27-1966.pdf

[83] President John Kennedy, September 13, 1962 / *Cuban Resolution Senate Joint Resolution 230 — Public Law 87-733, approved October 3, 1962*

https://www.jfklibrary.org/archives/other-resources/legislative-summary/defense-military

[84] Hancock, *NEXUS*, 86

[85] Americans freed in those negotiations included an extremely secret CIA covert action team that had been sent to Cuba to perform technical collections and hopefully steal code books from the Chinese embassy in Havana. The CIA technical directorate's chief audio specialist led the team. The Cubans had apparently not determined the actual value of the team – especially of David Christ – during his imprisonment, and the CIA concealed the importance of its release efforts by including other Americans in the negotiations, including John Martino. Martino had worked in the casinos in Cuba, then started his own small electrical company. Martino was eventually put into prison on charges of secretly assisting Cubans attempting to flee the island.

[86] Church Committee Interim Report, Section 3, 140

https://www.maryferrell.org/showDoc.html?docId=1156&relPageId=154

[87] "Kennedy Sought Dialog with Castro," National Security Archive, November 24, 2002

https://nsarchive2.gwu.edu/NSAEBB/NSAEBB103/index.htm

[88] Interview with William Harvey's Widow, JFK Facts, August 28, 2019

https://jfkfacts.org/a-true-sounding-of-the-politics-around-kennedy-when-he-was-assassinated/

[89] Jack Hawkins, Special Assistant for Counterinsurgency and Special Activities (SACSA), Joint Chiefs of Staff, Unconventional Warfare Plan Alfa

https://www.maryferrell.org/showDoc.html?docId=10310

[90] Meeting of the Special Group Augmented, May 23, 1963 (documents released Nov. 9, 2017), 8

https://www.maryferrell.org/showDoc.html?docId=189164

[91] Meeting of the Special Group, July 18, 1963

https://www.maryferrell.org/showDoc.html?docId=189164

[92] Remegio Arce appeared on the Miami scene only in 1962, as a freelancer associated with individuals such as Frank Sturgis, Gerry Hemming, Roy Hargraves, and the INTERPEN group. He was one of those arrested on an abortive boat raid on Cuba organized by Hemming. In that respect Arce appears quite unique, one of the only known individuals to make the transition to both JMWAVE operations, and Robertson's inner circle, without the experience of the Cuba project or the interim missions into Cuba during 1961/1962. Citation: William Turner, HSCA Interview Report 22-24, 1977, Part 5, 86

https://www.maryferrell.org/showDoc.html?docId=197034&relPageId=86

Also Hemming interview with Argosy magazine

https://www.maryferrell.org/showDoc.html?docId=110790&relPageId=8

[93] Cable, JMWAVE to Director, "Infiltrees"

https://www.maryferrell.org/showDoc.html?docId=29445

[94] Don Bohning, *The Castro Obsession*, 161-163

[95] Ibid, 164

[96] "Castro Says USA used Raider Ship," AP Wire Service, October 31, 1963

http://www.latinamericanstudies.org/pujol/NYT-11-1-1963-1.pdf

[97] CIA Cable from JMWAVE, Operation Involving Soviet Defectors which Mr. William Pawley Has Discussed, June 5, 1963

https://www.maryferrell.org/showDoc.html?docId=29002#relPageId=1

[98] Ibid, 3

https://www.maryferrell.org/showDoc.html?docId=29002#relPageId=3

[99] CIA Memorandum, Director Task Force W (Harvey) to CIA DDP, copy of memorandum for the Attorney General, September 3, 1962, also memorandum on contradictory information provided by Captain Eduardo Perez Gonzalez and a CIA informant report of April/May 1962 which evaluated Perez as unreliable, with inaccurate information and prone to excessive "small talk."

https://www.maryferrell.org/showDoc.html?docId=52403

https://www.maryferrell.org/showDoc.html?docId=55224

[100] Folder reviewed by the HSCA re the Bayo/Pawley Affair containing Ops CA; this folder includes an extensive operational description of the mission and is 254 pages in length, 38-47

https://www.maryferrell.org/showDoc.html?docId=105573

[101] Larry Hancock, *Someone Would Have Talked*, 21-22

[102] CIA Cable from JMWAVE, Operation Involving Soviet Defectors which Mr. William Pawley Has Discussed, June 5, 1963

https://www.maryferrell.org/showDoc.html?docId=29002#relPageId=3

[103] Internal JMWAVE memorandum, "Discussion TILT," Rip Robertson to Ted (Shackley) and Bob Bob Moore (pseudonym Fred Inghurst, Deputy Chief of Station; head of Maritime Operations).

https://www.maryferrell.org/showDoc.html?docId=28896

[104] Folder reviewed by the HSCA re the Bayo/Pawley Affair containing Ops CA, 30, 32

https://www.maryferrell.org/showDoc.html?docId=105573

[105] CIA Memorandum, JMWAVE to Director, Topic: Operation TILT, 4

https://www.maryferrell.org/showDoc.html?docId=28894

[106] TILT Photographs from Soldier of Fortune magazine article; Hancock Web site; *Someone Would Have Talked* reference materials

http://www.larry-hancock.com/documents/index.html

[107] Folder reviewed by the HSCA re the Bayo/Pawley Affair containing Ops CA, 6

[108] HSCA Volume 10, Section 4, "Cuban Revolutionary Council: A Concise History"

https://www.aarclibrary.org/publib/jfk/hsca/reportvols/vol10/pdf/HSCA_Vol10_AC_4_CRC_Hist.pdf

[109] Paulino Sierra JCGE / Junta – a chronology of the Junta's formation and activities:

Sierra officially announced the Junta on March 31, 1963, stating that he had pledges of 55 million dollars in funding from American banking and financial interests. He also stated that he had communicated via the owner of the King Ranch in Texas and had pledges of a base in Latin America via that connection.

Patricia Orr, HSCA numbered files, Anti-Castro activities, CIA, FBI, Administration

https://www.maryferrell.org/showDoc.html?docId=149157

In April Sierra traveled to Puerto Rico via New York, and in May extended an invitation to Manuel Artime and the MRR to join the Junta effort. In May he made an approach to several "action" groups including Commandos L, Alpha 66, etc. FBI investigation of Sierra's group revealed individuals associated with gambling, and casino businesses were involved with Sierra from the group's inception. Sierra was very much aware of the financial support coming from those syndicate connections. Claims were reported that some 12 million dollars had been committed by a Cleveland group (Jewish Mafia/Moe Daelitz/Meyer Lansky connected). Another 30 million was claimed to have been put forward from gambling interests in Miami. By June the Chicago FBI office had concluded the initiative was something of a con job, and had been unable to actually trace any syndicate money coming in to Sierra.

In June Sierra met with several mainstream, old line Cuba companies, in Chicago – United Fruit, Standard Oil, DuPont, ESSO, U.S. Steel and AT&T. He claimed that he had received pledges of major funding – as well as six hundred and fifty thousand dollars deposited in a Miami bank.

By October 1, 1963, Sierra had only purchased some six thousand dollars' worth of equipment. Lacking actual personnel, he paid to have material transported to Florida by freelance anti-Castro individuals out of Miami. Sierra did not even have enough volunteers to transport equipment purchases for the independent groups in Florida.

Steve Wilson, Denis Harber and Joe Garrman of Hemming's and Sturgis' earlier INTERPEN group were paid by Sierra to transport his purchases – and even offered money to make attacks against Cuba. Sierra appears to have been totally unable to line up actual exile fighters for his venture. The few followers he did have were in Chicago, and the FBI did interview one individual who on October 4 stated that he had planned a protest against JFK during his planned visit to Chicago on October 1; the protest was to be organized by Sierra supporter Jose Cordozo.

https://www.maryferrell.org/showDoc.html?docId=149157#relPageId=13

On October 14, Richard Lauchli was visited by Sierra, who stated he wished to buy weapons for exile group use. At that time, it appears that Sierra had turned his attention towards the DRE, and was offering financing to DRE military leaders who were visiting Chicago in the fall of 1963. Thomas Mosley served as one of the primary FBI sources on Lauchli's weapons sales, particularly to exile groups.

https://www.maryferrell.org/showDoc.html?docId=117734

The CIA continually monitored Sierra via its Cuban Intelligence/AMOT group sources, and concluded that he was acting as a front for gambling interests and should be avoided by CIA-associated individuals.

https://www.maryferrell.org/showDoc.html?docId=18256#relPageId=4

In December his employer, Union Tank Car, and other potential corporate donors backed off from Sierra due to apparent accounting and financial improprieties, costing the Junta its only real hope of financial support. By February 1964, Junta activities had ceased for all practical purposes.

[110] Julia E. Sweig, *Inside the Cuban Revolution*, Harvard University Press, 2002, 130-131

[111] Larry Hancock, *Someone Would Have Talked*, 2010, Appendix E, Student Warrior, 360-361

[112] HSCA Volume 10, Section 9, DRE, 82

https://www.maryferrell.org/showDoc.html?docId=1212#relPageId=86

[113] CIA memorandum, "Alpha 66; an Anti-Castro Organization," copies to FBI, Department of State (Security), DIA, INS, Army, Navy and Air Force, September 6, 1962

https://www.cia.gov/library/readingroom/docs/DOC_0000386756.pdf

[114] Memorandum, FBI Special Informant to Headquarters, Richard Lauchli / Counter Insurgency Council

https://www.maryferrell.org/showDoc.html?docId=116984

[115] FBI Memorandum to Headquarters, Richard Lauchli / Minutemen, September 9, 1970, 10

https://www.maryferrell.org/showDoc.html?docId=117734#relPageId=10

[116] FBI Memorandum, "Cuban Anti-Communist Army/Morua – Cordoso Plan to Acquire Arms," November 9, 1962

https://www.maryferrell.org/showDoc.html?docId=52381#relPageId=1

[117] FBI memorandum, Miami office to Director, "DRE / Cuba Neutrality Matters," April 5, 1963

https://www.maryferrell.org/showDoc.html?docId=81693

[118] Ibid, 10-11

[119] Jim Alcock, Assistant District Attorney to Jim Garrison, District Attorney, Interview at Christian Democratic Headquarters, Miami Florida, January 31, 1967

"ANGEL VEGA is a slightly built Cuban male appearing to be in his late twenties. He was one of the twenty Cubans who trained at a camp in the New Orleans area. VEGA arrived at the camp sometime near the middle or end of June, 1963. When he arrived, there were only four or five others at the camp site. The house and grounds where they stayed were completely run down, giving the appearance they had not been inhabited for quite a while. Their first task was to refurbish the house and its conveniences.

All personnel stayed in the house which consisted of three rooms, a kitchen and two baths. In addition to this, there was a screened porch on the front and back of the house. The grounds had a swimming pool which was constantly fed by an underground spring. Also, there was a stream or bayou running through the property. Within sight of the property was another house. The camp was served by a dirt road which VEGA recalls was never used by vehicular traffic during his entire stay at the camp.

Training at the camp was principally limited to a physical fitness program. Daily exercises were taken along with swimming lessons. The men at the camp also practiced fording the stream that ran through the property. At no time did the men stray farther than about 200 yards from the house. No shooting whatsoever took place at the camp. They had two or three old Springfield rifles and M-1 carbine. These weapons were never fired. The M-1 carbine was used to show the men how to disassemble and assemble the weapon. During the course of many of the exercises, the men would carry small logs to simulate the weight of a weapon. Also, these logs were used in mock hand-to-hand combat training. ...all Cubans at the camp returned to Miami. This was about August 1, 1963.Therefore, the camp was in operation for about five or six weeks."

[120] Garrison Committee Inquiries from the Justice Department, "Lake Ponchartrain Camp and Ricardo Davis"

https://www.maryferrell.org/showDoc.html?docId=8313&relPageId=6

[121] FBI Air Tel, Special Agent in Charge New Orleans to Director, Neutrality matters, September 27, 1963

https://www.maryferrell.org/showDoc.html?docId=136965

[122] Hancock research notes on McClaney / DRE bombing mission

[123] Warren C. DeBrueys, Bombing Raid Investigative Report, (112 pages), RIF Number 124-10217-10019, 65

https://www.maryferrell.org/showDoc.html?docId=136967#relPageId=65

[124] Larry Hancock, *Someone Would Have Talked*, 166-168

[125] Desmond Fitzgerald, Special Affairs Staff cable to Director, AMWORLD recruiting, November 23, 1963

https://www.maryferrell.org/showDoc.html?docId=53261&relPageId=67

[126] CIA Memorandum, AMWORLD Meeting in Washington CD 24 December, 1963, "Information on Ex-DRE Members," December 24, 1963

https://www.maryferrell.org/showDoc.html?docId=40547&relPageId=2

[127] Oswald's first letter to the Fair Play for Cuba Committee (apparently of some urgency to Oswald, who was normally quite frugal but sent this letter via Air Mail) expressed his interest in supporting Cuba and described having already demonstrated for Cuba in Dallas using a handmade placard; in response he was mailed 50 copies of the standard FPCC leaflet material. John Newman, *Oswald and The CIA*, 275. While the FBI did not confirm the incident described by Oswald in the letter, there is anecdotal information from the DPD that one officer may have observed such activity, but the individual fled upon seeing the officer approach so exact identification was not possible. It needs to be noted that in February the alias A. Hidell had been used to order a rifle, and Oswald would use that same alias in organizing his "virtual" FPCC chapter in New Orleans,

ensuring that "Hidell" was listed with the Post Office to receive mail at Oswald's PO Box.

[128] Ibid, 277

[129] There is good reason to suspect that Oswald's information was indeed collected and became part of an intelligence file on the Minsk Radio and Electronics plant. The HSCA developed information that in 1962 a contact report was routed to the Soviet Branch of the CIA Directorate of Intelligence, the information being provided by a former Marine who had returned from the Soviet Union after having been employed at the plant. That information became the subject of a news inquiry by reporter Daniel Schorr, and there is now documentary evidence that Schorr was stonewalled in his investigation, and that corroborative information was withheld from him. The ARRB obtained material showing that CIA Director William Colby even wrote a memorandum relating to the matter. Colby stated that he felt he had adequately deflected Schorr. But Colby remained concerned, so much so that he directed that Schorr must not be allowed to learn anything more prior to his broadcast – anything which would support the idea that Oswald had indeed been a source for the CIA.

Larry Hancock, *Someone Would Have Talked* 2010, 85-86 also Exhibit 7-A1, CIA memorandum of Colby conversations with CBS

[130] Warren Commission Volume 16, 422-3, and analysis in Andrew Kiel, *J. Edgar Hoover: The Father of the Cold War,* UPA, 2000, 146-147

[131] There appears little doubt that, during 1963, intelligence activities involving Lee Oswald, the Hidell alias, and the public image that developed around him over the summer were in progress. The ordering of a rifle under the Hidell alias in March, his March pro-Cuba/Castro communication with the FPCC, his initial outreach to the anti-Castro community in New Orleans – followed by highly visible pro-Castro public appearances and media visibility. That image would have been reinforced by his photograph with the rifle and both socialist and communist newspapers (both organizations staunchly defended and supported the Cuban revolution). Beyond that, he also repeatedly wrote letters to both groups, in one instance asking CPUSA about advice in possibly going "underground." In total, it is easy to see all these elements as combining to create the "image" of a young, radicalized former Marine being subverted by foreign propaganda.

Yet that image is dramatically inconsistent with the views expressed in his private memoire of late 1962 only months earlier, in which he expressed views undeniably hostile towards Soviet communism and in particular the Communist Party USA. In that context, it appears that, beginning in early 1963, Oswald either willingly or unknowingly was being crafted as a both a domestic intelligence "dangle" and a potential propaganda tool.

One scenario which appears likely is that information on Oswald collected by CIA's Domestic Contacts immediately following his return from Russia would have been shared with the Western Hemisphere directorate. At that point, a decision might have been made to monitor Oswald as a "dangle" in domestic collections regarding Cuba, and beyond that to begin developing him as a potential propaganda device. Oswald effectively served as a "dangle" simply by going about his interests and activities. Monitoring his mail, obtaining information on his activities though people in contact with him and if necessary conducting pretext interviews of his employers to determine his work status and activities could be done without his knowledge, while exposing persons of interest contacting him either privately or at work.

With anti-Castro and anti-FPCC propaganda reinvigorated within the new SAS group, it would not be surprising to find headquarters propaganda specialists such as John Tilton involved with the use of Oswald, as well as SAS staff at Miami Station – including both foreign intelligence officers and DRE case officers. When David Phillips was seconded to SAS as a propaganda asset he may well have been added to the Oswald project (Phillip's meeting in Miami with Tilton in October lends support to that idea).

However, despite the various usages pursued by the CIA, the bottom line in regards to conspiracy would be that a number of CIA officers would have been well aware of how entangled the CIA was with the Oswald identity by November 1963, not just for propaganda but in other respects which are discussed in this work – including penetration and fragmentation actions against Cuban diplomatic staff. For those involved in a conspiracy, that would have enhanced the use of Oswald, making him not only a pointer to Castro but making it likely the CIA would be forced to conceal information related to him for operational security reasons – not to mention neutering any real investigation of conspiracy that might be initiated internally within the agency.

[132] HSCA Volume 10, Section 9, DRE, 85

[133] Jefferson Morley, "Revelation 19.63", The New Times, April 12, 2002 https://www.miaminewtimes.com/news/revelation-1963-6353139

[134] Ibid

[135] Dan Hardway, "An Operational Sketch", 2014 https://aarclibrary.org/wp-content/uploads/2014/09/dan_hardway_aarc_9_26_14.pdf

[136] Ibid

[137] Larry Hancock, *Someone Would Have Talked* 2010, 40-41

[138] Jefferson Morley, "Revelation 19.63", The New Times, April 12, 2002

[139] Ibid

Morley determined that the CIA's archives contained no reports, receipts, memoranda, notes, or cables relating to the DRE (including funds supplied) for the entire 17-month period in which Joannides was its case officer. His personnel file only notes they were being paid for intelligence collection and propaganda. Of course, such reporting was standard administrative practice; reports for the officers preceding and following Joannides are in the files. Morley even notes that Joannides was commended in his 1963 performance review for his adherence to the rules for correct reporting.

Morley interviewed six separate, retired CIA operations officers who confirmed that Joannides was required to file written memoranda regarding anything reported as to Oswald and the DRE. All of which means that something was going on with Oswald and the CIA that had to be removed from the system following the president's assassination – or that the DRE was internally abuzz about Oswald but for some reason withholding everything about him from the CIA, including the sort of propaganda work for which they were retained and paid. The fact that the CIA has refused to disclose any contemporary documents or communications relating to Lee Oswald and the DRE during his time in New Orleans is quite suspicious. Either very relevant documents are still being withheld or both SAS and JMWAVE were ignorant of the DRE related contacts with Oswald that summer. A total lack of documents would also imply that the CIA's Domestic Affairs staff in New Orleans had totally failed to inquire into a highly visible American who had been in Russia, and had become a pro-Castro advocate – engaged with an activist Cuban exile group actively supported by the CIA itself.

[140] CIA document; Fitness Report on George Joannides, 1963, 1964

https://www.maryferrell.org/showDoc.html?docId=16078

[141] Personal communication with Jefferson Morley, January 2020 also Dan Hardway, "An Operational Sketch", 2014

https://aarclibrary.org/wp-content/uploads/2014/09/dan_hardway_aarc_9_26_14.pdf

[142] CIA Memorandum, Director to JMWAVE, Status of AMHINT-2 [Salvat], November 29, 1963

https://www.maryferrell.org/showDoc.html?docId=67663&relPageId=2

[143] The White House confirmed in a press release that U.S. President Kennedy would be making a trip to Dallas, Texas later in the year, though the specific itinerary was not complete, though the Dallas Times-Herald reported that Kennedy would have "a breakfast in Dallas, luncheon in Fort Worth, coffee in San Antonio and dinner in Houston." JFK Plans Whirlwind Texas Trip, AP report in Victoria (TX) Advocate, September 14, 1963, p3

[144] Larry Hancock, *NEXUS*, 106-107

[145] Warren Commission Report, Chapter 7: Lee Harvey Oswald: Background and Possible Motives, 413

https://www.archives.gov/research/jfk/warren-commission-report/chapter-7.html

[146] Odio was under considerable stress for several months in 1963; she had recently completed a divorce and was also pregnant and unmarried at the time of the reported visit. She was receiving treatment for an elevated nervous condition, but her doctor reported no other physical or psychological issues.

[147] Manolo Ray himself had been a perpetual problem for the CIA, refusing to even join the Cuban Revolutionary Council or the Cuba Project

until the very last weeks before the landings in Cuba. During the following years he expressed grave mistrust of the CIA – which because of his populist and socialist political leanings was reciprocated by CIA political officers from Howard Hunt to Henry Hecksher.

By the summer of 1963, JMWAVE operations had become increasingly concerned about the activities of the JURE group and Manolo Ray. The overall American relationship with Ray had been and continued to be described in CIA documents as "chaotic." Ray mistrusted the CIA; he made that clear with virtually everyone from Robert Kennedy to Desmond Fitzgerald. At the same time, JURE was collecting intelligence on JMWAVE activities, while Miami base had its own sources within JURE.

Emilio Rodriquez acted as case officer for the JURE group headed by Manola Ray, and the CIA had a number of sources inside JURE itself. The JURE/CIA relationship remained tentative at best in 1963, with an effort by RFK to get Ray and JURE to join the autonomous group effort along with Artime, but with Ray constantly mistrustful of the CIA as a whole, and with its own small offshore military group already carrying out its own efforts. The political jousting between Ray and Artime was ongoing, and JMWAVE determined that JURE had actually begun to obtain its own (highly negative) information about CIA attitudes within the Miami Station. By the summer of 1963, Ray was even expressing his personal opinion that CIA agents might try to assassinate him, and that certain of them were his personal enemies.

CIA mistrust of JURE became even higher during 1963 as JMWAVE began to question higher level decisions in regard to new Kennedy Administration / SAS projects such as AMTRUNK and AMWORLD. JMWAVE officers in particular were highly skeptical of the personal relationships between Robert Kennedy and exile figures such as Artime and Ray. Beyond questioning the effectiveness of Artime and Ray as leaders, there were specific concerns the two men were using the CIA and the U.S. government for their own agendas – and that their leadership styles would compromise not just the security of the new projects but overall CIA operations against Cuba.

The escalating concerns began with the RFK / SAS AMTRUNK regime fragmentation project. Other than at the highest levels, the longtime CIA officers were totally opposed to that idea. David Morales had attended the first organizing meeting and simply dropped out of any further participation. As early as April, Miami Station Chief Shackley recommended the whole AMTRUNK effort be cancelled, warning that it was either compromised or even very possibly being actively used by the opposition. Individuals including George Volsky (AMTRUNK-1) were cited as being particularly suspect as to their motives; Volsky was also known to be closely associated with Ray and JURE.

By August 1963, a CIA operational dispatch detailed JMWAVE concerns that Volsky had a history of using positions with the U.S. government to leverage JURE agendas. Certain of Volsky's associates were suspected of being Cuban intelligence plants. JMWAVE also learned that Ray had directed that a trusted JURE member be infiltrated to learn of CIA plans, and suspected that Volsky was performing that task. Beyond that, the report outlined an extended plan by Ray to collect intelligence from a variety of U.S. government agencies as well as the CIA. An AMOT intelligence operative had learned that Ray was specifically identifying CIA operatives active in Miami. The report indicates that the movements of both Ray and his second in command Eugenio Rogelio Cisneros were being monitored; the FBI was also following JURE's efforts to try and buy weapons.

One specific trip inside the United States was made in June, by Ray's number two in command, Eugenio Rogelio Cisneros. Cisneros later verified that he had specifically gone to Dallas to contact Sylvia Odio. Odio was to provide an introduction to individuals who might be willing to sell weapons to JURE. At that point in time there was no significant JURE organization in Dallas; a small group did begin to organize that summer, but based on a number of FBI informants, the group itself only met in small numbers, infrequently, and its only real activities were general fundraising. As of June, Sylvia Odio was the only direct contact with the JURE leadership in Puerto Rico, and the only individual in Dallas personally associated with Manolo Ray and his family.

Sylvia Odio had been active within JURE during her time in Puerto Rico, after leaving Cuba, and was personally acquainted with Ray. After arriving in Dallas, she had made contact with an individual who represented himself as having Latin American contacts for arms sales. She had advised Rogelio Cisneros (Ray's second in command, then living in Miami and using the "war name" alias Eugenio) of that by telephone. During a visit to Puerto Rico in the summer of 1963 (related to her divorce) she had met with Ray, and mentioned the possibility of weapons buys in Dallas. Following the assassination – and upon questioning by the FBI and INS – Ray and others would attempt to back away from their association with

Odio. Despite that, Odio's contacts with Eugenio and Ray certainly had been taken seriously enough in June for Ray to approve sending Cisneros from Miami to Dallas, specifically to work with Odio on weapons purchases.

Given that JMWAVE was very much engaged in an actual intelligence struggle with JURE by August of 1963, attempting to place its own sources – and attempting to deal with the JURE intelligence effort against it and other agencies in Miami – it is possible that sanctioned counter intelligence activities might have been conducted against individuals known to be associated with Ray. Especially individuals who might be involved in weapons purchases. It is also reasonable to speculate that the JURE case officer, Emilio Rodriquez, would have been the individual to direct intelligence collection on JURE's domestic activities.

We know that the FBI was monitoring JURE efforts to obtain weapons and carry out military operations from its base of operations in Puerto Rico. We lack sufficient information on what they might have been doing to uncover similar efforts inside the U.S. What is clear is that the FBI was diligent in obtaining informants and sources in virtually all groups, and was actively engaged in identifying their officers, members and activities.

Given that context, and despite all the confusion and debate over the Odio incident, it is likely that a "pretext" call was made on Sylvia Odio. JMWAVE's own JURE sources very likely would have had the "war name" used as an introduction in the Odio visit; her father had been a supporter of the anti-Castro resistance inside Cuba, imprisoned for aiding an assassination attempt against Castro.

In one sense, the possibility of a JMWAVE effort to entangle JURE in illegal activities makes perfect sense; we have no precise idea of exactly what they proposed to Odio, and it may well not have been as innocent as signing fund-raising flyers. It would have occurred at a time when both JMWAVE and the FBI were highly interested in JURE, a time when Miami base considered Ray as much of an adversary as an asset. Depending on Sylvia Odio's response, introductions might have been gained to JURE members in Dallas, discrete inquiries as to their success in obtaining weapons, contacts revealed, etc.

Sylvia Odio might have been considered an easier target than JURE's male leaders, most of whom were outside the country. Given her recent visit with Ray himself, and her history of social connections to his family (she was a good friend of his wife) she might also have been considered a valuable, independent source on how desperate JURE was for weapons, or simply on current attitudes within JURE, both towards independent military operations and towards the CIA.

Given that there was no obvious use of Oswald in the initial Odio contact (the young man was simply introduced and said little if anything), anything further would have depended on Odio's response to the dangle. As it turned out she proved to be quite suspicious and immediately rejected the approach. Guessing at what might have been in play given a different response from Odio is largely fruitless – as are her comments on a follow-up telephone call the following day in which the young man was described as loco and out of control, capable of anything. The call and those remarks failed to elicit any response from her (if anything making her more nervous) and she had no further contact with the men. It is certainly possible that the visit may have simply been exploratory, a wild card dangled to test her response – and possibly collect something which could be used against JURE. After all, Sylvia Odio was a personal friend of Manolo Ray and had been visited in Dallas by one of its chief military leaders – given those contacts surely Odio would not have expected unknown JURE members to show up at her door with no introduction or advance notice?

To some extent, the Odio incident is actually more important as an illustration of the extent to which the FBI was willing to suppress leads and actively mislead the Warren Commission. The Warren Commission had specifically requested the FBI resolve her report, especially since her doctor confirmed that she had discussed it with him before the assassination. Clearly it suggested some sort of conspiracy in play, so much so that the FBI was requested to subject it to an in-depth inquiry. That proved to be extremely challenging. Its first attempt to dismiss Odio was to demonstrate that her visitors had actually been local JURE members, whom she had not recognized; that effort – largely based on a very rough similarity in names – quickly collapsed. However by fall 1964, the FBI managed to locate three individuals (Loran Hall, Lawrence Howard and William Seymour), all out of Miami and with past associations to Hemming, Sturgis and INTERPEN, who had traveled to Dallas in 1963. Based on that, the FBI officially assured the Warren Commission that the issue was resolved.

Only years later would it become clear via internal FBI memoranda that was most definitely not the case. FBI interviews out of Miami determined that Howard had no knowledge of Odio, certainly not visiting her in Dallas. Miami also determined that Seymour was not in Dallas at the same time as Hall and Howard, and his employer confirmed he had been at work during the relevant time period. Beyond that, Sylvia Odio and her sister (who had seen the three men) were shown pictures of Hall, Howard and Seymour and stated that they were definitely not their visitors. None of that was shared with the Warren Commission. In the end, the best the FBI could do was to challenge Odio's story based on a negative assessment of her emotional stability – the same tactic it had used to discount the informant who had reported Roy Hargrave's involvement in the assassination.

In the end, we can only speculate that the Odio incident may have been a sanctioned counter intelligence dangle against JURE, possibly using JMWAVE assets associated with DRE (initially the visitors had asked for Sarita Odio, a college student with DRE friends). Several such individuals, including Carlos Hernandez, were still being used in JMWAVE activities at that point in time – Carlos and others had even been sent overseas to help disrupt a recent international student conference. However if that were true, it would add an interesting twist to the report of Lee Oswald with Mr. Hernandez, attempting to buy rifles from Robert McKeown in approximately the same time frame as that reported for the Odio contact.

[148] Jefferson Morley, "Revelation 19.63," The New Times, April 12, 2002

[149] Larry Hancock, *Someone Would Have Talked* 2010, 191

[150] CIA Dispatch, Chief Western Hemisphere Division to Chief of Station, Mexico City, Transmittal of Background Information on Dr. Rene Vallejo Ortiz, October 9, 1963

https://www.maryferrell.org/showDoc.html?docId=45080

[151] CIA Memorandum, Director to Mexico City / Information for JMWAVE, Dr. Rene Vallejo, Personal Physician Fidel Castro, October 12, 1963

https://www.maryferrell.org/showDoc.html?docId=45080

[152] Larry Hancock, *Someone Would Have Talked* 2010, 171-173

[153] Ibid, Chapter 12, "The Anti-Castro People," 171-175

[154] Jefferson Morley, "Revelation 19.63," The New Times, April 12, 2002

[155] Larry-Hancock documentation, website supplemental information, photographic comparisons – Oswald vs. Masen

http://www.larry-hancock.com/documents/index.html

[156] Larry Hancock, *Someone Would Have Talked* 2010, 198-199, also JFK Lancer Conference, 2003 presentation and panel discussion with James Hosty

http://www.jfklancer.com/dallas03/dallas03media.html

[157] There is very limited documentation related to this damage control planning, and no confirmation that it was actually established and in play at the time of the president's assassination. However members of the administration including RFK were aware of it and also aware of concerns that the president himself might be at risk. Larry Hancock, *Someone Would Have Talked* 2010, 194.

[158] There are a number of sources and incidents suggesting that both JFK and RFK were aware of a threat existing within the Cuban exile community. In addition, researcher Vince Palamara interviewed one Secret Service officer, John Norris, who stated that officers assigned to the Protective Service Detail were aware of people that wanted JFK dead and that a threat to his life did exist. It is also significant that on the afternoon of the assassination, RFK himself made two telephone calls, the second of which was to a contact who was working with Artime's group – in the call RFK expressed his concern that Cuban exiles had been involved in the attack on his brother. Larry Hancock, *Someone Would Have Talked* 2010, 194.

[159] Jilda Unruh, Exclusive: "JFK Death Threat Note from Nov. 1963 In Miami Revealed For 1st Time," CBS Miami, November 21, 2013

https://miami.cbslocal.com/2013/11/21/exclusive-jfk-death-threat-note-in-nov-1963-in-miami-revealed-for-1st-time/

https://flashbackmiami.com/2013/11/26/jfk-in-miami-1963/

[160] In the hours following the assassination, knowing that there were AMWORLD project meetings going on in Washington D.C. (he had attended at least one personally and knew that several of the senior Cubans he was working with at the time were in town) Robert Kennedy made a call to locate one of his closest personal Cuban friends among the exiles, Enrique Ruiz Williams. A journalist, Haynes Johnson, later related that following the brief conversation Williams had told him that Robert Kennedy had stated "one of your guys did it." Williams was shocked, however at a minimum the call does suggest that the Kennedy brothers were aware of a potential threat from among the more radical exiles. Haynes Johnson, Washington Post, April 17, 1981.

[161] Ray and Mary LaFontaine, *Oswald Talked*, Pelican Publishing Company, 1996, 300-306

[162] Personal research and communications from Ian Griggs, also *Someone Would Have Talked* 2010, 119

[163] Homer Echeverria / Chicago DRE Investigation:

The Echeveria incident surfaced in a report to the FBI by one of its ongoing sources (Thomas Mosley) as to weapons deals in the Chicago area, many involving Richard Lauchli, who was a long time supplier of explosives and weapons to the Minutemen, the DRE and other Cuban exile groups. The FBI passed the source report on to the Secret Service.

The report involved remarks made by a Cuban with whom Mosley had been in contact (Homero Sameul Valdavia Echeverria), regarding the sale of weapons and explosives. According to Mosley, while discussing a weapons buy Echeveria had remarked that "we have plenty of money, our new backers are Jews, as soon as they [or we] take care of Kennedy...," unfortunately at that point the conversation had been interrupted and there were no further comments about JFK.

It was certainly a suggestive remark and well worth investigation, and despite a good deal of what was later written, there was indeed an extensive follow-on investigation, involving multiple sources, ongoing contacts with Echeverria by Mosley, and FBI surveillance on Echeverria himself. In fact, the investigation extended to other individuals who were in contact with Mosley.

The reality is that neither the Secret Service nor the FBI dropped its investigation of the incident. They continued an effort to determine what exile group(s) Echeverria had been associated with, to develop the context of the remarks through additional meetings with Echeverria (and reports from Mosley) as well as pursuing whether or not an actual threat was in play and might extend to President Johnson. A detailed (albeit convoluted) synopsis of their report may be found at the Mary Ferrell Foundation.

https://www.maryferrell.org/showDoc.html?docId=10490#relPageId=363

In the end, the determination was made that no ongoing threat existed and that no illegal acts had actually been committed in regards to weapons or explosives sales. It was only at that point that the investigation ceased, simply because there were no grounds to refer the information for actual charges. While that is certainly unsatisfactory, it is consistent with a number of other investigations of exile weapons purchasing contacts (and even sales) in which the FBI appears to have determined that protecting ongoing sources and surveillance was more valuable than recommending charges – especially in incidents where sales might not have actually been illegal.

The chronology of the full FBI inquiry is as follows:

During September, Thomas Mosley approached Echeveria offering machine guns (Sten guns) and received no immediate interest or response.

On November 21, Mosley again approached Echeverria. It was at that point when the remarks about new backers, Jewish, with money and proceeding once JFK was out of the way, were made. During that conversation, Echeverria cautioned Mosley that his superiors would have to meet with and evaluate Mosley to ensure the weapons offer was not a sting.

On November 26, Mosley again tried to reach Echeverria, by telephone, but was unable to complete a call.

At that point in time active Secret Service and FBI investigation of Echeverria was underway, and attempts to place Echeverria under surveillance were initially made but discontinued on November 28th when it was deemed too risky, since the only approaches available were likely to be detected (and Echeverria had already expressed concern over Mosely's approach being a sting). However, Echeverria himself did respond to Mosley at his own initiative, and a meeting was scheduled for Nov 28.

On November 28, Homer Echeverria was brought into a conversation about JFK and characterized him as an intellectual who had not committed himself to the anti-Castro effort in the way that Johnson, described as a common man, would. It was felt that unlike Kennedy, Johnson would not stand in the way of direct Cuban exile military action against Cuba. Exile confidence in Johnson had grown following remarks attributed to the vice president that JFK had not been tough enough during the missile crisis. Christmas cards had been sent from exiles in Dallas to friends in Miami; enclosed with them were flyers touting LBJ as the savior of the Cuban exiles, essentially calling for something to happen to JFK so as to allow Johnson to come to their rescue.

Echeverria and Mosley, after a telephone call from Echeverria, left Homer's home in Mosley's car. After driving near Logan Square, Homer told Mosley to stop, and a man got into the car.

Mosley pitched his Sten guns to the man and in turn was given a shopping list for a much larger range of weapons and explosives…the Cuban began to vet Mosley – asking him how he felt about the death of JFK and then asking for references. Mosley brought up an association with Michael Ponce in earlier days and the man said he had known Ponce in Cuba. Ponce was an officer in the Cuban Navy under Batista and had been associated with Mosley in gun smuggling in the 1950s. Mosley suggested his Chicago arrests and CPD file would verify his experience. It should be noted that the "shopping list" related to Mosley was almost identical to the DRE shopping list which had earlier been submitted by the DRE to John Thomas Masen in Dallas.

Mosley talked sales details, partial payment and other logistics. The Cuban found it acceptable and remarked that Mosley would be further checked out by an attorney working with the Cubans. Future contact practices were outlined, using a classified ad and associated telephone number. It was a rather sophisticated contact and cut out communications process, and Mosley was told he would be contacted by the Cubans if they wanted to pursue the deal after checking him out.

An FBI informant identified the unknown Cuban as a DRE member, and Echeverria was also identified as a DRE member. The description of the unknown Cuban appeared to match that of Juan Francisco Blanco-

Fernandez, who had been observed by an FBI source at the same grocery store as Homer Echeveria only days earlier. Blanco had been in Chicago shopping for weapons and explosives on previous occasions. The FBI referred the Blanco inquiry to Miami, and the local FBI office used one of their sources to personally contact Juan Blanco Fernandez and establish that he was in Chicago during the period in which the Echevarria/Mosley meeting had occurred.

As of November 30, another meeting was being planned between Echeverria and Mosley. Mosley was also reported to be in contact with the potential buyers both via Echeverria and another individual referred to as Mannie. Mannie claimed to represent all the exile groups in the Chicago area. Mannie communicated the desire for a shopping list of items for an upcoming attack on Cuba – they were needed in a short time frame as attacks were planned to begin within 90 days – by March 1964. The urgency expressed in Chicago appears to be consistent with the DRE representatives discussions of imminent, upcoming attacks that had been going on in Dallas in late October/early November.

Several points suggests that "Mannie" was either Paulino Sierra himself or an attorney working with Sierra – and that by the fall of 1963 Sierra had established himself as the money man for exile group weapons buys. As noted before, while Sierra claimed funding from corporate backers, his initial and most significant source of funding was from underworld sources, out of Las Vegas (HSCA Report, p. 134).

A follow-on meeting occurred on December 1, 1963. That meeting, between Echeverria and Mosley, had been set for the Chicago Transit Authority building; the two met in Mosley's car behind the building. The meeting was intended to move the matter along to an actual sale (which could be prosecuted), and Mosley was instructed to offer major financing and support, indicating that Mosley had found backers interested in the exile cause who would assume support of Echeverria's group.

With funding on the table, on December 4 Echeverria contacted Mosley and proposed a public meeting (with passwords being exchanged by the participants) with Mannie in a public location, a bar. The meeting went down on December 5, at the Logan Square Terminal Tap room. Mannie told Mosley he needed to personally meet the head of the purported backers (fictional), and that his own backers were high level people with plenty of money. They were even buying boats (at the time Sierra had indeed bought both a boat and a small submarine).

Mannie also stated that Johnson's policies were not a concern to the exiles, but that JFK had been trouble for them as he "played both sides." Mannie related that his group had an office in Miami, he had been traveling a lot, but refused to comment on whether he had traveled to New Orleans. He said that before proceeding with the weapons buy, he would need to get an updated shopping list from Miami and wanted to meet Mosley's purported financial backer before placing an order for explosives. Mannie was described as a white male Cuban, very fluent in English, 48-52 years old, with short, wavy, receding hair, and sharp dresser. The FBI compared descriptions and confirmed that Mannie was not Juan Blanco. At that point the sting hit a wall because in January "Mannie" ceased all contact.

Given the remarks from "Mannie" about having plenty of money, buying boats, and needing to consult with his military guys in Miami, it seems almost certain that he was directly working with Sierra – or that "Mannie" was Sierra himself. At that point in time, Sierra was desperate to make something happen immediately. His employer (Union Tank Car) had already called him on the carpet for financial mismanagement, and during January his other major investors would all withdraw their support. Sierra's Junta essentially disbanded in February – which would certainly explain Mannie's disappearance from the Chicago weapons buying scene. It also appears that the initial Echeverria contact with the FBI informant was associated with DRE and Blanco Fernandez, who involved "Mannie"/Sierra only when money actually became an issue.

https://www.maryferrell.org/showDoc.html?docId=10490#relPageId=363

[164] Larry Hancock, *Someone Would Have Talked*, 2010 edition, 187

[165] "John Martino's Confessions", Mary Ferrell Foundation, also Martino's FBI Subject Files

https://www.maryferrell.org/pages/John_Martinos_Confessions.html

https://www.maryferrell.org/php/showlist.php?docset=1229

[166] Ibid

[167] Author's personal interviews with Edward Martino, also Edward R. Martino, PhD., "Events I witnessed July 1959 through November 1963"

http://www.larry-hancock.com/documents/chapter%2001/Events59-63.pdf

[168] Belford Lawson [longtime friend and business partner of John Martino] contact, HSCA memo Fred Claasen to Cliff Fenton, August 29, 1977

http://www.kenrahn.com/Marsh/Jfk-conspiracy/Martino.txt

[169] Larry Hancock, *Someone Would Have Talked*, 2010 edition, Chapter 1

[170] Edward R. Martino, PhD., "Events I witnessed July 1959 through November 1963"

http://www.larry-hancock.com/documents/chapter%2001/Events59-63.pdf

[171] Hancock, *Someone Would Have Talked*, 2010 edition, Chapter 1

[172] Nicholas M. Horrock, "Roselli Describes his Role in A CIA Plot on Castro," Special Report to The New York Times, June 25, 1975

https://www.nytimes.com/1975/06/25/archives/roselli-describes-his-role-in-a-cia-plot-on-castro-roselli.html

[173] Senate Select Committee to Study Governmental Operations with Respect to Intelligence Activities, Church Committee files on John Roselli testimony, Mary Ferrell Foundation

https://www.maryferrell.org/php/showlist.php?docset=1015

TESTIMONY OF JOHN ROSELLI, 22 SEP 1975
RIF#: 157-10002-10387 (09/22/75) SSCIA#: R-1360

TESTIMONY OF JOHN ROSELLI, 22 SEP 1975
RIF#: 157-10002-10386 (09/22/75) SSCIA#: R-1359

TESTIMONY OF JOHN ROSELLI, 23 APR 1976
RIF#: 157-10014-10000 (04/23/76) SSCIA#: 02-H-02

TESTIMONY OF JOHN ROSELLI, 24 JUN 1975
RIF#: 157-10014-10001 (06/24/75) SSCIA#: 02-H-01

TESTIMONY OF JOHN ROSSELLI, 23 SEP 1975
RIF#: 157-10002-10388 (09/23/75) SSCIA#: R-1356

[174] Jack Anderson, "Did Bobby's Plot Backfire?", March 3, 1967, California Digital Newspaper Collection

https://cdnc.ucr.edu/?a=d&d=MT19670303.2.90&e=-------en--20--1--txt-txIN--------1

[175] Hancock, *Someone Would Have Talked*, 2010 edition, 134

[176] Fred Black was close enough to Roselli to host him in Washington D.C. while Roselli was giving testimony to the Church Committee. He was also a close neighbor to LBJ and Bobby Baker, and Black had met with Johnson at his office in the Executive Office Building, a meeting which could well have seriously compromised Johnson had the Congressional Baker influence-peddling inquiry proceeded following President Kennedy's assassination. For details on Fred Black and his connections to Roselli and figures within Roselli's circle see *Someone Would Have Talked*, 2010 edition, Chapter 16, "Wheeling and Dealing."

[177] Ibid, 126

[178] Ibid, 126-132

[179] Ibid, Chapter 2, John Roselli: Strategist

[180] Gaeton Fonzi, *The Last Investigation: What Insiders Know about the Assassination of JFK*, Google Books excerpt:

https://books.google.com/books?id=nluCDwAAQBAJ&pg=PT583&lpg=PT583&dq=david+morales+robert+dorff&source=bl&ots=MTOQG9Kusy&sig=ACfU3U083GOipEV31QqTjxZuwa7yavryeg&hl=en&sa=X&ved=2ahUKEwj3pbTlxY7pAhVGRqwKHU5aAMoQ6AEwAHoECAkQAQ#v=onepage&q=david%20morales%20robert%20dorff&f=false

[181] The author worked extensively over a number of years with Robert Dorff, in collecting documents on David Morales and in personal conversations with Ruben Carbajal. That information is compiled and referenced in *Someone Would Have Talked*, 2010 edition, Chapter 8. "Well We Took Care of that SOB, Didn't We?"

[182] Larry Hancock, *Someone Would Have Talked*, 2010 edition, Chapter 8, 115

[183] Larry Hancock, personal communication with Ruben Carbajal, 2014

[184] Larry Hancock, personal communications by the author with Robert Dorff and Reuben Carbajal, 2014

[185] Larry Hancock, *Someone Would Have Talked* 2010, Chapter 8

[186] Larry Hancock, *Someone Would Have Talked*, Chapter 8, also Jeremy Gunn Memo, ARRB, March 7, 1996. In later years work by researchers including Robert Dorff and the author; as well as by the AARB; revealed the extent of Morales's CIA career and his various covers within the Army, State Department and USAID (end note: Jeremy Gunn, ARRB memo, March 7, 1996.

https://www.maryferrell.org/showDoc.html?docId=202942&relPageId=1

[187] Ibid, 107-108

[188] Ibid, Appendix I, "Echoes from Dallas"

[189] Bob Woodward, "IBEX Deadly Symbol of U.S. Arms Sales Problems," Washington Post, January 2, 1977, also Seymour Hersh, "Iran signs Rockwell Deal for Persian Gulf Spy Base," Seymour Hersh, June 1, 1975 also:

https://www.washingtonpost.com/archive/politics/1977/01/02/ibex-deadly-symbol-of-us-arms-sales-problems/be83dfc8-5998-441a-84c0-f376b240c83d/

https://www.nytimes.com/1975/06/01/archives/iran-signs-rockwell-deal-for-persian-gulf-spy-base-iran-signs.html

[190] The Wheaton Lead: An Exploration, Larry Hancock and David Boylan, Mary Ferrell Foundation, April, 2020

https://www.maryferrell.org/pages/Essay_-_The_Wheaton_Lead.html

[191] Larry Hancock, *In Denial: Secret Wars with Air Strikes and Tanks?*, 2020, Chapter 1, also The Wheaton Lead: An Exploration, a research paper by David Boylan and Larry Hancock, 2020

[192] Ibid, Chapter 7, "Hidden Measures"

[193] Wheaton was unable to offer any specific documents relating to the conspiracy given that he had simply heard conversations among individuals. However, he was able to specifically name at least two

individuals who could have been contacted for additional details, and he did provide various documents and materials corroborating his contacts with Carl Jenkins and Rafael Quintero, as well as the business relationship between Wheaton's company and Jenkins.

http://www.publicrecordmedia.org/wp-content/uploads/2015/09/whea/WHEA_pd_GW26004.pdf

[194] RIF 145-10001-10121 and 145-10001-10122, "Operational Plan Submitted to CIA by Quintero"

[195] Rafael Quintero, "CIA Agent Sent After Castro," Independent, 2006

https://www.independent.co.uk/news/obituaries/rafael-quintero-421370.html

[196] Larry Hancock, *Someone Would Have Talked* 2010, 71

[197] Ibid, 288

[198] Ibid, 72-73

[199] Hargraves on occasion volunteered information to the FBI. Actually many of the independent activists, including Gerry Hemming, did serve as voluntary sources – often providing information on each other's activities. The same was true for members of various exile groups, who served as sources for both the FBI and CIA. In some instances this appears to have been as much to undermine competitors as to seek some level of accommodation with the intelligence agencies.

[200] "JFK Suspect," Noel Twyman, *Bloody Treason*, 600-689. This document was originally located in the National Archives by Anna Marie Kuhns Walko.

[201] Larry Hancock, *Someone Would Have Talked*, 2010 edition, 73-74

[202] Ibid

[203] Noel Twyman, *Bloody Treason*, Roy Hargraves Interview, Tape 1, 2001, Side A, also *Someone Would Have Talked* 2006 spiral bound edition, with permission of Noel Twyman. Copy available online:

https://gregwagnersite.files.wordpress.com/2018/12/Roy-Hargraves-Interview.pdf

[204] "Kennedy Sought Dialogue with Cuba," The National Security Archive, November 24, 2003

https://nsarchive2.gwu.edu/NSAEBB/NSAEBB103/index.htm

[205] Larry Hancock, *Someone Would Have Talked*, 2010 edition, 276

[206] https://kennedysandking.com/john-f-kennedy-articles/the-mystery-of-red-bird-airport

[207] Larry Hancock and David Boylan, The Wheaton Lead: An Exploration, April, 2020

https://www.maryferrell.org/pages/Essay_-_The_Wheaton_Lead.html

[208] Larry Hancock, Someone Would Have Talked 2010, 206, also The Wheaton Lead: An Exploration

[209] Ibid, Chapter 11, "Cuba, the Guns, New Orleans and Everything," also 186-188

[210] Testimony of Mr. Jack Ruby, June 7, 1964, Dallas Texas

https://mcadams.posc.mu.edu/russ/testimony/ruby_j1.htm

[211] Treasury Department Memo, McBrien to Albrecht, "Reopening of Warren Commission," *Someone Would Have Talked*, Exhibit 5-6

[212] LarryHancock, *Someone Would Have Talked* 2010, 198-199

[213] Ibid, 199

[214] The Dallas Police, the FBI and the CIA were all notified of a witness who had observed an individual thought to be Oswald at the Harlandale street house. The FBI did carry out an investigation of the police lead, however it ultimately discounted it based on the statement from an unnamed source, who definitely stated Oswald had never been there at the house (strangely, the FBI report states that their source stated he himself had never been to the house). In retrospect, the dismissal of this particular lead is quite questionable, given that the confidential source cited appears to have been an individual who later left the United States for Puerto Rico (complaining bitterly about the lack of American support for actions against Castro). Given that Rodriquez Orcaberrio made a similar move at that time, it appears that the FBI accepted a potential suspect as the source

used to close out their inquiry – certainly a questionable practice. Also of note is the fact that Orcaberrio himself was separately reported as possibly having been in direct contact with Lee Oswald – and more importantly appears in Secret Service Protective Services files, listed as a potential threat to President Kennedy (unfortunately he only appears on a threat list and we have no further details). Larry Hancock, *Someone Would Have Talked* 2010, 79-80

[215] Dan Hardway, "An Operational Sketch," 2014, also personal communication with Jefferson Morley, January 2020

[216] Jilda Unruh, "Exclusive: JFK Death Threat Note from Nov. 1963 in Miami Revealed For 1st Time," CBS 4 Miami, November 21, 2013

https://miami.cbslocal.com/2013/11/21/exclusive-jfk-death-threat-note-in-nov-1963-in-miami-revealed-for-1st-time/

[217] Larry Hancock, *NEXUS: The CIA and Political Assassination*, 100

[218] Kennedy's turn towards covert action with highly trained military Special Forces – with the CIA held to an intelligence collection and analysis support role – anticipated the shift which actually occurred some four decades later following the attacks on America in 2001. Current American clandestine military action is carried out by Special Operations Command task forces similar to those which JFK was beginning to create in 1963.

[219] William Burr, "Why is Poodle Blanket Classified?", National Security Archive, April 7, 2010

https://nsarchive2.gwu.edu/nukevault/ebb310/

[220] Seth Jacobs, *Cold War Mandarin / Ngo Dinh Diem and the Origins of America's War in Vietnam, 1950-1963*, 136

[221] *The Battle of Ap Bac, Military Assistance Advisory Group – Vietnam* (1954-1963), 106-107

[222] Robert M. Gillespie, *Black Ops Vietnam / The Operational History of MACVSOG*, Naval Institute Press, 2011, 7

[223] While McNamara and JFK were enthusiastic, Maxwell Taylor (who had become chairman of the Joint Chiefs) was no fan of covert action, and delayed approving the plan for some two months. Taylor did not see

organizing covert action as a function of the military and gave it no special priority. Beyond that, there were no assets immediately available for the task, and a new organizational structure had to be established at MACV in Saigon. Even after the switch from CIA to the military occurred, the Army encountered the problem that its officers were trained for counter insurgency and counter guerilla operations – countering and defeating them, not organizing and managing them. Richard H. Schultz, Jr, *The Secret War Against Hanoi*, Harper Collins/Perennial, 1999, 35-37.

224 Robert M. Gillespie, *Black Ops Vietnam / The Operational History of MACVSOG*, 7

225 Larry Hancock, *Surprise Attack*, 273-276

226 Seth Jacobs, *Cold War Mandarin*, Rowman and Littlefield Publishers, 2006, 76-77

227 John Bartlow Martin, Third Oral History Interview with Robert F. Kennedy, April 30, 1964, New York, New York, for the John F. Kennedy Library

228 John M. Newman, *JFK and Vietnam*, Warner Books, 1991, 422

229 Lewis Sorley, *Westmoreland / The General Who Lost Vietnam*, Houghton Mifflin Harcourt, 2011, 77-78

230 We now know that General Westmoreland had already formed his own opinion – one which was in direct conflict with the strategy in play during 1963, under General Maxwell Taylor and with JFK's endorsement. Westmoreland would later write that Taylor and Kennedy were obsessed with "small wars," with counter insurgency operations to counter national liberation movements. Limited warfare was not something Westmoreland would endorse. And unlike JFK, Lyndon Johnson left the conduct of the war and the American strategy there to Westmoreland, advancing him to four-star rank in August, 1964. Westmoreland was determined to justify the new president's faith. In a message to all his senior staff he directed that they assume optimistic outlooks; they were to accentuate the positive and avoid showing any signs of frustration. Negativism would not be tolerated. Not surprisingly from that point on, up to the TET offensive of 1968, the military reporting out of Vietnam would indeed become far more positive.

At the end of 1964, President Johnson expressed a lack of faith in air strikes and bombing and called for the use of more Americans on the ground – Special Forces, Rangers or Marines. In response, Westmoreland would produce a study calling for 34 ground battalions, some 75,000 troops. Having placed his bet on his new general, Johnson was forced to comply – it would be only the first of an ongoing demand for troops as saturation artillery fire and air attacks into "free fire" zones became standard, and the sorts of ground sweeps into Viet Cong territory that Westmoreland had been warned about by senior officers with prior experience in Vietnam became standard practice. Ibid, 2011, 68-76.

[231] By the end of 1963 America had suffered 122 casualties in Vietnam.

[232] Historical research has now made it clear that JFK wished to, and had approved, the process of drawing down the numbers of uniformed, conventional American military forces deployed to Vietnam. The initial Kennedy administration surge of personnel to Vietnam had been in response to a 1962 request for a major increase (a surge) in training and advisory support for the ARVN. It had not been part of any strategy to deploy conventional ground forces to conduct an American ground campaign against the Viet Cong insurgency – that would have been in direct conflict with the strategy Kennedy was already pursuing in Laos.

In Laos, Vietnam, and the Congo, JFK supported the concept of Military Assistance Groups (MACV in South Vietnam). Kennedy's view of such military operations was clearly defined: American military personnel used as advisors, trainers – even small special operations forces in the field (as in the White Star deployment in Laos). Allowed to engage in combat if circumstances dictated, yes. Engaging in combat if circumstances dictated, yes. Preparating and equipping surrogate military forces, yes. Covert military action using indigenous surrogates or even small clandestine forces operating under cover (as with the CIA's Mikasi group in the Congo or its efforts in Tibet), yes. Limited clandestine and covert air support for government forces and surrogates, yes. Conventional American military forces going into combat on the ground – most definitely no. Certainly not under the conditions prevailing in the fall of 1963, and very likely not ever.

In early October 1963, JFK – responding to proposals from both Secretary of Defense McNamara and General Maxwell Taylor – approved the beginning of a phased withdrawal of the conventional American forces in-country in Vietnam, beginning with a routine downsizing of the force already there by some 1,000 men. However, plans for even that initial drawdown did not actually begin until October, and the drawdown was to be completed by the end of the year. The language associated with that directive specified that "The action will now be treated in low key, as the initial increment of U.S. forces whose presence is no longer required because (a) Vietnamese forces have been trained to assume the function involved; or (b) the function for which they came to Vietnam has been completed." In line with that move, on November 12, JFK publicly stated that his goal in Vietnam was to "to intensify the struggle" and "to bring Americans out of there."

Beyond that, both McNamara and Taylor secretly lobbied with the president for a longer term Vietnam exit strategy (and timetable) which would have brought the American military out of South Vietnam by the end of 1965 – if at all possible. There is no doubt that JFK was supportive of that position – putting numbers of uniformed conventional military personnel, much less full military units, into SE Asia, Latin America or Africa was clearly not something he advocated, nor did it fit with his overall geopolitical strategies.

JFK's support for an extended plan to withdraw conventional forces from Vietnam is now quite clear, described and supported in historical works by a number of authors including John Newman, Peter Dale Scott and others. An excellent synopsis of the withdrawal argument can be found in an article by James K. Galbraith in the following citation. However, this author offers the disclaimer that as a confirmed pragmatist and extremely savvy politician, over the next two years events and options would have determined President Kennedy's ultimate actions. As seen in his other decision making, from Angola to Cuban Missile Crisis, his final actions were often compromises, crafted at his direction rather than simply a matter of blessing specific positions advocated by his advisors. To that extent, my own speculation is that his success or failure in the new, highly secret dialogue with Fidel Castro, which could have led to a neutral Cuba, would have been a major factor in his ultimate approach to both Vietnam and Laos.

James K. Galbraith, "Exit Strategy in 1963; JFK's Complete Withdrawal From Vietnam," Boston Review, September 1, 2003

http://bostonreview.net/us/galbraith-exit-strategy-vietnam

[233] John Bartlow Martin, "Third Oral History Interview with Robert F. Kennedy," April 30, 1964, New York, New York, for the John F. Kennedy Library. The following candid discussion with Robert Kennedy reflects the challenges JFK faced in the fall of 1963; it simply represents his assessment of the dilemma (a blend of national security and political elements) which the Kennedy Administration faced at that point in time. Clearly RFK saw the situation in Vietnam as fluid at the time of his brother's death. We gain a sense of JFK's inclinations from RFK's remarks, but projecting President Kennedy's future actions months or years into the future based strictly on the situation as it was known to him in October/November 1963 seems to this author an exercise in historical speculation. The exchange which follows is offered simply as context for the reader.

http://mcadams.posc.mu.edu/vietnam.htm

Martin:

All right. At the beginning we seemed to have our lines crossed. I mean, the majority leader in the Senate, Mansfield, was saying this was not an American war, and he didn't think it was -- that our -- it should be -- not, not -- should not be an American war. He didn't think our heavy commitment there was justified. How'd you feel about it; how'd the president feel about it; and at what point did we get our lines straightened out? ......

Kennedy:

Yeah, but, you know, he's frequently taken that, those, that line or that position on some of these matters. I don't think that the fact he has an independent view from the executive branch of the government, particularly in Southeast Asia, indicates that the lines aren't straight. I, no, I just, I think every. . . . I, the president felt that the. . . . He had a strong, overwhelming reason for being in Vietnam and that we should win the war in Vietnam.

Martin:

What was the overwhelming reason?

Kennedy:

Just the loss of all of Southeast Asia if you lost Vietnam. I think everybody was quite clear that the rest of Southeast Asia would fall.

Martin:

What if it did?

Kennedy:

Just have profound effects as far as our position throughout the world, and our position in a rather vital part of the world. Also, it would affect what happened in India, of course, which in turn has an effect on the Middle East. Just, it would have, everybody felt, a very adverse effect. It would have an effect on Indonesia, hundred million population. All of these countries would be affected by the fall of Vietnam to the Communists, particularly as we had made such a fuss in the United States both under President Eisenhower and President Kennedy about the preservation of the integrity of Vietnam.

Martin:

There was never any consideration given to pulling out?

Kennedy:

No.

Martin:

But the same time, no disposition to go in all . . .

Kennedy:

No . . .

Martin:

. . . in an all out way as we went into Korea. We were trying to avoid a Korea, is that correct?

Kennedy:

Yes, because I, everybody including General MacArthur felt that land conflict between our troops, white troops and Asian, would only lead to, end in disaster. So it was. . . . We went in as advisers, but to try to get the Vietnamese to fight themselves, because we couldn't win the war for them. They had to win the war for themselves.

It's generally true all over the world, whether it's in a shooting war or a different kind of a war. But the president was convinced that we had to keep, had to stay in there . . .

Kennedy:

Yes.

Martin:

. . . and couldn't lose it.

Kennedy:

Yes.

Martin:

And if Vietnamese were about to lose it, would he propose to go in on land if he had to?

Kennedy:

Well, we'd face that when we came to it.....

[234] Remarks of Welcome to President Sukarno of Indonesia and President Keita of Mali at Andrews Air Force Base. The American Presidency Project, UC Santa Barbara, September 12, 1961.

https://www.presidency.ucsb.edu/documents/remarks-welcome-president-sukarno-indonesia-and-president-keita-mali-andrews-air-force

[235] Larry Hancock, *NEXUS*, "Going Nowhere" and "End Run," 97-101

[236] "Kennedy Sought Dialogue with Cuba", National Security Archive, November 24, 2003, also "Cuba and the U.S. Intimate Diplomacy," National Security Archive, April 20, 2018

https://nsarchive2.gwu.edu/NSAEBB/NSAEBB103/index.htm

https://nsarchive.gwu.edu/briefing-book/cuba/2018-04-20/cuba-us-intimate-diplomacy

[237] Richard Helms to Director, Interview with U.S. Newswoman with Fidel Castro Indicating Possible Interest of Fidel Castro in Rapprochement with the United States, May 1, 1963

https://nsarchive2.gwu.edu/NSAEBB/NSAEBB103/630501.pdf

[238] Lisa Howard, Draft Letter to John F. Kennedy, ca. May 1963

https://nsarchive2.gwu.edu//dc.html?doc=4444505-Document-04-Lisa-Howard-Draft-Letter-to-John-F

[239] Michael Beschloss, "When JFK Secretly Reached Out to Castro," The New York Times, December 17, 2014

https://www.nytimes.com/2014/12/18/upshot/when-jfk-secretly-reached-out-to-castro.html

[240] In 1964, Castro once again used Lisa Howard to carry an offer of conciliation, with a personal note from Castro stating that he realized that in order to be elected, Johnson would make strong statements and might even conduct some specific hostile action against Cuba. Castro accepted that and committed to no retaliation. He wished to continue the Attwood contacts and felt that there were no issues between the two nations which could not be resolved. He reaffirmed his trust in Howard and the need for secrecy, and promised to reveal nothing about the approach.

In response, McGeorge Bundy inserted himself to prevent Lisa Howard from delivering Castro's message, going so far as to distribute a memorandum to all White House aides which described Howard as a persistent and "self-important creature," and that under no circumstances must her message from Castro be allowed to be delivered. Larry Hancock, *NEXUS*, 100.

[241] Larry Hancock, *NEXUS*, 68-69

[242] Ibid, 166-167

[243] Noel Twyman, "Research Memorandum on William Harvey in 1963," *Bloody Treason*

[244] Interview with Ross Crozier, PM Section, Miami Base, June 2, 1961

https://www.maryferrell.org/showDoc.html?docId=148666&relPageId=10

[245] Project ZRRIFLE and QJWIN, Rockefeller Commission, May 5, 1975, 10

https://www.maryferrell.org/showDoc.html?docId=148666

[246] Harvey had claimed the missions were intelligence collection efforts, designed to obtain tactical information to support any American military operations into Cuba. But he was unable to point to any specific requests from the military, the Joint Chiefs, or DOD. In turn, none of those groups stepped in to his defense, confirming any request for missions. We do know the missions occured, at least one led by Rip Robertson. Whether they were actually for intelligence work or were related to something even more covert, such as the ongoing Castro assassination efforts (which had not been sanctioned by the President or RFK), remains a matter of debate.

[247] Cryptonym AMLASH, Mary Ferrell Foundation

https://www.maryferrell.org/php/cryptdb.php?id=AMLASH

[248] AMTRUNK Operation, Interim Working Draft, February 14, 1977. It should be noted that Morales expressed little faith in the beginning of the project, and JMWAVE supported it simply as a functional responsibility to SAS and CIA headquarters. Its failure proved to be one of several issues which left Shackley and Morales highly frustrated with the new Cuba Committee and SAS projects that were launched in 1963.

http://documents.theblackvault.com/documents/jfk/NARA-Oct2017/2018/104-10103-10097.pdf

[249] Alfonso Rodriquez SAS/SO, Meeting with AMBIDDY-1 [Artime], April 3, 1963

https://www.maryferrell.org/showDoc.html?docId=36963

[250] Memorandum for Director of Security, Chief Security Research Staff, Project AMWORLD, October 16, 1964

https://www.maryferrell.org/showDoc.html?docId=23439

[251] Larry Hancock, *NEXUS*, 99-101

[252] William Harvey had served as head of CIA counter intelligence and several of his former staff, both at Langley and in Mexico City, continued in that function as Harvey moved on to other assignments. Because of his role with Staff D, Harvey continued to receive counter intelligence information relating to potential collections targets, including the Cuban embassy in Mexico City.

[253] Cryptonym AMLAW-3, Carlos Lechuga, Mary Ferrell Foundation

https://www.maryferrell.org/php/cryptdb.php?id=AMLAW-3

[254] The CIA had also obtained information that Lechuga had actually offered to divorce his wife and marry Duran; the information was felt to be especially powerful leverage – although in the end the recruitment of Mrs. Lechuga failed.

[255] Bill Simpich, *State Secret / Wiretapping in Mexico City, Double Agents, and the Framing of Lee Oswald*, Chapter 3: "The Cuban Compound in Mexico City Was Ground Zero"

https://www.maryferrell.org/pages/State_Secret_Chapter3.html

[256] Chief Western Hemisphere Division to Chief of Station, Mexico City, Background Information on Dr. Rene Vallejo Ortiz, also Mexico City Cable Info JMWAVE Subject Rene Vallejo Ortiz, October 9, 1963

https://www.maryferrell.org/showDoc.html?docId=42941

https://www.maryferrell.org/showDoc.html?docId=45080&relPageId=1

[257] David Talbot, *Brothers: The Hidden History of the Kennedy Years*, 228

[258] Anthony Marro, "Helms, EX-C.I.A. Chief pleads No Contest to 2 Misdemeanors," New York Times, November 1, 1977

https://www.nytimes.com/1977/11/01/archives/helmsexcia-chief-pleads-no-contest-to-2-misdemeanors-case-tied-to.html

[259] Larry Hancock, *NEXUS*, 100

[260] Anthony Summers, *Not In Your Lifetime*, 307

[261] Citation: CIA Memorandum, "Arnesto Rodriquez, Anti-Castro Cuban, Knew Lee Oswald in New Orleans," November 26, 1963

https://www.archives.gov/files/research/jfk/releases/docid-32364528.pdf

[262] Mary Ferrell Foundation, CIA Cryptonyms Project: Arnesto Rodriguez Sr, AMJUTE-1

https://www.maryferrell.org/php/cryptdb.php?id=AMJUTE-1

[263] Warren Commission Report, Volume 22, page 189

[264] Emilio Americo Rodriguez, AMIRE-1, CIA Cryptonym Project, Mary Ferrell Foundation

https://www.maryferrell.org/php/cryptdb.php?id=AMIRE-1

[265] CIA Cover Request File, Emilio Rodriguez

https://www.maryferrell.org/showDoc.html?docId=157701#relPageId=14

[266] John Newman, *Countdown to Darkness*, 76-77, also CIA Dispatch JMWAVE Chief of Station to Director, Western Hemisphere,

https://www.maryferrell.org/showDoc.html?docId=157701#relPageId=4

[267] John Newman, *Into the Storm*, 80-81

[268] CIA Cover Request file, Emilio Rodriquez

https://www.maryferrell.org/showDoc.html?docId=157701#relPageId=16

[269] Memorandum to Convert Contract Employee to Career Agent, Emilio Rodriguez, January 21, 1965

http://documents.theblackvault.com/documents/jfk/NARA-Oct2017/docid-32371538.pdf

[270] Recommendation for Honor or Merit Award, Emilio Rodriguez, Service from April 1960 - June 1961

https://www.archives.gov/files/research/jfk/releases/104-10161-10131.pdf

[271] Oswald's first use of the Hidell identity occurred while he was still residing in Dallas, in the order for a rifle purchased by Alec Hidell. Active debate remains (and will continue) on the order of the rifle and the use of the Hidell alias. There is also some indication that Oswald was beginning to involve himself in promoting the FPCC prior to leaving Dallas. Oswald's first letter to the FPCC, requesting literature, was postmarked from Dallas on April 18, 1963. The FPCC reply letter notes that 50 pieces of literature were sent to Oswald. Source: Bill Simpich, "Fair Play for Cuba and the Cuban Revolution," Counterpunch, July 4, 2009.

https://www.counterpunch.org/2009/07/24/fair-play-for-cuba-and-the-cuban-revolution/

The FBI only began to speculate that "Hidell" was an alias being used by Lee Oswald when he became visible in FPCC-related activities in New Orleans in the summer of 1963. The outstanding question is whether or not Oswald could have become involved in a CIA intelligence/propaganda effort against the FPCC well before that point in time. It that were true, the "legend" of Oswald/Hidell as an American serviceman, subverted by communist and Cuban propaganda, could well have been in play as late as Oswald's "appearance" at the Cuban consulate in Mexico City in October 1963.

[272] Procurement of Domestic Documentation and Security Clearance Approval

https://www.archives.gov/files/research/jfk/releases/104-10161-10109.pdf

https://www.archives.gov/files/research/jfk/releases/104-10180-10225.pdf

[273] "Attempts to Locate Bank Accounts for Cuban Permanent Mission to the UN," Federal Bureau of Investigation, Interview Report, May 26, 1960

https://www.maryferrell.org/showDoc.html?docId=167707

"Political Action Operations in Cuba - The Proenza Case", House Select Committee on Assassinations, July 26, 1978

https://www.maryferrell.org/showDoc.html?docId=162401#relPageId=4

[274] Larry Hancock, *Someone Would Have Talked* 2010, 146-148

[275] CIA Dispatch, Chief Mexico City to Chief SAS, Operational / Eusebio Azcue

http://documents.theblackvault.com/documents/jfk/NARA-Oct2017/2018/104-10163-10014.pdf

[276] Chief of Station JMWAVE to Chief SAS, AMOT-106 Visit to Cuban Embassy [Mexico City]

https://www.maryferrell.org/showDoc.html?docId=21409#relPageId=2

[277] Larry Hancock, *Someone Would Have Talked* 2010, 99, also AMSANTA Crypt, Mary Ferrell Foundation

https://www.maryferrell.org/php/cryptdb.php?id=AMSANTA

[278] Larry Hancock, *Someone Would Have Talked*, "Oswald, Hot in Mexico City," 215-221

[279] Sullivan to Brennan, FBI Memorandum, September 4, 1964

https://www.maryferrell.org/showDoc.html?docId=10111#relPageId=323

[280] The CIA was unable to produce photographs of Oswald entering or exiting the consulate, photographs which should have been available from the surveillance cameras targeting the facility. The CIA's claim that an equipment failure had precluded such photographs at the time of Oswald's visit is inconsistent with a memorandum by David Phillips to the FBI in which Phillips provided photographs from September 27, which demonstrated that an individual the FBI was investigating had not visited the consulate. Phillips also provided photos of some 20 other individuals visiting the consulate during September and October. Beyond that, Phillips seriously embarrassed the CIA by supporting the claims of Gilberto Alvarado, an individual who reported actually observing Oswald discussing killing President Kennedy and accepting money from Cuban diplomatic staff – that story was quickly disproved in an FBI investigation, with the informant himself revealed as an intelligence asset. Gilberto Alvarado Allegation, analysis and documents, Mary Ferrell Foundation.

https://www.maryferrell.org/pages/Gilberto_Alvarado_Allegation.html

[281] David Josephs, Kennedy's and King, "Mexico City Parts 1 and 2," October, 2014 and January, 2015

https://kennedysandking.com/john-f-kennedy-articles/mexico-city-part-1

https://kennedysandking.com/john-f-kennedy-articles/mexico-city-part-3-the-trip-down-part-2

282 Jefferson Morley, "What Jane Roman Said," History Matters

https://www.history-matters.com/essays/frameup/WhatJaneRomanSaid/WhatJaneRomanSaid_1.htm

283 John Newman, Oswald, the CIA and Mexico City, PBS Frontline, November 19, 2013

https://www.pbs.org/wgbh/frontline/article/oswald-the-cia-and-mexico-city/

284 Bayard Stockton, *Flawed Patriot*, 114-115, also 160-161

285 Larry Hancock and David Boylan, "The Wheaton Lead: An Exploration," Mary Ferrell Foundation, April 2020

https://www.maryferrell.org/pages/Essay_-_The_Wheaton_Lead.html

286 Noel Twyman, *Bloody Treason: The Assassination of John F. Kennedy*, 1997, "Personal Interviews with Roy Hargraves." The following synopsis is reconstructed from a partial transcript made available by Noel Twyman; the entire interview session was taped but a transcript was prepared for only a portion of the many hours of dialogue involved in the session. Appendix A, Tape 2, Side A, 2001 Interview.

http://larry-hancock.com/roy_hargraves_interview.pdf

Noel Twyman conducted extended interviews of Gerry Hemming; Hemming was a highly visible figure in independent anti-Castro activism and the organizer of several abortive missions against Castro. For a time he also cooperated with Frank Sturgis in coordinating a group of independent anti-Castro American paramilitary activists; the group was promoted to the media under the name Intercontinental Penetration Force/INTERPEN. Hemming told Twyman that at one point that he had been knowledgeable of the early stages of a conspiracy targeting JFK, but dropped out before it developed beyond the talking stage. When Twyman asked for other sources, Hemming named Roy Hargraves and offered to make an introduction for additional interviews. Hemming was demonstrably close to Hargraves as well as to Felipe Vidal. Hemming had named one of his own sons was named after Vidal.

After considerable dialogue, and with Hemming's encouragement, Hargraves did agree to an interview by Twyman. Tyman allowed the use of a portion of that interview in the first edition of *Someone Would Have Talked.* The following narrative of Hargraves' remarks and involvement is based on that interview transcript, as well as extended personal conversation between Hancock and Twyman. The interview itself was confirmed in personal conversation with Hemming's brother Robert, a lawyer who sat in with Hargraves in the interviews.

Hargraves related to Hemming that he and Vidal had gone to Dallas but that he had no prior knowledge of a conspiracy, asserting that he had no idea of what was going to happen in Dallas, and was simply taken there to perform a specific job (building a bomb). Hargraves also repeatedly stressed that neither he nor Vidal were involved in the actual murder. He remained vague on Vidal's role, however, in the first phase of the interviews, he stated that he and Vidal were on Elm Street and Vidal acted as a signal man; in the second round of interviews he became much more circumspect about Vidal and their being on Elm Street at the time of the shooting.

Photographs do show two men (described respectively in JFK assassination literature as the Umbrella Man and the Dark Complected Man) who appear quite similar to Roy Hargraves and Felipe Vidal standing beside each other on Elm Street, then sitting quite close together before they walk away in different directions. One of them was wearing a beret similar in appearance to berets seen in other photographs of Vidal, and to many appears to have some sort of radio in his back pocket. It may be that Hargraves was not aware of those photographs in the first phase of the interview.

Hargraves was more specific about his own role. Being experienced with explosives (it can be confirmed that Hargraves was an explosives specialist; in later years after he and Hemming had moved to Los Angeles he built bombs which were used against the Black Panthers) he was to build an improvised explosive device (a car bomb). The bomb was placed in a car on the access ramp from Main Street to the Stemmons freeway (the route to JFK's scheduled speech at the Trade Mart), but was not used given the success of the rifle attack on Elm Street. Photographs do show a number of vehicles parked in the area described by Hargraves.

Two other names brought up by Roy Hargraves were John Martino and Bernardo De Torres. He expressed the opinion that Martino was directly connected to the individuals organizing the attack. In retrospect, it appears that Martino most likely involved both Hargraves and Vidal, through his close personal connection to Vidal. As for Bernardo De Torres, Hargraves went into some length as to how De Torres had inserted himself into the Garrison investigation, "burning money and doing damage control." As detailed in a separate end note, that assessment seems quite accurate and a bit ironic, considering that Hemming and Hargraves had also inserted themselves into the Garrison investigation; Garrison himself later commented that the two appeared to have been primarily interested in what information he was collecting, not in providing anything themselves.

Unfortunately, it can be shown that Hargraves was also passing along a great deal of misinformation – and intentional disinformation – in his conversations with Twyman – something not unexpected. Even Gerry Hemming's brother was open about the fact that Hemming, and presumably Hargraves, intentionally convoluted their stories so extensively that anyone dealing with them as potential suspects would simply give up and walk away confused. There is absolutely no doubt that Hargrave's information needs to be approached with great caution, considering only that which has some level of corroboration.

[287] Bernardo De Torres was a Cuba Project volunteer who landed with Brigade 2506 at the Bay of Pigs, and was captured. Upon his release in December 1962, he returned to Miami and joined his brother Carlos, who had a well-established detective agency in Miami. When a Brigade 2506 organization was voluntarily re-formed in Miami during 1963, he became its chief of intelligence. Photographs depict him as being personally involved with several former INTERPEN activists such as Roy Hargraves and William Seymour. Boat mission photographs also show him engaged with Felipe Vidal and Roy Hargraves in 1963, preparing a boat to be used on a mission into Cuba.

In December 1966, when New Orleans District Attorney began his confidential investigation into Lee Oswald and the Kennedy assassination (his initial suspicions were that the CIA had been involved in a conspiracy to kill the president), one of his first interests was a series of reports which placed Lee Oswald in the company of not only intelligence agencies, but also with unknown Cubans in New Orleans, not locals but possibly individuals from Miami. In pursuit of that lead, Garrison sent his investigators to Miami. After certain initial police contacts, the investigators were referred to De Torres. Given his connection to his brother's detective agency, and his familiarity with the Miami exile community, it appeared he was an ideal choice to pursue the lead. Garrison's interest did reach De Torres, who then volunteered his services directly to Garrison, becoming a paid investigator for him in January 1967.

It may well have been coincidence that De Torres' awareness of the Garrison inquiry coincides almost perfectly with the timing of John Roselli's outreach to principals in Washington DC (Earl Warren, the FBI, the Secret Service, and ultimately President Johnson and columnist Jack Anderson), in which Roselli affirmed a conspiracy to kill JFK. Roselli offered details on the conspiracy and raised concerns among key individuals in Washington, including President Johnson, at the same time De Torres elevated media attention to the Garrison's investigation. Larry Hancock, *Someone Would Have Talked*, 126-133.

Garrison had been making every effort to keep his inquiry out of the press; however, the combination of a payment receipt to De Torres and De Torres' own eagerness to speak to the press literally torpedoed Garrison's efforts. Without consulting with Garrison, De Torres talked openly about the investigation, giving his opinions that there definitely had been a conspiracy and that Fidel Castro was behind Lee Oswald and the murder. His press interviews and comments almost immediately led to full exposure of the Garrison inquiry, and to a very public media appearance by Jim Garrison. Garrison was left to face the reality that De Torres' involvement had fully compromised the confidentiality of his inquiry.

Garrison himself was already becoming suspicious of De Torres. As early as January 7, 1967, he had directed his own investigators to share no information with him, and soon afterwards began annotating memos from De Torres with notes stating that his reliability had not been established.

One of the sources referenced in this work, Rolondo Otero, told HSCA investigator Gaeton Fonzi that De Torres had intentionally penetrated Garrison's inquiry with the intention of directing him towards a conspiracy involving Fidel Castro and Cuba, rather than in any further interest in the activities of anti-Castro Cuban exiles.

Larry Hancock, *Someone Would Have Talked* 2010, 128, also The Dallas Action, "The Garrison Investigation and Bernardo De Torres," September 21, 2015

https://22novembernetwork.wordpress.com/2015/09/21/tda-71-september-21-2015bernardo-de-torres-and-the-garrison-investigation-with-larry-hancock/

[288] The lack of proper chains of possession for much of the material recovered by the Dallas Police, and the possibility that certain materials may have been planted, frustrates the effort to determine any actual participation by Lee Oswald in the conspiracy which killed President Kennedy. Worse yet, there is considerable anecdotal evidence to support the idea that certain pieces of evidence which would have exposed the fact of multiple shooters were recovered and later suppressed. As an example, the recovery of a bullet on the south side of Elm street is particularly well documented by both witnesses and photographs.

One of the less known and possibly significant indications that certain officers within the DPD were aware of more information than they ever acknowledged in public is revealed in a lead discovered by an HSCA staff member. During an interview with Starvis Ellis (a close friend of Dallas Police Captain Will Fritz, chief of the Homicide and Robbery Division) the unidentified staff person made notes about Ellis' comments in regard to his having observed a bullet (unaccounted for in the official shooting scenario) hit the street behind the president's limousine. In itself, Ellis's observation of the bullet strike would suggest multiple shooters, but more intriguingly the official interview summary sheet contains a totally unexplained handwritten note on the official interview summary sheet – "Martino (Marino) hired the shooter, ask Captain Fritz."

RIF 180-10109-10154 located and supplied by researcher Larry Haapanen, who brought the annotation to the author's attention.

There is no sign that any DPD knowledge relating to John Martino was ever pursued by the HSCA – although it did independently obtain information from two of Martino's close friends that he had indeed been involved in the conspiracy.

[289] Controversy and debate over Oswald's employment at the Texas School Depository, and its implication for the conspiracy, have been continual and will remain ongoing. Points that do have to be considered are the fact that Marina Oswald was living with Ruth Paine, next door neighbor to the Frazier family, whose son Buell worked at the TSBD. In addition, reports out of Dallas following the assassination relate an individual either using the name Oswald, or having a close physical match for Lee Oswald, inquiring about employment at various places along Main Street (the obvious route for a political motorcade) prior to Oswald's actual employment at the TSBD.

Oswald himself had made it clear that he was not pleased with his work at the TSBD and was looking for another job. Marina Oswald and others commented on his interest in finding other work. More specifically, based on documents and information now available, we know that the FBI itself was aware (from a local inquiry by Dallas newspersons) that Oswald had applied for work at the Devilbliss Company. While Oswald appears to have been first referred to that company in October (and according to the FBI, interviewed then), an independent inquiry at the company by a local news outlet found that Oswald himself had followed up on the initial application in person some two weeks prior to the assassination, while employed at the TSBD. The Devilbliss Company was not located in downtown Dallas, but rather in the vicinity of the Trade Mart. Larry Hancock, *Someone Would Have Talked,* 64-65, also FBI summary report, December 13, 1965, Hood College Archives.

http://jfk.hood.edu/Collection/FBI%20Records%20Files/105-82555/105-82555%20Section%20057/105-57c.pdf

The personal information on the Devilbliss application confirms the individual in question to be Lee Oswald, and has other points of interest, including the statement that Oswald did not own an automobile but did rent one.

What also has to be said is that any tactical plan is fluid, intended to be altered as field connections change. Since we simply do not know the details of the tactical plan for Dallas, we are left with speculation in regard to Oswald's employment; certainly, he could have been "framed" if he had been employed at a location other than the TSBD. While the plaza was a desirable location for a shooting attack, other locations could have been employed. Martino tells us that the team itself arrived in Dallas days before the attack, and it is likely the exact infiltration routes, shooting positions and exfiltration plans were not finalized until then. Reverse engineering the plan from what actually happened is tempting, but has to be approached with considerable caution.

[290] There is considerable debate in regard to the rifle belonging to Lee Oswald, or even having been ordered by him. Among other things, the debate is fueled by the fact that the rifle was ordered in the name of Hidell while being shipped to Oswald's Dallas post office box. The problem with that is there is no record of Oswald having designated Hidell to use the post office box or of the rifle being received by Oswald himself – records that would have shown both are missing and officially listed as destroyed. However, Oswald's post office box in New Orleans did have paperwork

designating it to be used by A Hidell, and there are indications that Oswald had begun a minimal level of FPCC activities while still in Dallas. Given that a rifle found in the Texas School Book Depository would have had no value to a conspiracy with the intent of implicating Castro via Oswald, the simplest explanation would seem to be that Oswald did use the Hidell alias in Dallas, and that it was either recorded on the post office paperwork or no questions were raised when Oswald presented a card placed in his box telling him he had a package. Ensuring that a rifle tied to Oswald was entered into evidence did not directly link the assassination to Castro, but it certainly did support speculation as to a Cuban linkage given the reputation Oswald had established that summer in New Orleans. Reference and issues with the rifle can be found Warren Commission documents in the National Archives and in an extensive and early research paper by Martha Moyer available at JFK Lancer.

https://www.archives.gov/research/jfk/warren-commission-report/chapter-4.html#purchase

291 A memorandum from FBI agent James Anderton was placed in the Dallas office FBI files, but never added to the central FBI file on the assassination. It was only revealed in a lawsuit filed by Harold Weisberg and is now housed in the Weisburg Archives at Hood College. The report states that Frazier *"recalls that on the morning of November 22, when Oswald rode to work in his car, he had something in a brown paper sack, the kind you would obtain in a dime store, specifically that the paper in the sack was of a flimsy, thin consistency. Frazier stated that he could not observe the sack very well since Oswald threw it in the back seat of his car, and upon arriving ...at work Oswald carried the package in a vertical position under his right arm, appearing to be holding the end of whatever was in the sack, which he recalled was about two feet in length. Mr. Frazier was questioned as to the ends of the sack and if two sacks had been placed together, but he could recall only seeing one sack described above."*

Most importantly it goes on to state something which never appears elsewhere in the evidence files pertaining to the crime scene materials: *"Mr. Frazier stated that between 11:00 PM and midnight, November 22, 1963, he was in the polygraph room of the Dallas Police Department and before taking the polygraph examination a police officer, name unknown to him, brought in a large paper sack, approximately three to four feet in length and the type a grocery store receives their five-pound bags of sugar in, specifically that the paper in the sack was very thick and stiff. He stated that this sack shown to him appeared to actually have been made by someone cutting down a larger sack. He said he told the police officer that this sack had never been seen by him before. He also said that this sack was definitely not the one he had observed in possession of Oswald the morning of November 22, 1963."* Pat Speer, Chapter 2, "An Investigation through the eyes of the all-seeing FBI.

http://www.patspeer.com/chapter2%3Alookingthroughtheeyesofanall-se

[292] The paper bag represented to be the device which Lee Oswald used to surreptitiously transport his rifle to the TSBD is actually the most important piece of evidence presented to connect Oswald to the shooting of the president. However the bag itself, unlike the rifle and hulls connected to it, was not photographed at the crime scene, and its location there is represented by nothing more than a dotted line box added to a photograph which purports to show the "approximate location" of the bag – and even that item was prepared not by the Dallas Police but at the request of the FBI. Beyond that, the crime scene unit notes and the police markings on the bag itself give no exact location nor the identity of the officer who first located or recovered it into evidence.

One individual, Detective Robert Studebaker (the crime scene photographer), testified to actually seeing the bag in place; he is the one who later added the dotted line representation to the photograph of the crime scene. Which means that the man responsible for filming all evidence in situ is the one who observed the sack in place, and then allegedly neglected to photograph it. Studebaker had been previously assigned to the auto theft bureau of the DPD, and on November 22 was not only new to the crime scene section (two months into that assignment) but virtually a trainee. As an aside, an eyewitness to the police work that day (Tom Alyea, a Dallas reporter) has long claimed that Studebaker was so new in his job and so apparently inexperienced that he actually moved materials at the crime scene in taking photographs, and those materials had to be repositioned to actually obtain the photographs that were later officially entered into evidence. Alyea also described the three bullet hulls which were so critical to the crime scene being picked up by a police captain so that he could film them, and then thrown back down on the floor – only then being filmed for the official evidence record.

Beyond that, the Warren Commission report itself notes that the area where the hulls were found was searched by police officer Luke Mooney (it being a relatively small area by a window in the NE corner of the

TSBD), but contains no record of Mooney observing a bag during his search of the area in which it was later represented to have been found. Statements from a number of officers on record as having searched the same area only adds to the confusion – some saw nothing resembling the sack, some saw other paper bags (lunch bags), two detectives described having seen a sack and actually recovering it into evidence (photographs show one carrying it from the building, fully extended to a four foot length and supported by something rigid inside it). Those detectives were not questioned in detail about their handling of the bag and its removal as evidence.

The issues with the paper sack, so critical in the evidence, go on and on. Researcher Ian Griggs records them in great detail in Chapter 18 ("The Paper Bag That Never Was") of his book *No Case to Answer,* and other researchers also present detailed studies of the issues with the bag as evidence connecting Lee Oswald to the shooting of the president.

Yet beyond all that work, one final fact appears to totally remove the paper sack itself from being of any value in that regard. We now know (only through an FBI agent's report) that on the night of the assassination, Buell Wesley Frasier, the man who had driven Oswald to work was shown the actual sack recovered from the TSBD during a police polygraph interview. At that point in time, as the FBI memo describes, Frasier stated (with the truth of his statement confirmed by the polygraph) that the bag in evidence was not the one which Lee Oswald had taken to work that morning.

Pat Speer, Chapter 4C, "Shining the Light on Day"

http://www.patspeer.com/chapter-4c

Gil Jesus, "The Bag Job"

https://www.giljesus.com/the-bag.html

Tom Alyea, "Facts and Photos," From Connie Kritzberg, *Secrets from the Sixth Floor Window*, pp. 39-46, also personal interview by the author with Tom Alyea

http://www.jfk-online.com/alyea.html

[293] David Wallechinsky and Irving Wallace, *The Peoples Almanac #2*, Bantam Books, 1978, "The Last Words of Lee Oswald," 47-52; compilation by Mae Brussell

[294] Larry Hancock and David Boylan, "The Wheaton Lead: An Exploration," April, 2020

[295] Patrick D. Marques, "Guerrilla Tactics in Urban Environments," U.S. Army Command and General Staff College, Leavenworth, Kansas, 2003

https://fas.org/man/eprint/marques.pdf

[296] Larry Hancock, *Someone Would Have Talked* 2010, 155-156

[297] Ibid, 157

[298] Ibid, 119

[299] An unnamed FBI source for reporter Scott Malone related that, during the investigation of John Roselli's murder, he had viewed Miami office FBI surveillance reports on John Roselli – reports which recorded Roselli meeting with Jack Ruby in Miami in 1963. The FBI source was recorded during his telephone call to Malone, however, he said that while he had seen written records of the surveillance, he did not have copies. Hundreds of pages of Roselli's FBI surveillance records do exist and have been reviewed, however the files covering his trips to Florida are not among them – it is known that the FBI was very much aware of Roselli's contacts with the CIA and his travels to Florida. Roselli himself certainly was aware of Ruby, telling reporter Jack Anderson that Ruby was "their boy" in Dallas. Ibid, 191.

[300] HSCA Report, 431-433

https://www.history-matters.com/archive/jfk/hsca/reportvols/vol9/pdf/HSCA_Vol9_5Fv_Gruber.pdf

[301] Hancock, *Someone Would Have Talked*, 2010, 201-202

[302] John William Touhy, *Johnny Roselli Gangster*, The Writers Site, 2016

http://mywriterssite.blogspot.com/2016/12/johnny-roselli-gangster.html

[303] Jim Magus, *Unspeakable Acts*, Magus Enterprises, 2011, 111

[304] Ian Griggs, *No Case to Answer*, JFK Lancer Productions and Publications, 2005, Chapter 19, "Jack Ruby's Carousel Club," 215-235

[305] Ibid, 222

[306] Testimony of Harry N. Olsen, Warren Commission Hearing, August 6, 1964, Los Angeles, California

http://mcadams.posc.mu.edu/russ/testimony/olsen_h.htm

[307] The skating party included Ruby, Olsen, Kathy Kay and Shari Angel, personal communication with Ian Griggs, based on Griggs Interview with Shari Angel, Ian Griggs, *No Case to Answer*, Chapter 20, "Search for a Stripper; the Kathy Kay Story," 235-255

[308] Ibid, 171-175

[309] Peter Dale Scott, *Deep Politics and the Death of JFK*, (University of California Press, Ltd, 1993, 179

[310] For reference, Eighth Street runs east and west from downtown Dallas – but it's considerably more distant from Stemmons Freeway than the two blocks Olsen described. More significantly, Eighth Street runs though Oak Cliff a distance of only a few a few blocks from the location of Lee Oswald's rooming house. Radio logs indicate that officer J.D. Tippit traveled down Eight Street the afternoon of the assassination. Given that Olsen described walking four or five blocks to his girlfriend's house (Kathy Kay), that places his actual location at the time of the assassination in the vicinity of a number of events involving both Oswald and Tippit. As Penn Jones pointed out decades ago, given the elevations in the area, Olsen's self-described location could actually have allowed him to observe Lee Oswald as Oswald crossed Eight, prior to his encounter with Officer Tippit. (Penn Jones, *Forgive My Grief*, Volume 1, 84). Strangely, the Warren Commission staff totally failed to map out Olsen's "estate" as being in proximity to any of the assassination-related locations in Oak Cliff, or pursue any interest in his proximity. Testimony of Harry N. Olsen, Warren Commission Hearing, August 6, 1964, Los Angeles, California.

It also should be noted that Harry Olsen and Kathy Kay encountered and talked with Jack Ruby in a parking lot in downtown Dallas for some period of time around 1:30 AM early on November 23, the day after the assassination. (Commission Exhibit 2318; FBI interview with Harry Olsen). Olsen had worked with the DPD for over five years and had been dating Kay for some time in December. Olsen was separated from the

Dallas Police, married Kay, and the two left Dallas and moved to California within a month or two following the assassination.

[311] While a number of early researchers, including Penn Jones, tried to track down the actual location which Olsen described, none were successful – nor has anyone else been so in later years.

[312] Ian Griggs, *No Case to Answer*, 243-244

[313] Chris Scally, "Dumb Cop or Man on a Mission," The Dealey Plaza Echo, Winter 2014, Volume 7 Issue 3

[314] Even Tippit's dispatch to Oak Cliff remains a matter of some mystery. The first copy of the DPD dispatcher recordings of that day did not contain any call to Tippit to move to Oak Cliff. When that was questioned, another copy surfaced which did contain a call to Tippit and another officer to move to Oak Cliff – yet the second officer never appeared in Oak Cliff, but instead has been determined to have actually moved downtown to the Plaza. Another point which makes the purported dispatch even more questionable is that there was already a DPD officer assigned to Oak Cliff – Officer William Mentzel. Yet Mentzel was never interviewed, no reports are on file from him, and his name is not even mentioned in the Warren Report. Joseph McBride, *Into the Nightmare: My Search for the Killers of Officer John F. Kennedy and Officer J.D. Tippit*, Hightower Press, 2013, 482.

[315] In addition to security work at a BBQ restaurant, Tippit had worked off-duty security at the Stevens Park Theater, owned by Manuel Avila. The theater reportedly ran Spanish language shows, attracting Latinos and Cuban exiles as well. Dallas rumors held that in addition to the movies downstairs, a prostitution business went on using facilities associated with the theater. Even more interesting is the rumor that Tippit himself had some problems involving one of the girls working that side of the business. It may also be significant that Manual Avila himself was very much connected to Cuban exile activities in Dallas, as well as to individuals associated with the house on Harlandale Street.

Avila's activities had included serving as a translator for Cuban exiles in Dallas, apparently including individuals newly arrived in the country. Amelia Diaz worked for Avila and was an active DRE supporter. Diaz had emigrated from Cuba in 1959, worked for Avila, and actually lived at the

Harlandale address during the relatively brief period in which the house was being visited frequently by both members of DRE and Alpha 66.

The individual who actually rented the Harlandale house was Jose Salazar, affiliated with Alpha 66, but perhaps equally importantly, a close friend of Oswaldo Aurelio Pino Pino. As of fall 1963, Pino Pino was under FBI investigation as a potential Castro agent. That investigation had begun in Miami and was transferred to Dallas when Pino Pino moved there. If Pino Pino was one of the visitors to the house, that would have been yet one more reason why the location would have been of interest to the FBI.

https://larryhancock.wordpress.com/2014/10/10/loose-ends-in-dallas-and-the-house-on-harlandale/

[316] Larry Hancock, *Someone Would Have Talked* 2010, 305

[317] The Frazier polygraph examination was never actually entered into evidence, and for some years various Dallas officers questioned if such a thing had even occurred. An FBI interview of the polygraph operator describes the fact that Frazier felt the nature of the paper and size of the sack he was shown that evening did not match the bag in Oswald's possession. There is no indication that the FBI re-interviewed Frazier on questions regarding his failure to confirm the sack as being the one carried by Oswald that morning. Special Agent Vincent Drain, FBI memorandum, December 1, 1963.

https://www.maryferrell.org/showDoc.html?docId=57689&relPageId=100

[318] Bill Simpich, JFK Facts, April 21, 2014

https://jfkfacts.org/oswalds-wallet-planted-at-the-tippit-crime-scene/

[319] "Photocopy of Personal Recognition Signal / used for contact with AMBIDDY-1 [Artime]," NARA Record Number: 104-10240-10338, Mary Ferrell Foundation

https://www.maryferrell.org/showDoc.html?docId=21223#relPageId=1

[320] During the 1990's, John Armstrong obtained a copy of a DPD document showing an evidence receipt which contained numbered references to "two half dollar bills." Armstrong has made an image available of that document. However the electronic version of that same document does not contain the annotation concerning the torn bill. Personal conversation with Jim Hargrave, May, 14, 2020. The image of

the original document recording the bills, as located by John, is presented on his web site.

https://harveyandlee.net/November/November_22.htm

[321] Oswaldo Pino's friend Jose Salazar had rented the house on Harlandale, and served as vice president of the Dallas Alpha 66 chapter. The FBI was particularly interested in Pino, as he had been an important figure in Cuba (Chief of the Fuels and Lubrication Department at the Institute of Agrarian reform) following the revolution. He was suspected of involvement with Cuban G-2 inside Cuba and being an informant on anti-Castroites and anti-Communists. After arriving in the US, he was investigated as being a subversive, a possible Cuban intelligence agent. That investigation began in June 1963 and was only completed in March 1964 – the investigation was delayed because Heitman was pulled for JFK assassination investigation work. Heitman concluded that Pino was not a Castro agent, largely based on his very public anti-Castro activism. Virtually none of Heitman's pre- assassination reports on his investigation of suspected subversives are available, yet he played the main role in FBI subversive investigations focused on Cubans in Dallas. This remains one of the most important and least pursued areas of JFK research.

[322] Heitman was involved in both the investigations of Marina Oswald and in the extensive FBI inquiry into the reported visit to Sylvia Odio by three men including Lee Oswald – as well as the possibility of other contacts between Oswald and Odio in Dallas.

[323] There is no doubt that a number of activities which occurred both before and during the attack in Dealey Plaza could be considered as security diversions. Simply watching a film of the shooting shows that the driver of the presidential limousine had his attention drawn to a man on the sidewalk pumping an umbrella at the time of the shooting. The attention of both witnesses and police was drawn to the area of the fence line by the grassy knoll, both by a loud noise at that location and a smoke flowing out over the fence at that point. With the crowd drawn to that location, other areas of the plaza received no attention at all.

Two lesser-discussed incidents occurred prior to the arrival of the motorcade. Whether innocent and circumstantial, or something more, both diverted police attention away from scanning the crowds or watching movements in the area of Elm and Houston Street. For almost two hours police officers were involved with a green and white pickup which apparently became stalled on the street at exactly that point on the motorcade route (a point which would have choked the street to a single lane under the bridge). Rather than immediately having it towed away, one officer actually left with the driver of the pickup, while another maintained a watch on the vehicle and occupant.

It was only shortly before the scheduled arrival of the motorcade that the driver and officer returned with another pickup which pushed the stalled vehicle away. The officer (patrolman Joe Murphy) was questioned by the FBI and stated that the pickup had belonged to a company doing construction work on a building in the area. No further inquiry was pursued (Josiah Thompson, *Six Seconds in Dallas*, 1966).

Further up Houston Street, police officers and the crowd near the intersection of Houston and Elm Street had their attention diverted for some twenty minutes immediately prior to the arrival of the motorcade. An individual in that area dramatically collapsed on the sidewalk and an ambulance was called. Ambulance attendants found the man, dressed in camouflage clothing – not common at the time – and noted that he showed no evidence of a seizure or any other medical problem; he was fully conscious but refused to talk to them. As a precaution, they transported him to Parkland Hospital. While in the Emergency Room at the hospital the man, despite the security following the President's arrival in the same area, simply walked away unnoticed. He was later located and briefly questioned, but offered no other explanation of the collapse than he had not felt well.

The ambulance itself only moved away just as the motorcade moved onto Houston Street. If it had not been behind schedule, the President's limousine would have come upon the ambulance still in the intersection. Most interestingly, one of the ambulance personnel, Aubrey Rike, later shared the fact that FBI agents had called on the ambulance company following the assassination, apparently interested in records recording that on several occasions in the week before the assassination the company had received false calls to the corner of Elm and Houston. The calls were all made at mid-day and requested an ambulance for "right in front of the fountain" at the intersection.

Those FBI visits are not recorded, but Rike himself observed and heard them discussed. Personally, he wondered if someone was making pretext calls to establish the timing required to put an ambulance in that particular intersection. *JFK: The Book of the Film / The Documented Screenplay*, Oliver Stone, Zachary Sklar, Interview with Aubrey Rike, 8. Also author's personal conversation with Mr. Rike.

All of these incidents tended to divert attention from different areas of the Plaza. Some may have been perfectly innocent and circumstantial. Others are much more suspicious, and at best the inquiries which followed were minimal, more recordkeeping in nature rather than true criminal investigation.

[324] Testimony of Sam Holland, Warren Commission, Volume V, 243-244

The smoke and sound triggered Holland and others to run towards the back of the fence. People throughout the area focused their attention on the knoll and the fence line, much more so than on the Texas School Book Depository.

The puff of smoke has often been discussed in terms of a shooter behind the fence line, but in tactical terms it could as easily been produced by a "squib," a type of firecracker serving as a signaling device, and specifically intended to divert attention and security response away from the actual location of shooters. Certainly the amount and density of the smoke does not correlate with the quality, well-maintained weapons or the modern ammunition most likely have been used in an attack on President Kennedy.

[325] Larry Hancock, *Someone Would Have Talked* 2010, 65-67; 69-70

According to a number of observers, Oswald's demeanor changed substantially over the course of a few hours on that Friday. He showed no particular signs of tension on his ride to work, appears to have joked with one co-worker about what was happening in Dallas that day (feigning ignorance of anything special going on in town when asked about a "parade" – as an inveterate newspaper reader and TV news listener he certainly knew the president was visiting Dallas and a motorcade was coming through downtown).

He made no effort to disguise his presence working on the sixth floor, yelling to fellow employees to send the elevator back up so he could come down for lunch. Beyond that, there certainly is a case to argue that Oswald was not on the sixth floor immediately prior or during the shooting – and that he had no idea a rifle linked to him was going to be found there and taken into evidence. What Oswald did not do is also important; certainly he made no appearance in a sixth floor window, nor did he do anything in real time to associate himself with the shooting (the official story portrays him as a total idiot, leaving iron clad evidence implicating himself while denying any connection to the rifle attack or the rifle itself – and whatever Oswald may have been, he certainly was not stupid). If he was being manipulated, there is no sign that he was a knowledgeable or involved patsy in the shooting itself.

After the shooting, he showed no signs of panic or immediate flight, calmly circulating at the front of the TSBD and stopping to talk with people – when he did leave, he walked several blocks to catch a local bus to his apartment. It was only on the bus, which came right back down the street towards the TSBD, when it became apparent something really serious had occurred on Elm Street, that he began to show some sign of concern. But even then when he got off and went back to catch a cab (the first truly unusual behavior for the notoriously frugal Oswald) he showed no signs of being rushed, in flight or working against a schedule (he calmly offered the first cab available to an older lady at the cab stand).

It was only in the cab, hearing the president had been shot, that he began to show real concern, ordering the driver to drop him off well away from his apartment and walking back, then picking up his revolver before moving off towards the nearest bus stop. At that point the only indication of his following instructions appears to be his appearance at the Texas Theatre.

All of which leads us exhibit grave caution – reverse engineering the full plan for what was supposed to happen in Dallas is purely speculative. We have details of what did happen after 12:30, but there is every reason to believe that at that point in time things began to go seriously off script.

[326] Ian Griggs, *No Case to Answer*, 287

[327] Marvin Robertson, CD 5:70; HSCA Volume 12:18, Roy Cooper of Euless, Texas

[328] Larry Hancock, *Someone Would Have Talked*, 225-228

[329] Larry Hancock, *Someone Would Have Talked* 2010, 236-237

[330] Ibid, CE 399, 224; other evidentiary problems, "Suppression," 230-238

[331] Jefferson Morley, JFK Facts, December 5, 2016, also Timothy Naftali and Alexsandr Furskenko's "*One Hell of a Gamble*." Naftali was later the director of the Richard Nixon Presidential Library and Museum in Yorba Linda, California.

https://jfkfacts.org/rfk-jackie-to-the-soviets-he-the-assassin-did-not-act-alone/#more-2298

[332] David Binder "Kennedy and Castro / Possible Cuban Links to the 1963 Killing Seen as Basis for Study," New York Times, June 25, 1976

https://www.cia.gov/library/readingroom/docs/CIA-RDP77-00432R000100400001-2.pdf

[333] Ibid, 124

[334] Ibid, 194

[335] "Are there records of Lee Oswald speaking?" Quora, also Oswald Radio Debate, Mary Ferrell Foundation

https://www.quora.com/Are-there-any-records-of-Lee-Harvey-Oswald-speaking

https://www.maryferrell.org/pages/Featured_Oswald_Radio_Debate.html

[336] Larry Hancock, *Someone Would have Talked* 2010, 144-145

[337] David Phillips endorsement of the Alvarado story remains especially questionable given Alvarado's details about a meeting in a public area of a Cuban diplomatic facility, and an open discussion of murder (including the public passing of money). The conversation was purportedly so visible that as simply a visitor to the embassy Alvarado was able to give detailed physical descriptions of all those involved. He was even able to quote their individual remarks – "I want to kill the man," and "You're not man enough I can do it."

Alvarado even described the passport, and gave an address for the girl involved in the conversation – as well as the exact amount of cash given to Oswald. That such a conversation would have occurred in a public area is highly questionable; the level of detail provided to support it is virtually beyond belief. As a former case officer and propaganda specialist, Phillips should immediately have raised numerous questions, challenging Alvarado.

Instead, Phillips and the senior Mexico City officers continued to support the story until it was totally disproven by the Mexican government and the FBI – after only 48 hours of investigation. Yet even in the face of the embarrassing deconstruction of Alvarado, Phillips continued to support the story, even repeating it in his autobiography, *The Night Watch*. In fact he elaborated on the story, maintaining Oswald had come back to the United States with a large amount of cash.

[338] Larry Hancock, *Someone Would have Talked* 2010, 111-112

[339] In more recent years, the speculation that the Oswald appearance at the Cuban consulate may have actually involved an impersonation, both physically and in related telephone calls, has received increasing support. If that were true, the CIA's initial support of the Alvarado story may have been at least partially driven by the urgency of covering up a pre-assassination counter intelligence/propaganda effort which had involved the Oswald "persona." Disclosing that level of involvement with Oswald prior to November 22 would have raised a whole series of questions which would have been extremely damaging. In later years, David Phillips himself would draft a fictional work based on Oswald being used by the CIA but going "rogue" and turning on Pesident Kennedy.

[340] FBI O'Connor Report re Oswald and Russia, December 3, 1964, Warren Commission document #59, 7

https://www.maryferrell.org/showDoc.html?docId=10460

[341] FBI letterhead memo of February 26, 1964, Warren Commission document #657

https://www.maryferrell.org/showDoc.html?docId=11056#relPageId=4

[342] Federal Bureau of Investigation, Miami Florida, May 8, 1964

https://www.maryferrell.org/showDoc.html?docId=11357#relPageId=2

[343] John Martino, Details of Investigation, United States Secret Service, Treasury Department, Protective Research, December 10/11, 1963

https://www.maryferrell.org/showDoc.html?docId=10490

[344] Federal Bureau of Investigation, Miami Florida, June 1, 1964

https://www.maryferrell.org/showDoc.html?docId=11565#relPageId=2

[345] Ibid, 4

https://www.maryferrell.org/showDoc.html?docId=10460

[346] FBI O'Connor Report re Oswald and Russia, April 4, 1964, Warren Commission Document #812

https://www.maryferrell.org/showDoc.html?docId=11210#relPageId=2

[347] Ibid, 2

[348] Larry Hancock, *Someone Would Have Talked* 2010, 380-381

[349] There were anecdotal remarks from both Ruth Paine and Marina Oswald that Lee Oswald was expected to go from New Orleans to Houston to look for work (where he reportedly did make a job inquiry), and then on to Dallas. The McKeown visit would certainly be consistent with that.

[350] McKeown would later tell author Dick Russell that he had actually recognized Hernandez as someone he knew from shipping weapons into Cuba during the revolution against Batista.

[351] Executive Session Testimony of Robert McKeown, Gun Runner, House Select Committee on Assassinations, Real History Archives

http://www.realhistoryarchives.com/collections/assassinations/jfk/mckeown.htm

[352] Larry Hancock and David Boylan, The Wheaton Lead: An Exploration, Mary Ferrell Foundation, April 20, 2020

https://www.maryferrell.org/pages/Essay_-_The_Wheaton_Lead.html

[353] David Talbot, *Brothers*, 10, quoting Haynes Johnson in Washington Post of 17 Apr 1981. RFK was on the telephone within hours of learning of his brother's murder. The remark was directed towards Cuban exile leader Harry Ruiz-Williams. Earlier that afternoon, RFK had directly

asked CIA Director John McCone if the CIA itself had been involved in the assassination.

[354] Personal conversation on July 1986 with Phillips by Kevin Walsh, a former staff member of the House Select Committee on Assassinations. The remark was made shortly before Phillips' death; up to that time he had totally rejected any talk of conspiracy. Anthony Summers, *Conspiracy*, 518

INDEX

A

B

C

N

O

P

Q

R

S

Y

Z

Printed in Dunstable, United Kingdom

67848760R10174